GHOSTS AND POLTERGEISTS

GHOSTS AND POLTERGEISTS

HERBERT THURSTON, S.J.

EDITED BY J. H. CREHAN, S.J.

James D. Johannes

Roman Catholic Books

A Division of Catholic Media Apostolate

Distribution Center: Post Office Box 2286, Fort Collins, CO 80522

De Licentia Superiorum Ordinis

Nihil Obstat: Eduardus Mahoney, S.T.D.
Censor Deputatus
Imprimatur: E. Morrogh Bernard
Vicarius Generalis
Westmonasterii: Die XI JULII MCMLIII

ISBN 0-912141-59-X

PREFACE

AFTER Fr. Thurston had written a full-length survey of the Poltergeist problem for the *Times Literary Supplement*.[1] he was immediately asked by one of the principal American University Presses to undertake a book on Poltergeists, though at the time, owing to the anonymity of the article, they can have had no idea of his identity. He was also approached by English publishers soon afterwards, and thanks to these promptings he did begin to collect and revise his various reports of such phenomena, pruning and discarding what no longer seemed reliable. It has been suggested by a reviewer of his *Life*[2] that " Towards the end of his life Fr. Thurston became more and more prone to believe the stories of spiritualistic phenomena printed in presumably reputable journals . . . Even *his* critical mind had failed to resist the barrage of suggestion and display of pseudo-science which was becoming one of the most marked features of psychical research."[3] On the other hand, it should be noticed that the story of the so-called Poltergeist of Battersea, which he had re-told in one of his earlier articles was rejected by him when he came to the work of revision with the remark, " I do not now believe in this story," even though it still has a chapter to itself in Mr. Harry Price's *Poltergeist over England* (1945), where it is described as " an amazing affair, exhibiting many unusual features." In fact, the tendency in that book to judge every manifestation by the standard of Borley Rectory and to regard the Borley case as " the best-evidenced, the best-witnessed, and the best-documented case of Poltergeist infestation in the annals of psychical research,"[4] would have seemed to Fr. Thurston unscientific, and it is significant that he did not, to my knowledge, write a single line on the subject of Borley, even when it was at the height of its fame.[5]

[1] 29 February 1936.
[2] Sheed and Ward, 1952.
[3] *Journal of the Society for Psychical Research*, November, 1952, p. 722.
[4] Price, *op. cit.*, p. 364.
[5] A letter from him to Lord Charles Hope, in the files of the Society for Psychical Research, disclaims any special competence about Borley, and refuses to give a verdict.

The fact remains, then, that even after the appearance of Mr. Sacheverell Sitwell's *Poltergeists* (1940), there is room for another collection of Chosen Instances and Conclusions, especially as the examples used by Fr. Thurston do not overlap those chosen by Mr. Sitwell. He set out some of the classical cases—Epworth Rectory, the Drummer of Tedworth and "musty Justice Mompesson," Willington Mill, Worksop, and the Great Amherst Mystery—with a wealth of poetry and imagination, but here one may find a wider range of examples in time and space, and what many have recognized as a sober caution of judgment. Fr. Thurston did at one time think of attributing these phenomena to special powers of the human person when he wrote :

That there may be something diabolical, or at any rate evil, in them I do not deny, but, on the other hand, it is also possible that there may be natural forces involved which are so far as little known to us as the latent forces of electricity were known to the Greeks. It is possibly the complication of these two elements which forms the heart of the mystery.

But when he came later on to gather his ideas together and formulate some tentative conclusions, he seems to have settled on two points only: some of the phenomena are genuine (*i.e.*, not all can be explained away as trickery), and in some cases at least diabolical interference seems to be excluded. He does not seem to have favoured the idea of the Gaelic *tàradh*, or unconscious human volition at a distance, which was the solution that Andrew Lang was most inclined to adopt, perhaps because of the apparent fruitlessness and lack of purpose in the phenomena.

Thanks are due to the Editor of the *Times Literary Supplement* for permission to reprint material which appeared in his issue of 29 February 1936, and to the Editor of *Studies* (Dublin) for several articles which are reprinted below. I have left Fr. Thurston to state his own ideas and have not tried to make him state mine. Any footnotes which I have found it necessary to add have been initialled; the rest of the work is his own.

While not being so extensive a searcher into psychic happenings as his Jesuit predecessors of the sixteenth century, Peter Thyraeus and Martin del Rio, Fr. Thurston had from his childhood an interest in these strange phenomena, having at the age of eight witnessed the hypnotizing of his father's laboratory assistant into a state of rigidity in which his body, supported on two chairs, could be made to support the weight of a man without crumpling up. Fr. Thurston published his findings about Spiritualism in a volume entitled *The Church and Spiritualism* (Bruce, Milwaukee, 1933) but his Poltergeist materials are here collected for the first time.

Heythrop.   J. H. Crehan, S.J.

28 *February* 1953.

CONTENTS

Herbert Thurston, S.J., 1856-1939

An authority on spiritualism, the falsity of which he combated, and a writer on this and ecclesiastical subjects, the Reverend Herbert Thurston, S.J., was a well-known British Jesuit scholar. Born in London, in 1856, the son of G. H. Thurston, M.R.C.S., he was educated at Mount St. Mary's College and at Stonyhurst, received his A.B. and was an Exhibitioner of London University. He took his vows in the Society of Jesus, served as Master at Beaumont College, from 1880 to 1887, and was ordained in 1890. The greater part of his life was spent at the Farm Street Jesuit Church in London and was devoted to writing.

Father Thurston was a frequent contributor to Catholic reviews and wrote numerous books. In 1898 he published *The Life of St. Hugh of Lincoln.* This was followed by a book on *The Holy Year of Jubilee* in 1900. *Lent and the Holy Week* appeared in 1904 and *The Stations of the Cross* in 1906. At the time of World War I he wrote *The War and the Prophets* and *The Memory of Our Dead.* He was a keen student of spiritualism, its frauds and deceptions, many of which he exposed. Admitting the possibility of genuine spiritual manifestations, he brought such phenomena into their proper perspective, and warned that the subject requires a cautious approach. He wrote *Modern Spiritualism* in 1919 and *The Church and Spiritualism* in 1933. Other books were: *Christian Science, The Church and the Confessional, The Eucharistic Fast, Indulgences for Sale, No Popery, Superstition, Beauraing and other Apparitions,* and *Miss Kate.*

One of his outstanding works was the revision of Butler's *Lives of the Saints,* which was enlarged and modernized. He also edited the folio edition of Bridgett's *History of the Holy Eucharist* and many of Mother Loyola's devotional works, and with Bishop Ward was co-editor of the Westminster Library Series of Catholic books. Many articles were contributed by him to the *Catholic Encyclopedia* and *Encyclopedia of Religion and Ethics.*

He died, after several months' illness, at Hampstead, near London, on November 6, 1939, at the age of eighty-three, a great loss to Catholic letters and to the Church he had so long and so well served.

CHAPTER I

A GENERAL VIEW OF POLTERGEIST PHENOMENA[1]

ALTHOUGH the German word " poltergeist " is now naturalized, and is often met with in the newspapers of both England and America, still an examination of standard dictionaries shows that it is a term of comparatively recent introduction. Few, if any, of those published in the last century will be found to contain it, and it is particularly noticeable that it is not recognized by *The Stanford Dictionary of anglicized words and phrases* (London, 1892), though this work was expressly compiled to register those foreign importations into the language which had acquired rights of citizenship. The word does appear in the great *Oxford English Dictionary* in 1910, but the earliest illustration there given of its use dates only from 1871. It is certainly older than that. Mrs. Crowe, in her widely-circulated book *The Night Side of Nature* (1848), makes frequent use of it—once in a chapter heading. When the Spiritualistic movement started in America, more attention was naturally directed to such matters, but the earliest American example I have met of the use of this term occurs in an article copied in 1852 from the *Boston Pilot* which speaks as follows:

The Germans have long been familiar with a mischievous devil called the " Polter geist," whose delight it appears to be to enter houses and turn everything upside down, doing more mischief in an hour than a thousand monkeys would do in a day. It is not well to listen to these things, but really some respectable witnesses have testified that this same monkey ghost has troubled several families in England and America within the few last years.

This article was reproduced in a book *Spirit Manifestations*, by Adin Ballou,[2] which may claim to be the first systematic treatise on

---

[1] *Studies*, March 1928

[2] Its full title is " An exposition of views respecting the principal Facts, Causes and Peculiarities involved in Spirit Manifestations together with interesting phenomenal statements and communications." Boston, Bela Marsh, 25 Cornhill, 1852. The passage quoted above appears in this, the first, edition, page 147. The word is misprinted " Polter giest."

Spiritualism ever printed either in America or elsewhere. As Ballou's little volume went through several editions, and was re-published on both sides of the Atlantic, appearing in London, and again in Liverpool, within less than twelve months, it may very easily have helped to give currency to a term previously unfamiliar to most writers of English. Moreover, the description supplied may be regarded as fairly accurate. A poltergeist is simply a racketing spirit, which in almost all cases remains invisible, but which manifests its presence by throwing things about, knocking fire-irons together and creating an uproar, in the course of which the human spectators are occasionally hit by flying objects, but as a rule suffer no serious injury.

In the last century several prominent members of the Society for Psychical Research—notably Mr. Frank Podmore from the sceptical standpoint and Mr. Andrew Lang in a more benignant vein—occupied themselves with poltergeist phenomena; but the most important contribution to the subject, definitely upholding the objective reality of these manifestations, is that published in 1911 by the late Sir William Barrett, F.R.S. Being himself then resident in Ireland, he had personally investigated two Irish cases, and he takes occasion to outline the features which are found to recur in other examples of the same type of disturbance gathered from all parts of the world. The points upon which he lays stress as characteristic of the poltergeist are the invisibility of the agents, the sporadic and temporary nature of the manifestations, and notably their dependence upon the presence of some particular individual—usually a young person and often a child—who must be assumed to possess strange, if unconscious, mediumistic powers. When telekinetic phenomena occur—and this is almost invariably the case—whether they take the form of missiles which seem to come from nowhere, or of crockery and even furniture crashing or flying through the air, the movement often seems to be controlled, tortuous and at variance with the laws of gravitation. Professor Barrett writes:—

The movement of objects is usually quite unlike that due to gravitational or other attraction. They slide about, rise in the air, move in eccentric paths, sometimes in a leisurely manner, often turn round in their career, and usually descend quietly without hurting the observers. At other times an immense weight is lifted, often in daylight, no one being near, crockery is thrown about and broken, bedclothes are dragged off, the occupants sometimes lifted gently to the ground, and the bedstead tilted up or dragged about the room. The phenomena occur both in broad daylight and at night. Sometimes bells are continuously rung, even if all the bell wires are removed. Stones are frequently thrown, but no one is hurt; I myself have seen a large pebble drop apparently from space in a room where the only culprit could have been myself, and certainly I did not throw it.[1]

In both the cases investigated by Professor Barrett, rappings and inexplicable noises played a prominent part. The earlier occurred in 1877 at a lonely hamlet called Derrygonnelly, nine miles from Enniskillen, in the house of a farmer who had been left a widower with a family of four girls and a boy, the eldest child, Maggie, aged about twenty, seeming to be the centre of the disturbance. Strange rappings and scratchings were first heard, then objects were seen to move, stones began to fall, and candles and boots were repeatedly thrown out of the house, Several neighbours urged them to send for the priest, but the family were Methodists and preferred to put an open Bible on the bed with a big stone on top of it. Some unseen power, however, displaced the Bible and eventually removed it from the room, tearing seventeen pages right across. The freakish disturber of their peace evinced a peculiar dislike for any source of artificial light; candles and lamps were mysteriously stolen or thrown out, and Professor Barrett recounts how the old farmer told him that " Jack Flanigan came and lent us his lamp, saying he would engage the devil himself could not steal it, as he had got the priest to sprinkle it with holy water." Nevertheless the lamp, in spite of the blessing, seems to have shared the fate of the Bible. When Professor Barrett visited the scene he heard the long continued knockings some of which were " like those made by a heavy carpenter's. hammer driving nails into flooring." He satisfied himself that the noises could not have been made by any of the inmates, who were all in view, and, as already mentioned, he saw a stone fall from the void. Moreover he challenged the mysterious agent of the knockings to echo by raps the numbers which he mentally indicated; which it did. Further putting his hands into the side pockets of his overcoat, Professor Barrett asked the spirit to " knock the number of fingers he held open." The experiment was repeated four times, with varying numbers, and in each case the answer was given correctly.

The disturbances which took place at Enniscorthy in July, 1910, were more dramatic, and though in this case Professor Barrett was

[1] *Proceedings of the Society for Psychical Research*, Vol. XXV, p. 378.

not personally a witness of the phenomena, still the depositions he obtained from those principally concerned are so explicit and so fully confirmed by independent testimony that it would be unreasonable to doubt the facts. Apart from hammering and other noises, the prank upon which the poltergeist seemed to concentrate his efforts was the pulling off the bed-clothes and the moving right across the floor of a heavy bedstead, which, lacking one castor, was a particularly difficult object to shift from its place. Three young men slept in the room, all of whom were reduced to a state of abject terror. The principal sufferer was a lad of eighteen, named Randall. According to his account, confirmed on one occasion by reliable investigators who sat up with them, the sheets and blankets were pulled off him, he himself was dragged out of bed on to the floor, " a chair danced out into the middle of the room without anyone near it," and when all three in their fright decided to get into one bed together, " the bed turned up on one side and threw us out on to the floor, and before we were thrown out, the pillow was taken from under my head three times. When the bed rose up, it fell back without making any noise."[1]

Since Irish cases are here in question, it may be noted that four others, located respectively at Upper Ballygowan near Larne, in Wexford, in Portarlington, and at Scotchforth near Ballina, have been recorded by Messrs. Seymour and Neligan in their book *True Irish Ghost Stories*. Even in Ireland alone the list might be greatly augmented. For example a particularly interesting poltergeist is said to have manifested at Tillymoan, near Claudy, Strabane, in 1866. According to information furnished to the *Derry Standard* in the early part of that year, showers of stones bombarded the house of a farmer named Speer who lived there with his wife and a little boy. We are told that " plates and dishes were smashed off the dresser, and the pots and cans began to *walk about* through the apartments." I venture to italicize the reporter's phrase, for it so plainly corresponds with what Barrett and Lang tell us of " the objects . . . which move in eccentric paths, sometimes in a leisurely manner." Numbers of curious people flocked to the spot from far and near, and one evening the crowd " distinctly saw a pot come flying through the door and fall in smashed pieces on the street." We may probably assume that the little boy was the nucleus of these precipitations, for it is mentioned that one morning " he was kindling the fire, when the coals were suddenly lifted off the hearth and scattered through the house in all directions."

[1] *Proceedings S.P.R.*, Vol. XXV, p. 389.

A year earlier a somewhat similar case had been reported from a farm in the townland of Lenagh, not far from Mountfield. The *Tyrone Constitution* printed a detailed narrative contributed by a police constable named Jeremiah M'Meilly, dated Mountfield, 15 February, 1865. The farmer, Peter M'Crory, a very respectable man, seems to have lived alone with his wife and a little girl whom they had adopted. The manifestations began with the throwing of turf-clods, seemingly inside the house, while the three were sitting round the fire in the evening. This was sufficiently disquieting, but next morning in clear daylight the attack was renewed in a more formidable shape. " Some bricks were lying at the corner of the kitchen fire, and these were thrown from all angles of the house at the inmates, until they were reluctantly obliged to beat a retreat." One Jemmy Carland, who came in by chance, was later on told the story. He listened incredulously, and shouted out: " Why the blazes do they not clod me now ? " The words were hardly uttered when three stones in quick succession struck him on the back. Whereupon, as he himself confessed, he promptly took to his heels. Peter's wife also decided to seek refuge for the night in the house of a friend who lived at a little distance, taking the child with her. They went, " but were assailed on their entire route by some invisible parties keeping up stone throwing," the child being the principal, if not the only, object of attack. After a day's interval, during which nothing happened, Peter's wife and her little charge returned. But no sooner had they entered the house than the girl was struck by a " hard turf " and knocked into a tub of water. Thus far the statement of Constable Jeremiah M'Meilly.[1]

Another Irish poltergeist case at Cookstown, Co. Tyrone, caused much talk at the time. *The Spiritualist* newspaper for 27 November 1874, and in subsequent issues, quotes at length from the *Belfast News-Letter*, the *Morning News* and other journals. It would appear that in the house of a Mr. Allen a process of window-breaking went on for months, which, though constant watch was kept, could be traced to no assignable cause. Some panes were broken by stones, others seemed to break of themselves. Then bowls, standing still on a table, began to rotate, shot off the table and smashed. Coats and hats, hanging upon pegs, were seized with a sort of ague and fluttered away. Other garments were torn to shreds. Potatoes boiling in the pot jumped into the fire or disappeared. Stones weighing three pounds or more, some wet and dirty, some clean, came slowly hopping down the stairs when not a soul was in the

[1] See *The Spiritual Times*, 18.iii.65; p. 87, etc.

upper part of the house.   Mr. Allen seems to have been an elderly man, but there were two youthful sons and a daughter living with him.   One of these was probably the medium.

Ireland, of course, has no monopoly in poltergeists, nor are the cases just recounted either exceptionally startling, or very satisfactorily attested.   On the other hand, no one can study the matter without being struck by the recurrence of certain features in these stories which undoubtedly could not have been suggested to their very simple-minded narrators by any familiariy with the literature of the subject.   I remember reading years ago—it was in *Chambers' Magazine*, if I am not mistaken—an account of a poltergeist in the Mauritius where a little girl's comings and goings were attended by an inexplicable precipitation of stones, though no great damage was done.   The writer was a lady whom I afterwards chanced to meet—she was a sister of the late Fr. William Humphrey, S.J.—and she assured me that the details, of which she had been an eye-witness, were absolutely accurate.   Quite on a par with this is a story which reached me in 1928.   A Jesuit Father, writing from Bratislava (*alias* Presburg), Czechoslovakia, sent me an account of an occurrence which was puzzling certain of the rural clergy in his part of the world.   The terms of his letter implied that neither he nor they had any idea that similar cases had ever been recorded elsewhere.   Assuming correctly that I knew nothing of Czech, his statement of the facts was written in Latin.   I may translate it as follows:—

On 11 August, 1927, a young man and a boy of thirteen had been fishing in one of the streams running from the Tatra range.   They were on the point of returning home when suddenly a stone fell near them.   It was followed by a second, and by others in succession.   They grew frightened and hastily decamped.   Then they seemed to encounter a continuous shower of stones which only came into view when they were 30 centimetres (*i.e.*, about a foot) away and which did not strike with any great violence (*non habebant ictum gravem*).   They took shelter in a tavern, but the stones pursued them there, and the pair were promptly ejected on the ground that they must be possessed by the devil.   When they reached home, there were further manifestations.   Stones seemed to fall from the ceiling.   In one of the rooms the boy's father had made a collection of curious pebbles and geological specimens.   These now started flying from one room to another and dropped on the ground.   The next day a piece of coal in the kitchen sailed out and broke a glass panel in the door. In the afternoon a pack of playing cards flew up from the table and scattered among the visitors who were present. Finally, on the third day some pieces of money dropped from nowhere— between ten and twenty coins in all—and there was also a twenty-kronen note in paper. It was afterwards discovered that this money belonged to one of the people in the house. The stones which fell were of a type common in the district. It is stated that the thirteen-year-old boy had taken part as a medium in various séances in other parts of the country; but these particular manifestations were new and had only occurred in this, his native village.

I was not in a position to check the accuracy of this statement of facts, but the points of resemblance between this and other polter-geist stories are striking; and most certainly the Slovak parish priest, who seems to have been the ultimate source of information, is not likely to have made acquaintance with any of the literature.

Furthermore, occurrences of this nature are no novelty. They belong to history at almost every period. Take, for example, an incident recorded by Giraldus Cambrensis, about the year 1191, in his *Itinerarium Kambriae*. A reference to the same occurrence seems to be found in the Margan Annals under the year 1184. In any case Giraldus states:—

In this part of Pembrokeshire it has happened in our own times that foul spirits have held intercourse with men, not indeed so as to be seen, but so as to make themselves sensibly manifest. For in the home, first of a certain Stephen Wiriet, and later in that of William Not, they rendered their presence known by the throwing of lumps of dirt (*jactu sordium*) and of other things meant to deride rather than to do bodily injury. In William's house, as both the host himself and his guests had repeatedly to deplore, they made rents and holes in garments both of linen and cloth, and against this mischief no amount of watchfulness, no locks or bolts, afforded the least protection. But what was stranger still, in Stephen's house the spirit used to talk with men, and when people bandied words with it, as many did in mockery, it taxed them with all the things they had ever done in their lives which they were least willing should be known or spoken about.

Giraldus goes on to express surprise that in hauntings of this sort the use of holy water, not only the ordinary holy water but even that of the font on Holy Saturday, seemed to be of no avail. Indeed no sacrament or sacred rite produced any effect. When the priests came in all devotion and seriousness, well supplied with holy water and carrying their processional cross, they were the first to get badly pelted. The Welsh scholar accordingly concludes that sacraments and sacramentals are meant to protect mankind against serious injury, not against mere mischief and illusion.[1]

It would, however, be a mistake to suppose that the activities of the poltergeist are invariably confined to whimsical pranks alternating on occasion with rather rough horse-play. Though Puck may be the predominating role, we sometimes come upon a Caliban, and it is this latter type of experience which most vividly recalls the physical outrages of which we read in the lives of saintly ascetics. Among the most remarkable scenes of violence, evidentially well-attested, which I have come across are those described in a paper read at the Warsaw International Congress of Psychic Research in 1923 by the Rev. Haraldur Nielsson, Professor of Theology in the University of Iceland. The incidents referred to took place in 1907, but they seem to have been recorded at the time in the minute book of the Icelandic Psychical Research Society, they were formally confirmed by the President of the Society who was himself a participant and who was present at the Congress, and they were also vouched for by three other gentlemen of standing concerned in the affair.

The central figure in the disturbance was a young professional medium Indridi Indridason, apparently little more than a boy. His normal controls seemed hardly able to protect him from the invasions of a spirit, here called " Jon," who was identified with the soul of a recent suicide. The medium lived in terror of Jon, since he was able to draw " power " out of other unconscious mediums without their sanction and showed himself hostile and vindictive. After an alarming séance, the experimenters came to the conclusion that it would not be safe for Indridi to sleep in a room by himself. Accordingly his friend Mr. Oddgeirsson agreed to share his bed-chamber with him, while Mr. Kvaran, the President of the Society, spent the night in the next room. According to Professor Nielsson's account—

During the night the medium shouts that he is being dragged out of bed and is very terror-stricken. He implores Mr. Oddgeirsson to hold his hand. Mr. Oddgeirsson takes his hand, pulling with all his might, but cannot hold him. The medium is lifted above that

[1] Giraldus Cambrensis, *Itinerarium Kambriæ* (Rolls Series), pp. 93-94.

end of the bed against which his head had been lying and he is pulled down on the floor, sustaining injuries to his back from the bedstead. At the same moment a pair of boots which were under Mr. Oddgeirsson's bed, were thrown at the lamp, breaking both the glass and the shade. The medium is now dragged head foremost through the door and along the floor in the outer room, in spite of his clutching with all his might at everything he could catch hold of, besides Mr. Kvaran and Mr. Oddgeirsson pulling at his legs. Mr. Kvaran and Mr. Oddgeirsson at last succeeded in getting under his shoulders, which they had great difficulty in lifting. They managed, however, to drag him into bed, but they could not make him stand upon his feet.[1]

Two nights later a similar scene occurred. Indridi on this occasion has a Mr. Thorlaksson and Mr. Oddgeirsson sleeping in the room with him. Ewers and other crockery were hurled about and smashed. The two watchers, while throwing themselves upon the medium and exerting all their strength, could hardly prevent him from again being dragged out of bed, and while this was happening " the table which was standing between the beds was lifted and came down on Mr. Oddgeirsson's back." They all determined to leave the house; but before this could be accomplished, we are told that the medium after partially dressing once more shouted for help.

Mr. Thorlaksson had been standing in the outer room, but now rushes in to the medium, and then sees that he is balancing in the air with his feet towards the window. Mr. Thorlaksson takes hold of him, pulls him down into the bed and keeps him there. Then he feels that the medium and himself are being lifted up, and he shouts to Mr. Oddgeirsson to help him. Mr. Oddgeirsson goes into the bedroom, but a chair is then hurled against him and falls down beside the stove in the outer room. Mr. Oddgeirsson swerved aside to avoid the chair, and went on into the bedroom. Mr. Thorlaksson was then lying on the medium's chest. Mr. Oddgeirsson threw his weight on to the medium's knees, who was at the moment all on the move in the bed. Then a bolster which was under the medium's pillow was thrown up into the air. It fell down on the bedroom floor. Simultaneously the candlesticks which were in the outer room came through the air and were flung down in the bedroom.[2]

All this sounds perfectly crazy. But Professor Barrett, who was

---

[1] *Congrès International tenu à Varsovie en* 1923, p. 155.

[2] Ibid, p. 157.

certainly neither crazy nor given to exaggeration, vouches, as we have seen, for the truth of happenings which were not very dissimilar. The Rev. Mr. Nielsson, the author of the account, who was a participator in other like scenes with the same medium, is professor of theology at Reykjavik.[1] Mr. Thorlaksson, described as " Senior Clerk in the Ministries of Industry and Commerce," Mr. Kvaran, who was president of the Society and custodian of its archives, and two other gentlemen who took part in the series of events narrated, all append their signatures and testify that the story is an exact record of facts. It is exceedingly difficult to believe that they can all have been hallucinated. The most curious part of the business is that the truculent Jon after being mildly remonstrated with and courteously encouraged, became a reformed character. Like a converted poacher turned game-keeper, he afterwards upheld the law and is said to have been most efficient in keeping the more unruly spirits in order.

It is a far cry from Reykjavik, Presburg and the Mauritius to Stratford, Connecticut; but it was in this last town that there was enacted, just a century ago, one of the most amazing poltergeist dramas of which we have record. The knockings at Epworth rectory in 1716-1717 were absurdly tame in comparison,[2] though John Wesley's correspondence has made these latter very famous. In Connecticut the scene of the disturbances was again a parsonage, but it was a Presbyterian clergyman, the Rev. Dr. Phelps, much honoured in his own communion and universally respected, who was the principal sufferer. For more than two years Dr. Phelps with a family of four children, of whom the eldest was a daughter of sixteen and the youngest a boy of three, had occupied the house without the occurrence of any untoward incident. But on Sunday, 10 March 1850, the troubles began which were destined, in varying phases, to continue for eighteen months or even longer. On the morning of that day the house was deserted and locked up. The Phelps family were all attending their own church, and the only servant, an Irish girl who is described as having shown herself " honest and trustworthy " during the six months she had been in their service, had gone to Mass in Bridgeport, three miles away. When the family returned the front door was standing wide open,

---

[1] A native of Iceland, later a Catholic priest working in Germany, told me that he had known Professor Nielsson, and, despite the divergence of their religious views, he spoke of him with respect as a man whose word might always be relied on.

[2] Still, as Mr. Andrew Lang reminds us (Cock Lane and Common Sense, p. 101), Nancy Wesley, as was averred in a letter from one of the family, was raised from the floor together with the bed she sat on.

and the furniture was strewn about the place in disorder. Nothing, however, had been stolen, and a gold watch in a conspicuous position had been left undisturbed. The family again went to church in the afternoon, but Dr. Phelps, remaining behind to keep watch, was conscious of no disturbance of any kind. None the less it was discovered that since their mid-day meal all sorts of new pranks had been played. Everything was out of place. Moreover in the principal bedroom " a sheet was found spread over the bed outside the counterpane, and beneath this were a nightgown and chemise laid out with the arms folded across the breast, with stockings placed in a position to represent, as it seemed, a corpse disposed as is usual before placing it in the coffin." Similar tricks were renewed next morning, and on that day the visible movement of furniture and other objects began. " An umbrella, standing in the hall, leaped a distance of at least twenty-five feet. Dr. Phelps saw the movement, and knows there was no perceptible agency by which the motion was produced. A bucket standing at the head of the stairs was thrown into the entry below." Smaller articles such as nails, forks, knives, spoons, bits of tin, iron and keys were thrown from different directions about the house. Further, " a piece of crepe was fastened to the knocker of the back door and the mirrors in the front rooms were covered with sheets and table-cloths, as is the custom in some parts of the country when a person lies dead in the house." As these uncomfortable disturbances continued, Dr. Phelps invited an intelligent and trustworthy friend, himself also a clergyman, to come and stay in the house. He remained for nearly three weeks altogether, and " became satisfied before the close of the second day that neither the girl in the kitchen, nor the children, had any agency in producing the strange movements." A large raw potato fell on to the breakfast table beside Dr. Phelps' plate. They experimented and decided from the concussion that it could not have dropped from a greater height than twelve or fifteen inches, but nobody could possibly have thrown it without instant detection. On numberless occasions both Dr. Phelps and his friend saw small objects rise from the place where they lay and sail into another position.

In one instance a chair was perceived to rise from the floor and beat down again, five or six times, with a violence which caused the house to tremble so as to be felt in all the adjoining apartments. A large plated candlestick, standing on the mantelshelf, was moved by some unseen power to the floor and then rose up and down beating the floor until the candlestick was broken. This was the first article which was damaged about the house. Several times during the day, loud noises, like someone pounding with an axe or some heavy substance on the floor, were heard in different parts of the house, and several times the loud poundings terminated with a frightful scream.

These and similar incidents were renewed hundreds of times. As the days went by and the news of these strange happenings circulated, numbers of people came to witness them. They could find no solution, but were agreed that neither the children nor the servant had any hand in their production. The mediumistic power seemed to centre mainly in the boy Harry aged twelve, but also in his sister Anna, who was four years older. On one occasion when Harry was taken for a drive by his father, twenty stones were thrown at intervals into the carriage. At times he was violently caught up from the ground until his head nearly struck the ceiling; once he was thrown into a cistern of water, and once also he was tied up and suspended from a tree. Under the eyes of a clergyman visitor the boy's trousers "were rent from the bottom upwards, higher than the knee, and were literally torn to ribbons an inch or more wide." Then, at another period of the manifestations, the poltergeist turned its attention to glass-smashing. No less than seventy-one panes were broken before the tormentor wearied of the sport.

Dr. Phelps saw a tumbler which was standing on a bureau rise from its place, fly to the window and dash out the only pane remaining whole, when no one was within twenty feet of it and the only persons in the room were himself and Harry, the latter standing by the Doctor's side in the doorway.

There were also written communications which suddenly appeared in unsuspected places, some of them bogus letters couched in facetious terms and signed with the names of neighbouring ministers. Dr. Phelps in fact averred that, when writing alone in his study he had for a minute turned his back to the table, and on resuming his task found written in large letters, the ink still wet, upon the sheet before him: "Very nice paper and very nice ink for the devil." But the most bizarre of all the reported manifestations was the following:—

On 16 March, soon after breakfast, two or three "images" appeared in the middle room; soon again another, followed by others still, numbering in all eleven or twelve. They were formed of articles of clothing, found about the house, stuffed to resemble the human figure. A lady's dress would be stuffed in some cases with a muff; again with a pillow, and sometimes with other dresses; a bonnet and shoes were aptly placed to complete the figure. These all but one represented females in the attitude of devotion, some having Bibles or prayer books placed before them. One formed of Mrs. Phelps's dress so much resembled the real that the little boy, scarce three years old, coming into the room with his sister whispered: " Be still, Ma is saying prayers."

Frankly the whole story is one which it seems extremely difficult to credit. But Mr. E. W. Capron, from whose book, *Modern Spiritualism its Facts and Fanaticisms* (Boston, 1855), I have borrowed the account just given, was by no means an uncritical writer. He knew Dr. Phelps well, and he states that he had been allowed to examine all the records kept by the Doctor himself. There can be no question that the disturbances were widely discussed in American journals while the phenomena were still going on, and that Dr. Phelps courted every sort of inquiry.[1] His own published letters dealing with this matter give the impression that he was perfectly honest and it is certain that he had nothing to gain, but on the contrary much to lose, by the sensation produced.

It would be premature at this stage to attempt any discussion of the nature of the agencies responsible for the phenomena here alleged to have occurred. I will only point out that we often seem to be confronted by evidence of a distinct conflict between these mysterious forces, some tending to protect and restrain, others violently aggressive and malevolent. On the other hand even the more brutal appear in some measure to be amenable to kindness, while execrations and words of scorn lead only to fresh disturbances in a still more outrageous form.

In the case of the Larne poltergeist, for example, Messrs. Seymour and Neligan record (p. 135): " On one occasion, after a volley of stones had been poured into the house through the window, a young man who was present fired a musket in the direction of the mysterious assailants. The reply was a loud peal of Satanic laughter, followed by a volley of stones and turf."

---

[1] See H. Spicer, *Sights and Sounds*, London, 1853, pp. 101-110; and the Swedenborgian publication the *New Jerusalem Magazine* (Boston, 1850), Vol. xxiii, pp. 225-226; *The Spiritual Telegraph* for 3 July, 1852; *The New Church Repository* (New York, Ap. 1851), Vol. IV, p. 162. Dr. Phelps was not a spiritualist.

CHAPTER II

GHOSTLY VISITANTS THAT BITE [1]

L ET me say at the outset that this chapter has nothing to do with vampires, though its title, I fear, might seem to lend itself to some such interpretation. The vampire superstition, though ancient and widespread, especially if we regard it as embracing the kindred belief in lycanthropy, does not offer much evidence that is capable of being tested. There was a curious epidemic of alleged English cases in the twelfth century,[2] but the vampire, as a rule, is a very shy bird which has a habit of locating itself in inaccessible places such as the Balkans or the islands of the Greek archipelago. What I propose to speak of here is a modern and actual problem of psychic research. The phenomena are not of very common occurrence, but they have recently been witnessed in England, and there is at least one other case, much older in date but of purely native growth, which might not unreasonably be described as one of the strangest stories of the preternatural ever recorded. To rescue this remarkable experience from oblivion is the main purpose of the remarks which follow. It will be well, however, to begin with what is recent and to work backwards.

Possibly some few readers will recall the name of Eleanore Zügun who, during the few weeks she spent in England in the late autumn of 1926, was the subject of a good many paragraphs in the London daily journals. She was a Rumanian child of peasant extraction, only thirteen years of age, though, to judge from her photograph, she looked older than she really was. She had been brought to this country by her patroness, Countess Wassilko-Serecki, in order that an investigation might be carried out at " The National Laboratory of Psychical Research," in Queensberry Place, London. Strange things were alleged to happen to the child, who seemed to be intermittently persecuted by an invisible agent known to her as *Dracu* (bluntly the Devil). In spite of the fact, however, that she

---

[1] *The Month*, August 1928

[2] Some account of these will be found in an article in *The Month* for November, 1897, under the title " Broucolaccas."

14

was repeatedly bitten and scratched in a way that apparently caused pain and made her wince, no permanent injury resulted; while in her presence curious movements of inanimate objects took place which could only be explained by the intervention of some freakish or mischievous outside intelligence. Of these telekinetic phenomena which are not only more inexplicable, but were more convincingly demonstrated than the physical lesions, I do not propose to speak; but it is well to note in passing that their genuineness was attested by a group of observers of whom Dr. R. J. Tillyard, F.R.S., was one. The supernormal character of one set of experiences seems to constitute a presumption that the other unwonted happenings had a similar causation. Without speaking of the vexations to which Eleanore is said to have been subjected by *Dracu* in her own country, let us come at once to the record of what took place in London in ordinary daylight under the eyes of competent witnesses. On the afternoon of Monday, 4 October, in the presence of Captain Neil Gow and Mr. Clephan Palmer, the former reports:—

3.20. Eleanore cried out. Showed marks on back of left hand like teeth-marks which afterwards developed into deep weals. I got Eleanore to bite her right hand and noted the kind of marks caused by this bite, but could trace no similarity between this and the first alleged stigmata.

3.25. Eleanore gave a soft cry and pointed to her right wrist. She undid the sleeve of her blouse and rolled it up. I saw several freshly-made red marks like scratches. There were several of these, about five inches long. After a few moments they rose up into heavy white weals.

4.12. Eleanore was just raising a cup of tea to her lips, but suddenly gave a cry and put the cup down hastily; there was a mark on her right hand similar to those caused by a bite. Both rows of teeth were indicated.

Mr. Clephan Palmer, the other witness, states:—

We were having tea in the laboratory and Eleanore was in the act of raising the cup to her lips when she suddenly gave a little cry of pain, put down her cup and rolled up her sleeve. On her forearm I then saw what appeared to be the marks of teeth indented deeply in the flesh, as if she or someone else had fiercely bitten her arm. The marks turned from red to white and finally took the form of white raised weals. They gradually faded but were still noticeable after an hour or so.

These apparent bitings which, we are told, had often occurred previously in Rumania were observed in London on three different days, viz., on 4 October as described, on 5 October, and 10 October. On the second of these occasions photographs of the marks were taken at the laboratory, and these are reproduced in Mr. Harry Price's statement from which I am quoting.[1]

Captain Seton-Karr, F.R.G.S., one of the eye-witnesses, contributes a formal attestation in these terms:—

I was present on 5 October when the so-called " stigmatic " markings appeared on the face, arms and forehead of Eleanore Zügun under conditions which absolutely precluded the possibility of Eleanore producing them by scratching or other normal means. The marks were photographed in my presence.   H. W. Seton-Karr.

Colonel W. W. Hardwick, another witness, similarly states that as Eleanore was tying up a box " she gave a gasp " and that " distinct teeth-marks appeared on her wrist." He adds that " the girl was under close observation and could not have produced these herself by any normal means."

This is the sum of the evidence, and it seems to me that there cannot be any reasonable question that these " stigmatic " markings appeared as described. It is, no doubt, conceivable that they may have been the result of some sort of auto-suggestion. Mr. Harry Price himself propounded the hypothesis that when in Eleanore's early childhood certain " poltergeist " phenomena made themselves manifest " the simple peasants threatened her so often with *Dracu* (the devil) and what he would do to her, that her subconscious mind has become obsessed with the idea of whippings, bitings, etc., which these ignorant people said would be her lot at the hands—or teeth —of *Dracu*." This is in itself not impossible, though Mr. Price admits almost in the same breath that he cannot lay claim to have unravelled the companion mystery of the telekinetic movements of the coins, the " apports " and the other strange happenings which occur in Eleanore's presence. Discussion of the problem, however, is here precluded, for my immediate purpose is not to provide explanations but to draw attention to the fact that, however produced, these biting phenomena are not without precedent.

[1] *Proceedings of the National Laboratory of Psychical Research*, Vol. I (1927), pp. 8-9, 14-15, 26, etc.

For two of the earlier examples to which I would make appeal I can afford little space. The first of these has been cited by Mr. Andrew Lang in his book *Cock Lane and Common Sense*. The case is that of a Madame L. who was plagued by a persistent spirit at Toulouse in 1853. Madame L. detecting some uncanny presence, threw holy water under the chair and " her thumb was bitten and marks of teeth left upon it. Presently her shoulder was bitten, whether on a place she could reach with her teeth or not, we are not informed."[1] This information is meagre enough, but it is plainly a manifestation of the same nature as those observed in the hands and arms of Eleanore Zügun. Of the Schuppart case, however, which is more than a century older, a very full record is provided in a formal statement made by the sufferer himself before a Lutheran theological academy and confirmed by him most solemnly on oath. Dr. Schuppart, of Giessen, the victim of this poltergeist invasion, which lasted for six years, seems to have been a professor of theology of the highest character, much respected by his contemporaries. The story of his experiences is full of interest. He declares that every pane in his study window was repeatedly smashed, stones from six to ten pounds in weight were aimed at him but seemed designedly to miss him by a hair's breadth, his wife was struck with blows which resounded all through the house but which nevertheless inflicted relatively little pain. What, however, is most to our purpose is the following passage:—

Often (he writes) I have been for four weeks together without taking off my clothes. It has struck me in the face, it has pricked me with pins, it has even bitten me so that both rows of teeth could be distinguished. The two big fangs stood out plainly and they were as sharp as pins.[2]

And now we come to the case, a Bristol poltergeist, which more specially concerns us. The account we possess was evidently drawn up by the author, Mr. Durbin, from notes made at the time, though it was not printed until after his death. What kind of man

---

[1] *Cock Lane and Common Sense*, 2nd Edition, p. 309. Not many people, it seems to me, would be able to bite their shoulder with their teeth. A first-hand account of the incident was printed by M. Bénézet, the editor of the *Gazette du Languedoc*, in his booklet *Les Tables Tournantes*, pp. 29-34.

[2] Oft bin ich in 4 Wochen nicht aus den Kleidern gekommen. Da hats mich in Angesicht geschlagen, mich mit Stecknadeln gestochen, ja gebissen, dass man utramque seriem dentium gesehen hat. Die zwei grossen Zähne stunden da und waren so spitz wie Stecknadeln. Horst, " Dämonomagie." Vol. I, p. 244; and cf. " Zauber Bibliothek," IV, 252.

the narrator was we learn from a friend of his who contributed a preface to the little book.   The Durbins seem to have been people of some consideration in the western capital, and in the year 1800 when the account appeared a nephew of the author, Sir John Durbin, was an alderman and knighted.   Of the uncle, Mr. Henry Durbin, a highly-respected citizen of the same town, we are told that:—

His inviolable attachment to truth, his unblemished uprightness, his widely extended charity (for he invariably, from the time he entered into business till his decease in 1799, gave a tenth of his ample annual income to the poor), his probity in the concerns of his calling, and his genuine and unaffected piety to God, rendered him deservedly dear to all who had the happiness of his acquaintance.   When he first heard of the strange transactions at Lawford's Gate, he went, through a principle of critical curiosity, to detect and expose what he deemed to be imposture.

His conscientious researches, however, continued for many months, convinced him that fraud was out of the question.

The result was, what every man of sense must expect, that Mr. Durbin was firmly persuaded the whole business was the effect of supernatural agency; and as such he fully believed it to his dying day.   But Mr. Durbin was not the sole examiner in this business. Several clergymen of learning and piety, and gentlemen of considerable abilities, some of whom were professed Deists, searched into these matters also; and Mr. Durbin has been often heard to say, that they were fully convinced that there could be no imposture in the case.[1]

Probably the Deists of Bristol at the close of the eighteenth century, who presumably knew nothing of poltergeist literature, would have been harder to convince than the average reader of the present time who has at least met with such stories in the newspapers.   At any rate Mr. Durbin's editor explains his withholding the account from publication by the following statement:—

Durbin did not publish in his lifetime, though urged to do so, because—" the present is an age of infidelity; men scoff at spiritual

---

[1] *A Narrative of some extraordinary things that happened to Mr. Richard Giles's Children*, Bristol, 1800.   Preface, pp. 4-5.

things; if they believe not Moses and the Prophets, Christ and the Apostles, they will not of course believe my feeble testimony concerning a work which it may be their interest to discredit. When I first engaged in the examination of this business, I was abused in the public papers for what was termed my credulity. Should I publish the Narrative, the same abuse would be revived, and I wish to live and die in peace with all men. It will doubtless be published after my death, and the matter will then speak for itself."[1]

The writer of the account was probably a sensitive man who shrank from the ridicule which his narrative would undoubtedly have provoked. His manuscript, however, was preserved and it will help the reader to understand the situation if I reproduce its first paragraphs unaltered.

AN ACCOUNT OF DISTURBANCES, ETC. AT THE LAMB, WITHOUT LAWFORD'S GATE

18 Dec 1761, hearing that Mr. Giles's children, Miss Molly and Dobby, were afflicted in an extraordinary manner for a fortnight past, I went there this day, and saw Molly sewing, and she had marks on her arms given on a sudden, like the marks of a thumbnail; which I am satisfied she could not do herself. As I watched her, I saw the flesh pressed down whitish, and rise again, leaving the print of a finger-nail, the edges of which grew red afterwards. The girl complained that it came with the force of a finger, hurted her much, and smarted after. I inquired of Mr. Giles when this first took place; he said: " On Friday, 13 Nov. last, the children being all in bed in the morning, something scratched violently at the window and bed's head, and they were so frightened that they jumped out of bed and ran downstairs." As nothing of the kind occurred till about three weeks afterwards, the father and mother thought it was the pigeons that had made a noise at the window.

On Sunday, 6 Dec., this became more violent and continued every day, scratching and knocking. Several persons said they saw the finger of a hand near the children. Mr. Giles told me he then thought it to be tricks of the servants and would find it out, as it began about five in the morning, and when they went to bed it was more violent than in the day-time. He went into the children's room once, to detect the servants if possible. He first saw the cover of a box move up and down several times, which he examined, but saw no cause of it. While he was observing it, the cover moved again

[1] *A Narrative*, etc., p. 6.

until it fell to the ground; then the box with the child's clothes in it moved several times, till it turned over and threw the clothes on the floor. This startled him. At night he determined to take Molly from the maids, to be with himself in a room not commonly used. He told me he looked under the bed, and took a hanger with him. As soon as he was in bed with his daughter, she cried out she was pinched on her legs and feet; and the clothes he found were pulled off the bed several times, and the child said she saw the hand that did it. He then put the hanger into her hand to cut it; she cried out it was pulling the hanger out of her hand, and he saw it pulled out of her hand and thrown on the floor. He then made her hold it with both her hands, and it was pulled out again and thrown on the floor. He was then fully convinced it was preternatural, and took the child to the maid's bed again.[1]

Molly Giles, we learn, was thirteen years of age, and Dobby eight. A great deal of the poltergeist phenomena recorded in the case was of a surprising kind and would be quite incredible if it were not for the fact that well-attested examples in our own day—I might refer in particular to the experiences of Indridi Indridason, mentioned in the previous chapter[2]—furnish accounts which are precisely similar. At Bristol a great table which it would require two men to move was turned upside down, things were thrown about, and furniture and fire-irons moved of themselves. One of the most graphic, and to me convincing, incidents is Mr. Durbin's description of how he saw a wine glass " flung " at a nurse by an invisible hand. We may probably assume that the wine-glass of 1762 was a rather formidable missile.

On the chest of drawers (says Mr. Durbin) stood a wine-glass which I saw glitter in the sun, and was astonished to see it rise from the drawers without hands. It rose gradually about a foot perpendicularly from the drawers; then the glass seemed to stand, and thereupon inclined backwards, as if a hand had held it; it was then flung with violence about five feet and struck the nurse on the hip a hard blow.

One of the maids to whom the nurse next day showed the bruise said that the place was black and blue. Mr. Durbin, who had witnessed the whole incident, goes on to explain:—

[1] *A Narrative*, etc., pp. 9-10.
[2] See p. 8 above.

There was no person near the drawers when it rose; the children were standing near me, who saw it and ran to the other end of the room, fearing that it would be flung at them, as things generally were . . . This was about nine in the morning (the date was 5 January), in clear daylight, close by a sash-window.

This incident, not unnaturally, seems to have made a considerable impression on Mr. Durbin. He kept the glass, which, he tells us, " was quite whole, except that the foot of it was broken as if pincers had pinched it all round." In the preface his editor states that " the glass, which was an old-fashioned one, has been shown to several and it was nipped round at the foot in the manner described." It would seem that Mr. Richard Giles, the father of the children, was the landlord of " The Lamb " Inn. The place must have been fairly commodious and servants were not lacking. As a further introduction to the biting phenomena we may note the following passage:—

2 January 1762. I went and met there Mr. —— and several other gentlemen. We went into a room called the George and saw the children pinched with the impressions of nails, and the children said they saw the hand that did it. There was a loud knocking against the table and I saw a chair move in which Molly sat so as almost to throw her down. Dobby cried the hand was about her sister's throat, and I saw the flesh at the side of her throat pushed in, whitish as if done with fingers, though I saw none. Her face grew red and blackish presently, as if she was strangled, but without any convulsion or contraction of the muscles. We went to her, and I touched her head. It went off in a moment and she was well, which could not have taken place had it been the effect of a natural disorder. Soon after Molly was struck twice on the head and we all heard it.[1]

Four days later, on 6 January, we have a further development:—

After that, seven of us being there in the room, Molly said she was bit in the arm, and presently Dobby cried out the same. We saw their arms bitten about twenty times that evening. Their arms were put out of bed, and they lay on their backs. They could not do it themselves, as we were looking at them the whole time. We examined the bites and found on them the impression of eighteen

[1] *A Narrative*, etc., p. 12.

or twenty teeth, with saliva or spittle all over them, in the shape of a mouth, almost all of them very wet, and the spittle smoking (*sic*), as if just spit out of the mouth.   I took up some of it on my finger to try the consistence of it, and Mr. — did the same, and we found it clammy like spittle, and it smelt rank.[1]

I must ask the reader's pardon for the introduction of these rather revolting details, but it is important to notice that this unpleasant clammy liquid does not seem always to have been associated with an actual bite; for we read at a later stage:—

We bid Molly put her arms out of bed, and we put the petticoat on them to prevent, if possible, the cuts, but could not hinder it. As we looked on, she cried out her arm was rubbed with nasty stuff; Mr. — took off the coat (petticoat)?, and saw about a teacupful of spittle rubbed over her arm, all in a lather.   We were certain she could not put her hand to her mouth.   Soon after she said someone was washing her arm.   It was out of bed and her arm was again daubed over with spittle.[2]

On another occasion Mr. Durbin mentions: " I stopped a little to talk with Molly, and saw a dab of spittle fall on her forehead; it was smoking, as if just spit out of the mouth, and ran down her face."[3]   It would occupy much space to give full details, but the observers were convinced that the bite marks were not produced by the children themselves.   The following passage supplies some indication of their reasons for arriving at this conclusion:—

Thursday the 7th (Jan. 1762).   I was there with three gentlemen, when Molly and Dobby were in bed; it again began beating and scratching as usual, and bit them about ten times, leaving the spittle on the bite . . . Their backs and shoulders were bit while they lay on them, which put it out of doubt they did not do it themselves. I heard the slaps on Molly's breast several times.   She cried out that she was hit on her breast; I could hear the slaps of a hand very loud, but I could not see anything that did it . . . After we had seen sufficient to convince us it was not done by any physical power, and the children were roaring out for the pain of the pinches and bites, I begged the gentlemen to assist in screening (*i.e.* protecting) the children from their torments . . . Their hands being out of bed, I took a petticoat and covered over their hands and arms with it,

---

[1] *Ibid.*, p. 15.   [2] *Ibid.*, p. 26.   [3] *Ibid.*, p. 31.

and held it down close on them to defend them if possible; but they cried out that they were bitten worse than before under my hand. I pulled off the petticoat, and we saw fresh bites with the spittle in several places, though we covered them so closely. Dobby was bitten most and with deeper impressions than Molly. The impression of the teeth on their arms formed an oval, which measured two inches in length.[1]

These biting phenomena continued for a long time and under all sorts of conditions. The following is a good specimen of some casual incidents of the same nature:—

The 30th at noon I called there and saw Molly bit on the arm, while she was rubbing a chair. I saw Dobby wiping her hands on a towel. While I was talking to her, she cried out she was bitten in the neck. I looked and saw the mark of teeth, about eighteen, and wet with spittle. It was in the top part of the shoulder close by the neck; therefore it was impossible for her to do it herself, as I was looking on all the time, and nobody was near her but myself.[2]

There were two other forms of physical vexation to which the children were often subjected—cutting, as with a blunt knife, which marked but did not always pierce the epidermis, and pricking with pins. The latter seem generally to have been taken from their clothes or from the pincushions they each carried about with them. These pins were almost always bent, or, as Mr. Durbin phrases it, " crooked," into the most extravagant shapes. He kept a large collection of them and his editor, who had often seen them, remarks in the Preface that " it would have tortured the ingenuity of man to have invented the vast variety of fantastic figures which several scores of these pins exhibited." A single extract will suffice to give an idea of this curious form of vexation.

Monday afternoon (15 Feb.). I went with — and called on Mr. —. We found all the pins had been taken out of Molly's clothes and crooked and stuck in her skin. As I had many reflections thrown on me in the public papers, I was determined to try an experiment, in order to have a certain fact to convince the world, if possible. I made Molly sit down in a chair in the middle of the parlour: I took a large pin and marked it at the top with a pair of scissors; I put her hands across, and bid her not move. I desired

---

[1] *A Narrative*, etc., p. 6.   [2] *Ibid.*, p. 22.

the above gentlemen to watch her narrowly; none were in the room besides ourselves. I then put the marked pin in her pincushion in which the other pin was; I put the pincushion that hung at her side into her pocket-hole and pulled her clothes over it. As I moved one hand (my watch being in the other to see the time), she cried out she felt somewhat at her pin-cushion, and directly was pricked in the neck (her hands being still across). The identical pin I had marked was run through the neck of her shift, and stuck in her skin, crooked very curiously. It was not a minute from the time I put the pin in to her being pricked in the neck. Those two gentlemen were witnesses of the fact. We then marked four other pins, and I put them in her pincushion singly, as before; and all of them were crooked and stuck in her neck. I examined the pincushion (after we took every pin out of her neck) and found the pins gone from the pincushion. Some of them were crooked in half a minute, in such a manner as no human hand could do in the time.[1]

With regard to the cuts, I must content myself with citing one short paragraph.

The 9 Feb. I dined there (presumably at the " Lamb " inn) with the Commissioners of the Turnpikes. Two gentlemen were accidentally holding Molly's hands, and a fresh cut came on one of her arms. She had above forty cuts on her arms, face and neck, with the blood dried on them and very sore. They looked very bad, and were all about the thickness of a shilling deep; the skin not jagged, but smooth, as if cut with a penknife.[2]

At a later stage in the history physical phenomena seem to have developed of quite extraordinary violence. There is nothing in the experiences of Indridi Indridason which can have involved a greater expenditure of energy than the following:—

I went again (19 Feb.) and found there Messrs.—. The children had been pulled out of bed several times, as it were by the neck, in their sight. The children lay on their back, and I saw very strong gentlemen hold each child under their arms as they lay on their back: they soon cried out they were pulled by the legs. Major D— held Molly with all his might, and put his knee against her bedstead, but cried he could not hold her, the force was so great that he

---

[1] A Narrative, etc., p. 32.
[2] A Narrative, etc., p. 27.

thought three hundredweight pulled against him. They were both pulled to the foot of the bed and the Major fell on the bed. The children then were pulled up again, and the Major for a *certain* experiment (for he did not believe that there was anything supernatural in the affair) tried again about ten times. I saw the children as often pulled to the bed's foot, and both the Major and the other gentlemen pulled after them, though they held them with all their strength, the children crying with pain. They felt hands pull them by their legs, and I saw black and blue marks on the small of their legs, as if hands had done it. I held Dobby myself under the arms, as she lay on her back, but I found my strength nothing to the force which pulled against me, and she was pulled to the bed's foot and then it stopped. This so confounded the Major that he could not help cursing it, and as we had observed, if anyone cursed or called it names, it was worse, and they suffered for it. The Major took a candle to look under the bed, to see if he could find out any trick, and he said he felt three or four fingers catch hold of his wrist and pinch him so hard that the prints were very visible and grew black next day, and were sore for some time. He was *now* very certain, no visible power did it, and was fully convinced that the whole was supernatural.[1]

Durbin left at midnight but the Major afterwards saw the children dragged about the room by the neck.

There are many other interesting details in this history which lack of space prevents my touching upon. Clergymen from the neighbourhood came and asked the spirit questions in Latin and Greek to which correct answers were returned, not in this case by raps, but by the repetition of a curious scratching noise. In spite of the vexations to which the children were subjected, a certain consideration, as has often been noticed in other poltergeist manifestations, was shown by the spook to prevent their sustaining serious injury to health. It was also remarked that the power developed in the dark was greater than that which was exhibited in daylight. No doubt many readers will be tempted to dismiss the whole narrative as a silly fiction, but I do not think that it can be quite so easily disposed of, even though there was an obvious tendency on the part of some of the principal actors in the drama to associate the phenomena with old witchcraft superstitions of a very debased type. The children, responding no doubt to the folk beliefs still widely prevalent in 1762, were inclined to romance about " a

[1] *A Narrative*, etc., p. 36.

woman dressed in a dirty chip hat with a torn ragged gown " and attributed to her a prominent part in the troubles which had befallen them. This is true and it ought to be taken into consideration, but it does not affect the substance of the narrative. On the whole I am distinctly disposed to believe that Mr. H. Durbin was a conscientious and truthful reporter of the phenomena he claims to have witnessed.

CHAPTER III

GHOSTS THAT TEASE [1]

URING the twenty or thirty years that I have taken an interest in poltergeist phenomena I have read or listened to many accounts of the disturbances commonly classified under this heading. As we have already seen, some of the manifestations appear to have been extremely violent and in particular there are a number of stories which recount how invisible hands caught the victim by the throat, tightening their grip until the very verge of strangulation was reached. The curious thing, however, is that these apparently homicidal attempts never actually result in the death of the person so assailed. Failing memory warns me to be cautious about general statements, but I cannot at the moment recall a single instance, barring perhaps the famous Amherst (Nova Scotia) mystery, in which the human subject in such a case has sustained any serious or permanent injury. The damage to property is often considerable. Windows are broken by flying stones until not a sound pane of glass is left in the house. Chairs and tables are rendered unserviceable; plates, dishes and china ornaments are shattered wholesale; wearing apparel is torn to shreds or disappears mysteriously just when the owner wants to use it; but, however unpleasant this form of horseplay may be to the parties concerned, life and limb are apparently always respected. No doubt it may be urged that if anyone were strangled by a poltergeist, he would not be in a position to explain to his family what it was that had happened to him. But there are such things as inquests, and the medical expert would probably be able to satisfy himself that the catastrophe was due to something more than heart failure. There would be a verdict of wilful murder against persons unknown, and a good deal of publicity would result. "Death by Poltergeist" is not a formula sanctioned by coroners, but it would make a good newspaper head-line, and if any suspicion of this sort were aroused the world could hardly fail to hear of it.

All this by way of introduction to a curious story which is almost

[1] *The Month,* September 1928

typical of the more innocuous variety of poltergeist phenomena. It is recounted by that earnest Catholic savant and politician, John Joseph von Görres, in his well-known work, *Die Christliche Mystik*.[1] Though Görres was uncritical in dealing with the events of past history, no one ever doubted his absolute sincerity. We may trust him for reproducing without exaggeration the terms of the documents he had before him, and he was too shrewd a judge of character and too widely conversant with men and affairs to be easily imposed upon by a mere charlatan. The details he publishes were derived from the written statement of an eye-witness, a certain H. J. Aschauer, a competent teacher of mathematical physics, who afterwards became professor of that subject at the Johanneum of Gratz. Görres describes him as a keen observer and as a man without bias, though it is not quite clear how far this estimate is derived from personal knowledge. In any case the affair produced a considerable sensation in the neighbourhood, resulting further in some sort of police inquiry and the drafting of a report. This report, a copy of which Görres apparently had before him, corroborated in all essential details the narrative of Aschauer, but it deprecated the exaggerated rumours and the superstition to which such alleged phenomena gave occasion. The official who drafted it recommended that a scientific investigation should take place and three professors of the Johanneum were accordingly nominated for the purpose. They, however, regarding this matter of spooks beneath their dignity, refused to act; with the usual result that, the manifestations having come to an end, what had been a nine days' wonder soon ceased to be spoken of and was then forgotten.

The incidents with which we are concerned took place at Münchhof, a village in Styria (Austria) about nine miles from Gratz. In October 1818 a house occupied by one Obergemeiner, who was a son-in-law of the above-mentioned H. J. Aschauer, was repeatedly struck by stones which broke some of the windows on the ground floor. As this happened only in the afternoon and evening, never after the house was closed for the night, Obergemeiner concluded that the trouble must be due to some trick of mischievous schoolboys who were playing pranks. He kept constant watch but could not succeed in detecting the culprits. In a few days, however, the case began to be further complicated by mysterious knockings which

---

[1] See *Die Christliche Mystik*, vol. III, pp. 361-368. Görres was the most distinguished of the Catholic political leaders at that period, and he was one of the founders of the *Historisch-politische Blätter,* which long remained an influential organ in Germany. The literary society which carried on the *Historisches Jahrbuch* and other undertakings, was named in his honour the " Görres Gesellschaft."

were heard both at the front and at the back doors of the building. What added to the puzzle was that the dog never barked as he would certainly have done if any stranger had approached the house.[1] Some members of the family began to be frightened and Obergemeiner determined to end this state of suspense. One day without giving previous notice to anyone he obtained the assistance of two or three dozen of the neighbouring peasantry and got them to form a cordon round the house, gradually closing in upon it and allowing no one to pass between them in either direction inwards or outwards. He himself, meanwhile, with a man named Koppbauer, after assembling all the members of the establishment in one room, searched every corner of the building from garret to cellar. No clue of any kind was discovered, but at the very time that this programme was being carried out stones began to strike the kitchen windows. Koppbauer, putting his head out of one of them, looked anxiously to discover from what direction these missiles came, when suddenly a big stone broke a pane of the very window out of which he was craning his neck. As he had seen nothing move within his field of view he was convinced that the stone must have come from inside and that it was a trick played upon him by one of the people in the room. He turned round furiously to protest, but Obergemeiner and the others assured him that they had had nothing to do with it. In point of fact it would seem that the stones *were* coming from inside, though no one present could tell how, and they continued to fly at intervals until half-past six in the evening, when the manifestation abruptly ceased.

Next morning the stone-throwing was resumed about eight o'clock, by which time a crowd of sixty people had gathered round the house. Further observation convinced the proprietor and his friends that the stones came from under the settle which ran along part of the wall on the same side of the room as the windows themselves. There was an accumulation there of " die sogenannten Sechsteine," fragments of a substance which seems to have been used like soda for washing purposes. Some of these " stones " were small, others weighed several pounds. The reason why the household did not discover earlier where the missiles came from was, no doubt, the apparent impossibility of any inanimate object moving in such a path. They flew out from under the settle and

---

[1] Other cases could be cited in which it was noted that the dogs were not disturbed by poltergeist manifestations. They neither barked nor showed any sign of alarm. This is mentioned, for example, in M. Perrault's account of the spook at Mâcon. On the other hand one meets with instances in which dogs, and even horses, seem to have been thrown into a frenzy of terror.

doubled back in a semi-circular course against the window, precisely as an imprisoned bird might have done.[1]

This, however, was only the beginning of disturbances of a much more violent character. Other windows of the house were broken, and in the kitchen on the ground floor, which seems throughout to have been the starting point of the manifestations, a perfect pandemonium began to be enacted. Spoons, dishes, saucepans, fire-irons and almost every moveable object were seen to fly about as if endowed with life. A good deal of damage resulted, but it was noticed with some surprise that no one present was seriously hurt, even when struck by a big " stone " which seemed to be deliberately aimed and to be travelling with great velocity. Many of the moving objects upon contact with a living person or with a resisting surface fell dead as if a hand had arrested them in their flight.[2] None the less almost every breakable thing in the kitchen was destroyed, and when attempts were made to rescue some of the crockery by removing it to a table in the hall, those who carried it declared that plates, etc., were snatched from their grasp and eventually shattered like the rest. On the table just mentioned a crucifix stood with two lighted candles beside it. The candlesticks were violently thrown down but the crucifix itself was not interfered with. The disturbance lasted only some two or three hours, but a curious detail is recorded of the mid-day repast of the family. Obergemeiner had before him an empty decanter with a ground-glass stopper. Suddenly the stopper jumped out of the neck of the decanter and fell upon the table. It was replaced, but twice subsequently went through the same performance, until they took the decanter and locked it up in a cupboard.

So far Aschauer had only heard a second-hand report of these occurrences; but towards the end of October fresh phenomena occurred, and Obergemeiner invited his father-in-law to come and see for himself. On his arrival at Münchhof he found the mistress of the house and Koppbauer alone in the kitchen picking up the fragments of a piece of earthenware which he had heard fall with a crash as he approached the door. As the three stood conversing at some distance from each other, a big iron spoon suddenly left the shelf on which it was lying and came straight at Koppbauer's

[1] Görres illustrates the curved path of the stones by a plan, which is not reproduced in the French translation of his work.

[2] " Menschen, die vom Werfen grosser Steine getroffen wurden, empfanden zu ihrer Verwunderung, trotz der grossen Wurfgeschwindigkeit, den Anschlag nur leicht, und auch an ihnen fiel der Körper dann senkrecht herunter." Görres, *Mystik*, III, 362.

head. Weighing about a pound[1] and travelling with great velocity it might have been expected to inflict a serious bruise, but the stricken man declared he felt only a light touch and the spoon dropped perpendicularly at his feet. Aschauer, as a student of physics, was keenly interested. He tried to investigate the electrical conditions, etc., but could find no natural explanation of such extraordinary movements. Nothing further however happened in his presence until the afternoon of the next day. On that occasion as he was standing at one end of the kitchen with nothing to intercept his view of a shelf opposite to him on which his gaze for the moment was resting, a big copper soup-tureen standing on the shelf flew off and whizzed past his head with such force that his hair was blown about by the draught it created. It crashed on to the floor but was not damaged. Several other people who were in the room at the time were like himself witnesses of what had happened. A few minutes later when a maid who had been rasping some loaves laid the loaves and the bread rasp upon a wooden tray, the tray proceeded to float gently across the room, grazing the surface of the big stove, after which it suddenly dropped on to the floor so that the tray rebounded and the bread was scattered about. Aschauer declares that he is prepared to vouch for all these facts upon his solemn oath and that it was absolutely impossible that anyone present could have had a hand in them.

Evening was now upon them and in view of previous experiences it was deemed safer to evacuate the kitchen. They left it bare except for three objects which it seemed to them could come to no harm—a " Nudeldurchschlag " (which I imagine to be a sort of metal colander), a heavy wooden bucket and an iron saucepan full of water which had its place beside the stove. Four people remained behind to watch developments, but nothing happened, and they were on the point of retiring early to bed when the colander, standing near the wall, was suddenly flung horizontally into the middle of the group. Ten minutes after, the bucket, which had been left upon the floor, fell perpendicularly from the ceiling without their having the least idea how it got there, for there was nothing whatever to support it. It fell amongst them without doing any injury, but the slightest deviation to right or to left could hardly have failed to have serious consequences for one or other of the party. Finally the saucepan gently tilted up and discharged all its contents on to the floor. It was, they said—and, as they were

---

[1] Görres says " three-quarters of a pound," but the Austrian pound at that date was notably heavier than the English.

then seated in a semi-circle, each one holding a candle, they could
see plainly that no one was touching it—just as if a careful dairy-
maid was very deliberately emptying one of her milkpails.

It may readily be admitted that this would not be a very convincing record if it stood by itself. The police report would seem
to afford some corroboration, but we have not the text of that
report before us. Though Görres speaks very positively of
Aschauer's sound judgment and scientific competence, the latter
was not an eye-witness of all that occurred, and an interval of
fourteen months had elapsed before he wrote down the statement
which has just been summarised. The real strength of the case for
the genuineness of poltergeist phenomena lies in the confirmation
afforded by a multitude of similar examples often well attested and
of quite modern date. Let me take, by way of illustration, the
case of the Austrian maid-servant, " Hannie." She visited London
in 1922 and was apparently accompanied by her "Kobold" who
even in this country did not desist from his embarrassing attentions.
We first hear of Hannie in November, 1921, when she was employed
in an inn at Lieserbrücke (Carinthia) and was fifteen years of age.
A local newspaper, the *Karntner Tageblatt* for 15 February, 1922,
devoted an article to the extraordinary things which had been
taking place in the vicinity of this girl. Terrifying noises were
heard, horses reared, bells rang without any ascertainable cause
and even windmills were said to have been set in motion. What
was more definite, the reporter, who had investigated the matter
on the spot, states that:—

Towards the end of December the phenomena seemed to gather
round smaller articles and became destructive in tendency. Domestic utensils were the objects of attack. Glasses, cups and bottles
were thrown about, beer casks were sent rolling; wood, potatoes
and ropes were treated as if they were feather balls. The enamel
was scraped from a pot, panes of glass and lamps were broken.
An attempt to fix it with a chain did not prevent it being moved.

The innkeeper hoped that the disturbances would cease as
quickly as they had arisen, but the damage grew to such an alarming
extent, that he could not keep the girl Hannie any longer. She
was discharged and from that day the haunting of Lieserbrücke
ceased.

Naval Commander Kogelnik, a gentleman who with his wife is

much interested in psychic research, heard of the case, and decided to take the girl into his own service, though he was by no means blind to the risk he was running. He issued what seems a temperate and trustworthy report of his experiences, a report which is at least indirectly confirmed by the testimony of other witnesses to the phenomena which subsequently occurred in London. To give a résumé of his whole statement would be impossible here, but a few specimens may be quoted. Commander Kogelnik's wife reported to him that during a short absence of his she had herself witnessed the movement of various objects in the kitchen whilst the girls were engaged upon their work. He goes on to state that on the same day, 6 May, 1922:—

About 5 p.m. I chanced to be in the kitchen giving some orders to Hannie, and even as I was speaking to her, I heard something fall to the floor, and saw that a small iron box which was kept on a shelf was lying beneath my feet. I cannot say that I had observed this box to be standing in its ordinary place when I entered the kitchen, and consequently I did not see how it was seized and thrown. I only heard the noise and then observed the box lying on the ground. But I can vouch for the fact that Hannie was not moving either hand at the time, and I was looking at her whilst I spoke to her. The cook was not in the kitchen with us. Neither did I on any subsequent occasion see how things were thrown, because the phenomena always happened at unexpected moments, and I have never yet outwitted the mysterious agent, though I have done my best to that end, and have never relinquished my attitude of suspicion for a moment. I finally received the impression that my thoughts were in some way guessed beforehand and that a superior intelligence was at work in the production of the phenomena and was able to make a fool of me.

This inability to notice the initial stages of poltergeist phenomena frequently recurs in the accounts preserved to us. The reader will remember the incident of the bucket falling from the ceiling which has been recounted above. In the case of flying stones many observers speak as if these missiles could never be perceived until they were less than a yard off. It would almost seem as if the agency at work, whatever its nature may be, possessed the power of rendering them invisible, just as there is much evidence which suggests that the same agency is able to introduce material objects into a room through closed doors. I am not affirming this, of course, and still less do I wish to touch upon the philosophical and theological problems involved. I am only saying that apparently reliable witnesses speak in such terms that one can only vaguely conceive, in accord with old-fashioned views of the impenetrability of matter, that certain objects may have been dematerialised and then built up again by the spiritual forces concerned. However, to return to the servant Hannie, Commander Kogelnik, after replacing the iron box in its accustomed position asked the poltergeist to repeat the performance so that he could see how it was done.

I waited for five minutes—for ten minutes—life has taught me patience; and suddenly a smart " bang " and the fragments of a porcelain cup were on the kitchen floor! This cup was kept on the same shelf as the iron box. Who could have thrown it ? Not Hannie, for she was seated at the window under my eye, at no more than four yards distance. Or myself ? I must ask this preposterous question, for there was no one else in the room. Between 5 and 6 p.m. on 6 May it would hardly be dark, and there were no shutters to the large window. So I must suppose an Invisible Third.

It was natural enough that Hannie's fellow servant, the cook, should not take kindly to the poltergeist who not only broke things but interfered with her special work. For example, " a ladle and a spoon which the cook had laid on the upper part of the stove were thrown into pots standing on the hearth, and these throws were made with precise aim, and never failed of the target. So both ladle and spoon went straight into the sauce." Again a noise of moving furniture was heard in the servants' bedroom at night, and the cook came to Mrs. Kogelnik to complain that " after she and Hannie had gone to sleep she was awakened by certain movements, and that when fully awake she saw, with the greatest horror, that her bed was slowly sliding hither and thither about the room, Hannie being all the time sound asleep." It will be remembered that the late Sir William Barrett, in his paper in the proceedings of the Society for Psychical Research " recounts how at Derrygonnelly he saw " a large pebble drop apparently from space in a room where the only culprit could have been myself, and certainly I did not throw it," and how at Enniscorthy, in 1910, a heavy bedstead lacking one castor, with young men sleeping in it, was dragged right across the floor.[1]

[1] *Proceedings S.P.R.*, vol. XXV, pp. 370-389.

At the Kogelniks, in 1922, after many stories of things broken, or disappearing when they were wanted, we have a solitary instance of a more friendly attitude on the part of their tormentor. The Commander reports:—

The same afternoon, our teabox lid was missing, and on discovering the loss I said: " Now wouldn't you be kind enough for once to bring back what you have taken away? " After some minutes the said lid came rolling in from the hall! At this time there were with me in the kitchen both the cook and Hannie, and I had both under observation.

All the same, the spirit's general attitude was distinctly vindictive. The following was the most striking manifestation of the kind:—

The cook's resentment had been increasing, and towards evening she could no longer refrain from cursing the thing. But the grievous words had hardly escaped her lips when a sharp hissing sound was heard in the air, followed by the frightened cry of the girl, who fled with both hands to her head. Though present, we heard nothing fall, and though we thoroughly inspected the kitchen and the rooms adjoining it, we discovered no object which could have been thrown. It must have been heavy and sharp, for we found her head swelled in one place, and a small cut in another which was bleeding. This was the end of our cook's occult experiences, for she straightway left the house, minus her overcoat, two pairs of stockings and one pair of boots—all discovered some days later in different parts of the house.

A particularly objectionable trick of this poltergeist was his spiriting away of keys as well as of much-needed articles of wearing apparel. On one occasion when the cellar key had disappeared, the wood and coal which were kept there became inaccessible and cook had to go out of doors to obtain some. " She went to her room for another pair of boots, and we saw the key of that apartment flying away before our eyes, too quickly for pursuit. The cook's attempts to find it, as she eventually did, involved a further disappointment, for as she opened her room, she found her boots gone!" This game of hide-and-seek seems to have affected all the members of the household as the following incident will show. Commander Kogelnik reports:—

I must now relate that for a fortnight I had been unable to find an inkstand, which always stood on my desk. All search for it had been in vain . . . Whilst my wife was up under the roof, and Hannie close by her was engaged in cleaning and sweeping, suddenly there was a whistling sound from the further end of the large space where no one had been standing. Then came a crash, and the inkstand fell at my wife's feet, shivered to fragments, the ink it had contained running about over the floor. Shortly afterwards, pieces of coal were thrown, and as my wife and Hannie were not daunted, but continued their sweeping, an old, unused flower-pot came hurtling through the air from a corner in which it had long rested, the earth with which it had been filled being sprinkled over the newly-swept part of the floor. After this the work of cleaning was stopped, and as my wife saw an axe suddenly disappearing before her eyes, she quitted the room. All this had happened between ten and twelve noon, and the light was good for exact observation.[1]

A more friendly poltergeist was that at the Lutheran parsonage at Gröben in 1718 of which a very full account has been left us by the Pastor Jeremias Heinisch.[2] For a long time, though showers of stones were rained upon the roof of a cowshed, and though other mischievous tricks were played, no damage was done to property. Even when the stones were directed at the house and began to break windows, consideration was shown to prevent the inmates and curious observers from being injured by these missiles. If a group of people were standing near the window assailed, then, the pastor tells us, the stones, after breaking through the panes, fell perpendicularly to the ground close to the wall as if they were spent and some force checked them ("wie ermüdet und zurück-gehalten"). If the observers moved far back near the opposite wall, then the stones would penetrate right into the middle of the room. There were also stones flying in the contrary direction from inside the room into the open air. When a group of curious visitors stood looking on in the courtyard outside, the stones always fell short of them, never amongst them. It may be noted, too, that in this case, more than two centuries old, the worthy pastor, Heinisch, writing

---

[1] See Commander Kogelnik's article in *Psychic Science*, vol. I (1922), pp. 272-287, and in the same journal for January, 1923, an account of the phenomena subsequently observed in London.

[2] " Das Zeugniss der reinen Wahrheit von den Sonder- und wunderbahren Wurkungen einer insgemein sogenenannten *Kobolds* oder unsichtbaren Wesens in den Pfarr-Wohnung zu Gröben . . . abgestattet von der Orts Predigern Jeremias Heinisch," Jena, 1723.

mainly for the benefit of his ecclesiastical superiors, comments on the curved path of many of the missiles, which sailed round corners in a semi-circle contrary to the laws of motion, a course, as he phrases it, " welcher nach der Ordnung eines natürlichen Wurffs unmöglich bleibt." During the time that these disturbances at Gröben were at their height the pastor's wife was confined, and her babe was baptised the same day in defiance of the presumably evil agencies at work. But the spirit showed a certain consideration and for three days after this event the family were left in peace. Similarly on one occasion a large stone seemed to be falling perpendicularly and with great velocity right on the minister's head. One of the maids who was looking on shrieked in terror, but the stone turned aside in full career, though at the cost of a pane of glass through which it passed into the court outside.

One final illustration may be cited from the report printed by the Society for Psychical Research[1], concerning an abnormally gentle poltergeist at Durweston, on the estate of Lord Portman, in 1894. The following forms part of a statement made by Newman, one of his gamekeepers.

On Tuesday (18 December, 1894) between 10 and 11 a.m. Mrs. Best sent for me and told me that Annie (the elder girl, about 13 years of age) had seen a boot come out of the garden plot and strike the back door, leaving a muddy mark. I went into Mrs. Best's, and I saw a bead strike the window; and then soon after a big blue bead struck the window and broke it, and fell back. Then a little toy whistle struck the window, but did not break it. Then I sat down . . . and was looking at the door opening into the garden; it was wide open leaving a space of 15 inches between it and the inner wall, when I saw, coming from behind the door, a quantity of little shells. They came round the door from a height of about five feet. They came one at a time, at intervals varying from half-a-minute to a minute. They came very slowly and when they hit me I could hardly feel them. With the shells came two thimbles. They came so slowly that in the ordinary way they would have dropped long before they reached me. They came from a point, some, I think, a trifle higher, and some no higher than my head. Both the thimbles struck my hat. Some missed my head and went just past, and fell down slanting-wise (NOT as if suddenly dropped). Those that struck me fell straight down. The two children were all the time in the same room with me.

[1] *Proceedings*, vol. XII (1897), p. 91.

There were other similar phenomena, and among other things an old boot, before the eyes of the witness, came sailing in horizontally a foot above the ground through the door; Mrs. Best threw it out.   But for the final incident I will quote the condensed statement and comment of the late Mr. Andrew Lang:—

Newman went and put his foot on the boot and said, " I defy anything to move this boot."   But his story goes on thus: "Just as I stepped off, it rose up behind me and knocked my hat off. There was nobody behind me."   Gamekeepers are acute observers, and if the narrative be untrue, malobservation or defect of memory does not explain the fact.   In this case at Durweston, the Rector, Mr. Anderson, gave an account of some of the phenomena.   He could not explain them and gave the best character to (Mrs. Best) the Nonconformist mother of the child with whom the events were associated.   No trickery was discovered.[1]

In the absence of cross-examination and of any great mass of corroborative testimony, it can hardly be pretenced that any of the incidents above recounted, can be regarded, taken singly, as conclusively proved.   The curious fact is that in these and in scores of other cases, some of them centuries old, the same type of phenomena should be recorded by simple and apparently honest people who had no knowledge of psychic literature and who believed their own particular experiences to be unique.

---

[1] *Encyclopaedia Britannica* (1911) XXII, p. 15.   This article by Mr. Andrew Lang may still be recommended as the best brief statement of the poltergeist problem at present available.   It has unfortunately been suppressed in later editions.

CHAPTER IV

A POLTERGEIST AMONG THE HUGUENOTS [1]

IN the majority of the cases of disturbance with which we are here concerned no attempt appears to be made by the spook to open communication with the victims whom he plagues. But there are also a number of exceptions to this rule. Occasionally, as in the Phelps household, written messages are found left on scraps of paper; at other times threats are chalked up on the walls. A very notable instance of the latter procedure will meet us in the account of the hauntings which made Mr. Pillay's life a burden to him at Nidamangalam in Southern India. Sometimes again the tormentor, though without showing himself, speaks at considerable length in a voice audible to all present. Perhaps the most remarkable instance of this kind which I have come across is that of the " devil of Mascon " whose antics I propose to describe in the present chapter.

Not least distinguished among the eminent men born on Irish soil in the seventeenth century was the Hon. Robert Boyle, the youngest son of Richard, first Earl of Cork. As one of the founders of the Royal Society, as the discoverer of that working hypothesis regarding the pressure of gaseous bodies which among writers of English speech is most commonly known as Boyle's Law, and as a man of genuinely scientific temper, he deserved in large measure the prodigious reputation he enjoyed with his contemporaries. While wholly wedded to the cause of Protestantism, he seems to have been a sincere Christian, abstemious, charitable, and conscientiously devoted to the furtherance of biblical studies. In the course of his early wanderings on the Continent he was at two different periods resident in Geneva, in which Calvinistic atmosphere he spent close on four years. It was probably on the second of these occasions (1642 to 1644) that he came in contact with a Huguenot minister, one Francis Perrault. The date is of some interest; for Perrault presented him with a copy of his poltergeist narrative, and

[1] *Studies*, June 1928

Boyle was so impressed with it that he persuaded Dr. Peter Du Moulin to translate it into English.[1] The tractate must therefore have been completed at least as early as 1644, though the French original was not printed at Geneva until nine years later. This lends confirmation to Du Moulin's definite statement (made in his preface to the English translation) that the account was drawn up shortly after the events it records. It was certainly not a story concocted by an old man in his dotage regarding an experience which had happened to him forty years earlier. In view of the references made by Perrault himself to certain sermons of a famous Capuchin, Father Marcellin, and to other documents, there can be little doubt that the incidents of this diabolical visitation, as it was then judged to be, were widely discussed in Burgundy and Savoy at the time when they occurred. In a letter to Du Moulin, Robert Boyle himself says:—

I must freely confess to you that the powerful inclinations which my course of life and studies hath given me to backwardness of assent, and the many fictions and superstitions, which (as far as I have hitherto observed) are wont to blemish the relations where spirits and witches are concerned, would make me very backward to contribute anything to your publishing, or any man's believing, a story less strange than this of Monsieur Perrault.

But the conversation I had with the pious author during my stay at Geneva, and the present he was pleased to make me of this treatise before it was printed, in a place where I had the opportunity to inquire both after the writer, and after some passages of the book, did at length overcome in me (as to this narrative) all my settled indisposedness to believe strange things.

We further learn from the same letter that " that great scholar and excellent person," Dr. Peter Du Moulin's father, had a very high opinion of François Perrault, and Boyle considers that this commendation will go far " to make wary readers believe even the amazing passages " of the narrative thus introduced to them.

---

[1] The title of the little book runs as follows: " The devill of Mascon, or a true Relation of the chiefe things which an Uncleane Spirit did and said at Mascon in Burgundy, in the house of Mr. Francis Perreaud, Minister of the Reformed Church in the same Towne; Published in French lately by himselfe, and now made English by one that hath a particular knowledge of the truth of this story. Oxford, Printed by Hen. Hall, printer to the University, for Rich. Davis, 1658." The French original is entitled *L'Antidemon de Mascon*, etc., *en la maison du Sieur F. Perreaud*, Genève, 1653; the modern annotated edition was edited by Philibert Le Duc, Bourg en Bresse, 1853.

With regard to the Huguenot minister whose experiences are recounted, both internal and external evidence present him in a very favourable light.   His descendants in course of time reverted to Catholicism, and one of them, who in 1853 was partly responsible for an annotated edition of what had become a very scarce booklet, is able to supply much documentary evidence of the esteem in which his ancestor was held.   The Perraults were of ancient lineage, and were already landed proprietors in the fourteenth century. The grandfather of François had fallen under the personal influence of Calvin, but the younger generation, though still Huguenots, seem to have laid aside much of the fanaticism which was characteristic of the Genevan reformer.   Be this as it may, it is in the following terms that the evangelical minister, François Perrault, begins his narrative.   I quote Du Moulin's translation, modernising the spelling:—

The 14th day of September in the year 1612, I went with one of the Elders of the Church of Mâcon to the meeting held at the Borough of Couches, and five days afterwards we returned.   Being come home, I found my wife and her maid in very great consternation, apparent in their face and countenance, and when I inquired the cause of that great alteration, my wife told me that the night after I went out of town, she being in bed, her first sleep was broken by something, she knew not what, that drew her curtains with great noise and violence.   That her maid that lay in another bed in the same room, hearing that, arose in haste and ran to her to see what it was, but saw nothing; yea, that she found the doors and windows of that room very close as she had shut them before she went to bed. My wife told me also that the night following she made the maid lie with her by reason of that accident; that as soon as they were in bed they felt something that pulled off their blankets; that then the maid, getting out of bed, went from that room, which is on the back side of the house, but that she found the door bolted, not within only, as she had bolted it herself, but without also, which before she could perceive, after she had unbolted the door and would open it, she felt resistance, as if a man had been on the other side thrusting against her; that the maid finding herself shut up, called a youth that lay in another room on the foreside of the house, who rose to open her the door, to whom she would say nothing of that disorder lest he should be frighted, but lighting the candle, she found in the kitchen the pewter and brass thrown about, wherewith the same night and the following nights the evil spirit made such a noise as they use to make when they give a *charivary*[1] or when they will hive bees.

M. Perrault protests that he found it extremely difficult to credit this story. He thought that some malicious person or practical joker must have secreted himself to play pranks upon two timid women. Accordingly, before retiring to rest himself on the night of his return, he searched every corner and saw to the fastening of every door and window, " stopping even the very cat-holes of the doors " (*jusques à boucher les chattières qui estoyent aux portes*). He seems, however, to have gone to bed early and left his wife and her maid " spinning by the fire, with a lamp upon the table." But he had not long to wait before events developed, for, to quote once more from the seventeenth century translation, which I have compared with the French original:—

Scarce was I in my bed, but I heard a great noise from the kitchen, like the rolling of a billet thrown with great strength. I heard also a knocking against a partition of wainscot in the same kitchen, sometimes as with the point of the finger, sometimes as with the nails, sometimes as with the fist, and then the blows did redouble. Many things also were thrown against that wainscot, as plates, trenchers and ladles, and a music was made with a brass cullender, jingling with some buckles that were at it, and with some other instruments of the kitchen. After I had given attentive ear to that noise, I rose from my bed, and taking my sword, I went into the room where all that stir was kept, the maid holding the candle before me, and did search narrowly whether I could find somebody hidden, but finding nothing, I returned to my bed. The noise beginning again, I rose again and searched again, but all in vain. Then did I begin to know indeed that all this could not proceed but from a wicket spirit, and so did I pass the rest of the night in such an astonishment as any man may imagine.

Early the next morning M. Perrault made a report of what had happened to the Elders of his Church, and he also gave an account to M. Francois Tornus, a royal notary and a procurator of Mâcon, " although he was a Roman Catholic and very zealous of his religion." The result was that a number of these gentlemen came that night to see for themselves, but nothing happened. I think we

---

[1] " A *Charivary* is a mad kind of serenade music of pans and kettles (might we say 'jazz'?) given to old widows when they marry."—Note of Dr. P. Du Moulin.

may infer that the Huguenot minister's word was trusted, for in spite of a succession of disappointments the same friends continued to visit him on several subsequent evenings.

In the end, upon the 20th of September, about 9 o'clock, the wicked spirit made himself openly known for such as he was. For in the presence of us all, Mr. Tornus being one of the company, he began to whistle three or four times with a very loud and shrill tone, and presently to frame an articulate and intelligible voice, though somewhat hoarse, which seemed to be about three or four steps from us. He pronounced these first words singing *Vingt et deux deniers*, a little tune of five notes which whistling birds are taught to sing.[1] After that he said and repeated many times the word " Minister," " Minister." Because that voice was very terrible to us at the first, I was long before I would answer anything to that word, but only " Get thee from me Satan, the Lord rebuke thee."

It is curious that in the accounts that are given of " direct-voice " séances at the present day it frequently happens that new communicators are said to be indistinct or hoarse in their first attempts to make themselves understood. As the sittings are continued, and more especially with the same group of intimates, the voices gain greatly in strength and distinctness. M. Perrault's experience at Mâcon three hundred years ago seems to have been in every way similar, for he goes on to tell us of what were evidently long and bantering conversations between the spirit and the visitors who night after night assembled at his house. But the Mâcon communicator made little or no attempt to disguise the fact that he was amusing himself at their expense, and though sometimes he told them things which were true and which they were afterwards able to confirm, he did not scruple to make all sorts of ridiculous pretence which they were evidently very far from crediting. For example:—

Then he (the spirit) did offer to transform himself into an angel of light, saying of his own accord and very loud, the Lord's prayer, the Creed, the morning and evening prayers and the ten commandments. It is true that he did always clip and leave out some part of it . . . Then he said many things which might be true, as some

[1] This seems to be a French equivalent of " Pop goes the weasel," which is often nowadays used in this country for a similar purpose.

particular passages belonging to my family, as among other things that my father had been poisoned, naming the man that did it, and why, and specifying the place and the manner of the poison.

There were a number of other mischievous stories of the same kind about wives who had murdered their husbands, unfriendly neighbours who kept intending visitors away, and so on. It would be useless to go into details here. The astonishing fact is that for two months or more a group of townspeople seems to have gathered together almost every evening to converse and exchange badinage with this denizen of another world, who never showed himself to their bodily eyes, but whose voice was audible to all. It may be remembered that the conditions described closely reproduce those recorded by Giraldus Cambrensis in the case of the Pembrokeshire goblin four centuries earlier. If anyone were disposed to conjecture that some member of the company was practising ventriloquism, this solution seems barred by the fact that the spirit did on many occasions manifest a knowledge of past and distant things which could not naturally be known to any of them. Moreover, the physical phenomena, which were numerous and which continued to the end, still remain unaccounted for. M. Perrault is quite precise in the description he gives of many of the tricks performed by the alleged demon. Thus he remarks :

As his words were strange and admirable, so were his actions; for besides those which I have related, done in my absence, he did many more of the same kind, as tossing about very often a great roll of cloth of fifty ells which a friend had left at my house to be sent to Lyons by water. Once he snatched a brass candlestick out of the maid's grasp, leaving the candle lighted in her hand . . .

One afternoon a friend of mine, one M. Connain, a physician of Mâcon, bestowed a visit upon me. As I was relating to him these strange passages,[1] we went together to the chamber where the demon was most resident. There we found the feather-bed, blankets, sheets and bolster laid all upon the floor. I called the maid to make the bed, which she did in our presence, but presently, we being walking in the same room, saw the bed undone and tumbled down on the floor, as it was before . . . Sometimes he would be the groom of my stables, rubbing my horse and plaiting the hair of his tail and mane, but he was an unruly groom, for once I found

---

[1] As often in Shakespeare, the word " passages " is used by Du Moulin in the sense of experiences, incidents.

that he had saddled my horse with the crupper before and the pommel behind.

There can be little doubt that the medium in this case was no other than the maid to whom M. Perrault so often refers. Her remarkable courage in going before him with a candle on the occasion when he first had personal experience of these disturbances seems to suggest that she was not unused to such happenings. She was a girl from the neighbouring province of Bresse, a name then given to what is now the department of Ain, and she spoke only the Bressan patois. Her master himself tells us that many of his friends " attributed the coming of that demon " to her presence in the house, for she was the daughter of parents who had been suspected of witchcraft, and she was believed by some to be a witch herself. In accordance with this view, M. Perrault mentions one or two facts which seemed to him to suggest that the maid was very much at her ease with the cause of all the uproar. The spirit delighted in chaffing her, " *l'appelant à tout propos Bressande*," calling her his Bressan girl and " mimicking her patois."

The truth is (the Minister goes on) that she would jest and be familiar with him. For besides what I have mentioned before,[1] she once expostulated with him that he brought her no wood, whereupon he presently threw down a faggot for her at the stairfoot; and whereas, upon her offering to leave our service, another came to serve us in her place and lay in the same bed with her, the demon who never hurt her (the Bressande) used to beat that new maid in the bed and to pour water upon her, until he forced her to go away.

The climax of the physical phenomena is recounted as follows:—

His last actions at my house were the most troublesome of all, as they say that the devil is always more violent at the end than in the beginning, and is then most fierce when he must be gone. He threw stones about my house continually the ten or twelve last days from morning to evening, and in great quantity, some of them of two or three pounds weight.

One of those last days Mr. Tornus, coming to my house about noon, would know whether the devil was there still, and whistled

---

[1] Perrault says elsewhere: " He would throw our shoes about the room, those of the maid especially who, feeling him once taking one of shoes, laid hold presently of the other, and said smiling, ' this thou shalt not have.' "

in several tones, and each time the devil whistled to him in the same tone.[1]   Then the devil threw a stone at him, which being fallen at his feet without any harm to him, he took it up and marked it with a coal, and flung it into the back yard of the house, which is near the town wall and the river Saone, but the devil threw it up to him again; and that it was the same stone he knew, by the mark of the coal.   Tornus taking up that stone found it very hot, and said he believed it had been in hell since he had handled it first.

I may confess that I have conceived a very good opinion of M. Perrault's truthfulness and sobriety of judgment, and it seems worth while to point out that the statement regarding the heat of the stone comes to us only on the authority of the notary Tornus and not on that of the Minister.   Similarly, it should be noticed that Perrault is not personally responsible for the story that *the day after* the demon took his departure " a very great viper was seen going out of my house, and was taken with long pincers by some nail-makers, our neighbours, who carried it all over the town, crying " here is the devil that came out of the Minister's house."   Apparently such a snake was caught, and eventually left with an apothecary in the neighbourhood, but Perrault tells us no more than that it was found to be " a true and natural viper, a serpent rare in that country." After all the talk that had been going on regarding the diabolical manifestations in the home of the Huguenot, the tendency amid a superstitious and not too friendly population would undoubtedly be to connect any such unusual incident with the visitation of the evil spirit.   It must be remembered that this was a period when the witch mania was at its height.   Almost any unusual manifestation was liable to be construed as a presumption of sorcery.   We shall probably, then, be justified in regarding it as a high tribute to M. Perrault's reputation that not only the procurator Tornus père, but M. Fovillard, the Lieutenant-General, and Monseigneur Gaspard Divet, then Bishop of Mâcon, seem all to have taken his side against the misrepresentations of the Capuchin, Father Marcellin.   The Bishop, he tells us, sent his secretary, M. Chambre, " to learn the particulars of these passages from mine own mouth, to whom I related all without concealing or disguising anything." Perrault was afterwards informed, both by Tornus and Chambre, that the Bishop had been much impressed by the story, and had had a record of the facts drawn up in writing.   Undoubtedly the

---

[1] This seems to dispose of the ventriloquism hypothesis, unless indeed M. Tornus, the Catholic, was himself the ventriloquist.

Minister was no fanatic, and, though he himself had written a book on demonology, he was far from sharing the extravagant prejudices of his age. As his modern Catholic editor, M. Le Duc, points out, he has left on record his congratulations addressed to the magistrates of Berne upon a decree which they had recently issued safeguarding the citizens of that town against frivolous accusations of witchcraft. He also manifests a spirit of sincere gratitude to God for the protection afforded, as he believed, by Divine favour, during the time of his own visitation.

All the time (he writes) that the demon haunted my house God permitted him not to do us any harm, neither in our persons nor in our goods. Those bells which he did so toss and carry about, he hanged at a nail over the chimney of the room where he was most conversant the day that he left the house. He had not so much power given him as to tear one leaf of my books, or to break one glass, or to put out the candle which we kept lighted all the night long. Wherefore I bow my knees, and will, as long as I live, unto my gracious God, to give Him thanks for that great mercy.

Here again we have a feature which is in curiously exact accord with Giraldus's previously quoted description of the Pembrokeshire poltergeist in 1184. The spirits, says Cambrensis, who threw things about " meant to deride rather than to do bodily injury " (*quibus illudere potius quam lædere videntur*). At the same time M. Perrault and his Huguenot friends seem none of them to have had the least doubt that their unseen visitor was in truth a myrmidon of Satan, though this did not prevent them from exchanging the liveliest badinage with him whenever the opportunity presented itself. The " demon," on his side, seemed equally to delight in such encounters, and he loved in particular to banter one Michael Repay, a young man who came to the house almost every night with his father, when the ghost used to greet him playfully, shouting " Michael, Michael," and reminding him of ludicrous misadventures which had lately happened to him.

He put him in mind that the Sunday before, going to church with one Noel Monginot, to the village of Vrigny, he was saying that the way to catch the devil was to spread a net for him, and then he told him, " Wilt thou now spread thy net to catch me ? " At the same time he did so lively counterfeit the voice of Michael Repay's mother that the lad said laughingly to his father, " Father, truly he speaks just like my mother."

This counterfeiting of voices is another curious detail the bearing of which upon the phenomena of modern Spiritualism is full of significance. Mr. H. Dennis Bradley and Sir A. C. Doyle were convinced that they really were in communication with their departed friends, because they recognised their voices and the mannerisms peculiar to them in life. But it is plain that, if any credence is to be given to the record with which we are here concerned, there may be excellent mimics—whether diabolical or not I do not pretend to say—upon the other side, who find a quite particular amusement in mystifying the curious and in pretending to be what they are not. There were times, we are told, at Mâcon, when the spirit openly " mocked God and religion," and the strongest impression left by Perrault's narrative is that all the communications made were pervaded by some bantering purpose. For example, we read:—

He then desired us with great earnestness that we should send for M. Duchassin, the popish parson of St. Stephen's parish, to whom he would confess himself, and that he should not fail to bring holy water along with him for that, said he, could send me away packing presently.

It is perhaps worth noticing that the word " popish " does not occur in Perrault's original. He simply speaks of the " Sieur Duchassin, Curé de la paroisse dite Sainte Etienne "; and throughout his narrative there is hardly one unfriendly or disparaging word used of his Catholic fellow-countrymen. As for the mocking and deceptive character of the spirit, the following passage will perhaps illustrate it as clearly as any other:—

A while after, he counterfeited that he was not the same spirit that had spoken before, but his servant only. That he came from waiting on his master, who had charged him to keep his place in his absence while he was on his journey to Chambéry. And when I rebuked him in such words as God put into my mouth, he answered with much seeming lenity and respect: " I beseech you, sir, to pardon me. You are mistaken in me; you take me for another. I never was in this house before. I pray, sir, what is your name ? " As he was thus speaking, one Simeon Meissonier, that used to resort often to my house upon that occasion, rushed suddenly to the place whence the voice seemed to come, and having searched it again and again, as others had done before him, and found nothing, he returned to the place where we all were, bringing with him several things from the place where the voice sounded, among other things, a small bottle. At which the demon fell a-laughing, and said to him: " I was told long ago that thou wert a fool, and I see now that thou art one indeed, to believe that I am in that bottle. I should be a fool myself to get into it, for one might take me by stopping the bottle with his finger."

The late Mr. H. Dennis Bradley was persuaded that " direct-voice " communications from space were hardly known before the period of his own sittings in 1923 with the American medium Valiantine, and he consequently congratulated himself upon this experience of his as " the deepest probing into the secret problem of life that has ever been made."[1] It seems a little difficult in the face of the Mâcon record and a number of other similar narratives to justify this claim to pioneer exploration. The Mâcon spirit seems never to have grown weary in his mimetic performances, " counterfeiting the voice of jugglers and mountebanks, and especially those of huntsmen crying aloud ' ho lévrier! ho lévrier! ' as hunters use when they start a hare." So again we are told of him:—

Another time he informed us in a faint and moaning tone that he had a mind to make his will, because he must needs go presently to Chambéry, where he had a law suit ready for the trial, and that he feared to die by the way; wherefore, he bade the maid go for a notary, naming M. Tornus, father to that Tornus of whom we spoke before. Of his family he said many particularities, of which, as also of all the passages of this demon acted in his presence, the said Tornus, the son, a royal notary like his father, hath left a relation, written and signed with his own hand, which I have in my keeping for confirmation of all that is here related. And it was to have such authenticated testimony that I addressed myself to him when this vexation came upon me.

That the intelligence which was responsible for all these manifestations was certainly not a spirit of light seems to be clear not only from his many unblushing deceptions, but also from the fact that " he sang profane and bawdy songs, amongst others that which is

[1] Bradley, *The Wisdom of the Gods*, p. 68, and cf. pp. 197, 231, etc.

called '*Le Filou*'."[1] On some occasions the intruder seemed quite untroubled when he was called a demon, and even jested about it, as we have seen, but at other times he manifested great anger. When M. Perrault addressed him once in the words of the Gospel, " Depart, thou cursed, into everlasting fire," the spirit replied: " Thou liest; I am not cursed; I hope yet for salvation by the death and passion of Jesus Christ." Perrault conjectures that he said this to make us believe " that he was the soul of a woman deceased a little before in that house "; and in fact it seems possible that, as is assumed to be the case in modern mediumistic seances, there was not a single communicator, but several, who all acted as " controls " of the Bressande girl. On this particular occasion, however, the spirit after indignantly denying that he was accursed,

went on (says M. Perrault) to tell me in great wrath that he would do this and that to me. Among other things, he said that when I should be in bed he would come and pull off my blankets, and pull me out of bed by the feet.

Now there can be no possible question that this was all in print in a rare little booklet nearly three centuries ago, and yet this is exactly the phenomenon which, as the reader will remember, is declared by such sober authorities as Sir William Barrett and the Rev. Professor Nielsson to have occurred in our own day under the eyes of unexceptionable witnesses. It is all very puzzling, and I am far from pretending to be able to supply any satisfactory, solution of the mystery. But in view of the character of M. Perrault of the contemporary observers, of Robert Boyle, etc., and more particularly when we recall the multitude of more or less similar relations which come to us from every part of the world and every period of history, an obstinate scepticism as to the facts seems to me the most desperate expedient of all.

But let us turn now to a curious medieval story in which the spook, though not presenting the phenomena of the racketing type of poltergeist, caused a good deal of disturbance, and while remaining invisible, conversed freely with a crowd of bystanders.

---

[1] I have never heard of this ditty, but the minister presumably knew what he was talking about.

CHAPTER V

THE GHOST OF GUY [1]

SPEAKING generally, it must be admitted that the modern ghost, and especially the type that frequents old country houses, is rather a tame sort of being and distinctly lacking in originality and enterprise. Even overwrought nerves have no special reason to be disquieted by the old gentlemen in snuff-coloured coats, or the sad-faced ladies in sun-bonnets, who occasionally revisit, apparently with quite peaceable intentions, the haunts they frequented in life. Of course, there are exceptions. For example, the Rev. Mr. Tweedale's Aunt Leah, though no doubt a most charming old lady when she lived upon earth, would in most households hardly be regarded as a welcome visitor when she appeared five years after her death at a children's Christmas party. If I seem to be taking an unwarrantable liberty with the private concerns of the family in question, I can only plead that it is Mr. Tweedale himself who has published all the details at considerable length in his book, *Man's Survival after Death*.[2] He tells us how Aunt Leah, whose demise took place on 13 August 1905, presented herself unannounced in his dining-room on the afternoon of 25 December 1910.

Dressed in white, she suddenly appeared from behind a curtain and " *walked clean through the Christmas tree*, neither overturning it, nor displacing a single toy suspended thereon." The italics are Mr. Tweedale's. Previously to this Aunt Leah had manifested with, or as, " a winged figure something like a cherub in appearance." There were also loud scratchings at the door like those of a big bird or animal, and a long growl ending in a wail or moaning sound. The growl apparently came from Aunt Leah's short-haired terrier who sometimes accompanied her in visible form when she paid her visits from the other world. Although the dog had died

---

[1] *Dublin Review*, July 1921

[2] *Man's Survival after Death*, by Charles L. Tweedale, Vicar of Weston, Otley; second edition (1920), pp. 146-61. Only the second edition contains these experiences.

several years before its mistress, its ghost seems to have been of more solid texture than that of the old lady. At any rate it sprang at Mrs. Tweedale " as though leaping upon her shoulder " while she was going upstairs with a lamp in her hand. " It seemed to knock off the lamp-glass and burner, which both fell on the stairs, the glass being broken, while the oil was splashed all over the wall." She (Mrs. Tweedale) " was a good deal shaken and startled by this experience "—as well she might be. On another occasion the dog, in the full view of Mrs. Tweedale and their servant Ida, jumped up and rang the dinner-gong by knocking against it. In fact, both the gong and all the bells sounded the whole of one afternoon at frequent intervals, no one being near them. Further, Aunt Leah used to shout the Christian names of members of the family from all parts of the house, but by preference from the top of the stairs, " in a most wonderful, indescribably sad, wailing tone." She also upset the contents of bedrooms, left doors open which were meant to be shut—a most objectionable habit even in the young and thoughtless—startled the servants when passing up the staircase until they nearly broke their necks with the speed of their precipitate descent, carried on long conversations with her sister Marie (Mr. Tweedale's mother) in so loud a tone that " Marjorie, Sylvia and Herschel heard every word," and was so forgetful of the proprieties, that when she wanted her sister, the elder Mrs. Tweedale, she remarked to the young servant-maid *tout court!* " Tell Marie to come up." Mr. Tweedale himself, apparently, never saw the ghostly form of his aunt, though he heard her voice; but his wife, mother, three children and two servants both heard, and also saw. Indeed, he informs us " The witnesses signed the various statements in my presence, and on oath, which I am also prepared to do independently where my own testimony is concerned."

Perhaps the most curious feature connected with the case, is the reason assigned for this visitation, which lasted almost continuously for five months. When asked whether she was happy, Aunt Leah, by raps, replied, " No." On further inquiry it appeared that the cause of her unhappiness was the fact that her name had not been inscribed on her tomb. On a later occasion she shouted to her sister, " her wonderful voice seeming to come from the ceiling," in these words, " Marie, Marie, I want my name on the vault," and when the request was at last carried out, a new demonstration followed. No wonder Mr. Tweedale found himself constrained to draw the conclusion: " This experience . . . showed in an unmistakeable manner how terrene interests loom largely in the early days, or even years, of the spirit life." Moreover, although the tomb grievance seems to have been the principal cause of the old lady's interest in her nephew's household, the carving of the inscription did not entirely bring the apparition to an end; for we read that:—

My Aunt Leah continued to manifest wonderfully for several months, appearing to the various members of the household, and also speaking in the direct voice audible to all present. She was last seen and heard on 9 February 1913, when, appearing suddenly, tall and white, the face plump and clearly visible, she took out of my wife's hands an article she much used when in earth life, saying: " It's Leah's, it's mine." The dog continued to be seen from time to time, notably on 25 December 1911 [another sociable Christmas visit!] when it was seen in our bedroom, and again on 8 October 1914.

It seemed worth while to deal with this illustration at some length, partly to show what the modern ghost—or should one, perhaps, say the modern ghost-hunter—at his best, is capable of, but still more to mark the contrast between the " spiritualism " of a Church of England clergyman at the present day and the belief in the spirit world as exemplified by the clergy of the Middle Ages. Some few years ago, M. Charles-Victor Langlois, *de l'Académie française*, delivered a *conférence* before a select audience connected with the Académie des Inscriptions et Belles-Lettres. He took for his theme the story of an apparition which has left its mark upon the early literature of most of the countries of Europe, and the purport of M. Langlois' discourse was to rehabilitate the spectre, or at any rate to show that the narrative depended upon very much better evidence than has hitherto been supposed. The tale is sufficiently famous to have claimed a paragraph in Raynaldi's continuation of Baronius. In Great Britain it obtained currency by means of a long Middle-English poem still preserved in two or three different manuscripts, and the hero developed into an almost proverbial personage to who we find allusions not only in the somewhat ribald verse of the " poet laureate " John Skelton, but also north of the Tweed in the writings of Dunbar. Moreover, Sir David Lindsay,[1] Lyon king-of-arms, tells us in the preface to his poem *The Dreme*

[1] It is curious that Sir David Lindsay was himself the authority for one of the most famous ghost stories in history. While Lindsay was standing beside the king in St. Michael's Church, Linlithgow, the weird spectre of an old man appeared and warned the young monarch against the campaign which ended at Flodden. Buchanan declares that he heard the story from Lindsay's own lips.

54 GHOSTS AND POLTERGEISTS

(1528) how he used to amuse the infant James V, by dressing himself up sometimes as a goblin or a demon,

And sometyme like the greislie Gaist of Gye.

So far as England is concerned, perhaps, the first mention of the
" grisly ghost of Guy " is to be found in an allusion which seems to
have escaped M. Langlois' researches. It occurs in the annals of
the anonymous chronicler of Bridlington, and as the late Bishop
Stubbs, in editing the text for the Rolls Series, had here to depend
upon a seventeenth-century transcript, the names have been trans-
figured almost beyond recognition. The brief entry, as it stands
in the chronicle, runs thus:

Likewise in the same year (1324) a certain brother John Coby
[read *Goby*], of the Order of Preachers, Prior in the convent of
Mestum [read *Alestum, i.e., Alais*], in the province of Provence, at
the request of the principal inhabitants of Mestum [*Alais*], taking
with him some of his brethren and a number of other persons,
visited the house of a man recently dead, one Gilbert de Corno
[read *Guy de Torno*]. Here for eight days continually, after the
date of his demise a certain voice was heard by many of the inhabitants of Mestum [*Alais*] which being interrogated by the friar replied
very pitifully to the questions asked, and said that he was a good
spirit, as you will find written in another book under the heading
" spirit " amongst the *Incidentia Chronicorum*.[1]

Other chroniclers, like the famous Florentine Villani and the
Dominican Archbishop, St. Antoninus, make brief reference to the
same incident. In Hermann Corner the whole tale is narrated in
its most developed and uncritical form, occupying no less than six
folio pages in the edition of Eckhart. As a separate work the
treatise *De Spiritu Guidonis* exists in a number of manuscripts, it was
translated into many languages, including Catalan, Swedish and
Welsh, and was printed for the first time in its Latin form at Delft
in 1486. At the same time no modern critic who reads the story
in the expanded version, in which it reaches us in all these widely
circulated redactions, could possibly regard the incident as having
any serious historical value. M. Barthélemy Hauréau, who dealt
with the subject in the thirty-third volume of the *Notices et Extraits*,
was fully justified upon the evidence before him in pronouncing

[1] See *Chronicles of the Reigns of Edward I and Edward II*, ed. Stubbs, ii, p. 85.
Bishop Stubbs, in the preface, deplores the loss of this work, the *Incidentia
Chronicorum*. He also expresses his regret that he could find no Dominican house
called Mestum in the list of the Dominican priories of Provence.

that the long dialogue between the prior and the ghost, a dialogue in which both parties displayed their skill in subtle scholastic distinctions, bore every mark of having been fabricated with a tendential purpose. Moreover, in the available text, the names, owing to some primitive misreadings, which are even now not quite cleared up, left the reader in uncertainty as to the identity of the place where the ghost appeared. In many manuscripts Bologna or Verona seem to be indicated, and naturally with a false starting-point of this kind the whole account seemed to abound in contradictions. The first step towards a better understanding was made by a German scholar, Gustav Schleich, who in 1898 edited for the second time the Middle-English poem on the subject and printed with it, not only the expanded Latin relation so widely known, but also a much more compendious version which was incorporated by Walter Bower in his continuation of Fordun's *Scotichronicon*. That this latter document, concise and comparatively sober in tone, was the kernel of the tractate *De Spiritu Guidonis* becomes practically certain upon careful comparison. But M. Langlois from Spanish and other sources has now been able to contribute further evidence and I cannot do better than follow him in trying to set the story in its proper light.

The earliest information we possess upon the subject comes to us from a letter of the Dominican, Bernard de Ribera, who on 23 April, 1324, wrote to Bishop Guy of Majorca in the following terms:—

Reverend Father and Lord, I want to send you an account of an astonishing manifestation which has just occurred here. So far as I have been able to read or hear, there is no fuller or better ordered narrative than that contained in the little roll I send herewith. It contains the whole truth, just as it was set out before the Sovereign Pontiff and their Lordships the Cardinals.

Some other information communicated in the letter will find a more fitting place further on. Be it noted, however, that the same Father Bernard de Ribera seems also to have dispatched another copy of the document with another covering letter, in the course of which he says:

You may like to know that Peter Gautier, the Procurator of our Order, told me on 10 February, that the Lord Pope has commissioned

Brother John Goby, the Prior of Alais, with the best people of the town, to conduct an inquiry at the request of those who have heard the Voice, to know if there is any imposture in the matter. The truth of the account I send you herewith is now established by an immense number of credible witnesses. Some of our Brothers have left Avignon to present the official investigation to the Lord Pope and the College of Cardinals. Meanwhile the Voice still continues to make itself heard, and whether it be questioned by barbarians from England, Scotland or Germany, it answers every one in his own language.

The copy of the same relation which is contained in the *Scotichronicon* is introduced by a statement that it was attested by the common seal of the town of Alais and that the Pope and cardinals then, of course, resident at Avignon, forty miles off, had been greatly impressed by it. The writer who transmitted the account seems further to imply, like Ribera, that the phenomena still continued after the report was drawn up. In all our copies the document begins in the first person, and the first few sentences may as well be given entire:

On Christmas day in the year 1323, I, Brother John Goby, Prior of the Order of Preachers, in our friary of Alais, in the province of Provence, was requested by the principal inhabitants of Alais to go to the house of Guy de Torno, in which house, for eight days together since his death, a certain voice had been heard by many people of consequence in the town. Although I went reluctantly, still, to see whether it was an imposture or some diabolical illusion, I set off, taking with me three of the community (names given). Besides these there accompanied us more than a hundred laymen, to wit, the Lord of Alais, William de Cadoena, etc. When we came to the dwelling, in order to take precautions against fraud, we very carefully searched the house and even under the tiles, and not only that, but all the neighbouring buildings. And in all those which we examined we left the best of the townsmen to keep watch, men whom we could thoroughly trust, turning out all the usual occupants. Further, in two places of the house itself which might offer facilities for fraud, that is on the flat roof (*solarium*) over the room in which the said voice was heard, and also in the middle of the rafters, we stationed other picked townsmen. And lest perhaps the wife of the said dead man might play us any trick, we arranged that a worthy and elderly woman should sleep in the same bed with the aforesaid wife of the deceased. The doors then being shut, I asked the wife at which of the beds the voice was particularly heard. She answered that, so far as she could tell, it was at the bed in which he had died. And so I, with my three companions, each of us having his lantern lit, sat down upon the bed of the said dead man. Let me add, however, that I, as I always clung to the idea that it was all mere deceit of the devil, had brought away with me, when I left the friary, but so secretly that no one but myself knew it, a pyx with the Body of Christ, and I carried it about me with such devotion as I could; but none of my companions knew anything of the matter.

It would almost seem as if Prior John Goby could give points to the Society for Psychical Research in the thoroughness of the precautions he had taken against fraud. But the rest of his story must be told more succinctly. The four friars upon the bed recited the three nocturns of the Office for the Dead, together with the Litany, when suddenly they were conscious that some invisible presence was passing in front of them. It advanced towards the bed of the wife and made a noise like the sweeping of a broom. The wife thereupon, in a panic of fear, cried out aloud: " There it is! There it is! " The friars were themselves somewhat shaken, but one of them induced the wife to ask the spirit whether he was Guy de Torno. At once a feeble and pitiful voice answered, apparently from the middle of the room, " Yes, I am he." The friars then stood round the spot from which the voice seemed to proceed and the laymen of the party apparently pushed their way into the room and crowded round. The prior, recovering all his courage, greeted the spirit with many forms of adjuration and then went on to put a number of questions. The ghost was asked whether he was a good or an evil spirit. He answered that he was a good spirit; he said further that he was assured that he would ultimately reach heaven, but that at present he was performing his purgatory. Asked why he haunted that spot, he replied that it was because his sins were committed there; amongst these sins was the grief he had caused his mother. He added that there he was enduring his particular purgatory, but that during the daytime he suffered in the common purgatory (*purgatorium commune*), further that it would be his lot to have to return continually for two years to the places where he had sinned unless others came to his aid by their prayers. Asked what kind of prayers helped most, he replied masses, especially, and the seven penitential psalms. In reply to further questions he declared that it would take a hundred masses to procure his release, that he was enduring the pain of fire, that indulgences were beneficial and that the living could divest themselves of their indulgences for the benefit of the dead—this last is theologically an interesting statement in view of the date at which it was recorded. Further, it is noteworthy that the ghost, when asked concerning the fate in the next world of those he had known during life, replied that he could disclose nothing regarding the lot of others. God did not permit it.

Extravagant as this account must appear in many respects to the religious sceptic, M. Langlois seems thoroughly justified in his favourable opinion both of the authenticity of the document itself and of the good faith of the writer. Let me hasten to add that in the view of the same distinguished French Academician the whole phenomenon is explainable as an ingenious piece of ventriloquism on the part of Guy de Torno's widow. She was, he thinks, hysterical and possibly a victim of fits and starts of that curious mental condition which we call duplex personality. No doubt if we further call to our aid those gifts of lucidity or telepathic sensibility which in some rare cases we find associated with hystero-epilepsy, there is nothing in the story of Guy which cannot be explained away. Still the difficulties are not inconsiderable. To begin with, ventriloquism is not a novelty in the world. It was known to the ancients, it is known by many savages. Prior John Goby and his brethren, the members of a learned order, living close to the papal court at Avignon, are not likely to have been quite unsophisticated; while the whole story shows that they were evidently on the alert to detect trickery. Again, the art of ventriloquism requires a great deal of practice.[1] We can hardly suppose that an hysterical subject, generally keen to attract notice, would successfully conceal such an accomplishment from her neighbours in the hope of mystifying them ultimately if her husband happened to die. On the other hand, if the neighbours knew, the imposture could hardly have been maintained. Hardly less serious is the difficulty created by a point upon which I have not yet touched, *viz.*, that the spirit, under pressure, admitted that the abject terror exhibited by his wife was due to her consciousness of the sins committed between them in their marriage relations. "We have both confessed it," said the ghost, "but she has not expiated it; let her make expiation now." If Prior John's account of what happened is accurate (and the frank

---

[1] I think I am also right in saying that a ventriloquist finds himself particularly hampered in the dark.

admission of points making against his own view, as well as the generally sober tone, give an impression of conscientious accuracy), it is hard to believe that a woman in her state of hysterical excitement could at the same time have kept up the ventriloquism without faltering. Other difficulties may be found in the fact that the spirit, as we read, openly declared that the prior was carrying the Blessed Sacrament about him, though this was unknown to everyone but himself; and also in the gentle breath of wind (*sibilus aurae levis*) which fanned them and which all present were conscious of when the ghost finally took its departure.

I do not think that we can safely lay much stress upon the statements contained in the concluding portion of Friar Bernard de Ribera's letter of 23 April, from which I have previously quoted. John Goby writes from personal experience, and is drafting a formal report to be submitted to the Pope. Ribera only repeats what has been told him by friends and correspondents. Still, what he says is interesting. After mentioning that Goby's narrative was read before the Pope and Cardinals in consistory and that directions were consequently sent to the Archbishop of Aix (a Dominican) to inquire still further into the case, in concert with the King's officers and the magistrature, the investigation, he adds, was duly made and Goby's report was in every way confirmed. Then he goes on to say that in the course of this inquiry,

The spirit showed itself for the first time in a luminous form. A Carmelite in the crowd exclaimed, " What is the meaning of this appearance ? So far you have only manifested through the sound of a voice." The spirit replied proudly: " The light you see is my good angel who, when I have finished my term of penance, will conduct me to the joys of paradise." And this is not all. Two of our friars sent to Alais by the Pope have, along with the chief men of the town and religious of all Orders, questioned the spirit on three different nights in the presence of three hundred people. One of them said to the spirit: " I conjure thee by the Body of Christ to tell us under what form thou art speaking to us." Everybody heard the answer: " Under the form of a dove." Then said the Brother, " Prove it." The spirit answered, " Willingly," and at once (it was the hour of cock-crow and there was not a trace of a feather in the house) the whole room was covered with white feathers. Every one was stupefied. The Brother in question is named Arnold of Perpignan. He is a student of good reputation who preaches very well. For the rest, questions and answers have continued from

Christmas down to Holy Week. If anything new happens, I will let you know.

Nothing further, it seems, need here be added by way of comment upon this curious tale. It is a matter upon which everyone may be left to form his own opinion. But the text of Prior John Goby's report at least makes it clear that the ghosts of the Middle Ages, whether genuine or fictitious, were preoccupied, not with the inscription to be carved on their tombstone, but with the things of the spirit and the thought of heaven. " Terrene interests " seem to have troubled them but little, except in so far as they could help men still living to avoid their own mistakes and make their salvation more secure.

CHAPTER VI

AN INDIAN POLTERGEIST[1]

AS a pendent to these ancient stories in which it was believed that spirits conversed in the direct voice with a whole group of listeners, let us turn to a modern disturbance in which communcations by writing formed perhaps the most striking feature of the manifestations.

The scene is Southern India and the narrator is a native official Mr. A. S. Thangapragasam Pillay, Deputy-Tahsildar and Sub-Magistrate in the town of Nidamangalam (Tanjore district). He bears the reputation of an honourable and conscientious Catholic and is well-known to the Bishop and clergy of the district. His narrative was not written for publication or to court notoriety, but it was drawn up by Mr. Pillay from his diary in response to the request of Lt. Col. O'Gorman, M.D., C.M.G., who had seen some account of the case in a local journal. I am much indebted to Col. O'Gorman for allowing me to make use of the document. Unfortunately the statement is too long to be reproduced entire. The account here given is an abridgment, but wherever possible the somewhat quaint phraseology has been faithfully preserved. Where passages have been introduced to link up disconnected incidents in the narrative or to comment on the statements made, such interpolations have been enclosed in square brackets. Mr. Pillay repeatedly has occasion in his manuscript to quote Tamil words and sentences, adding his own translation. It would be useless, even if it were feasible, to print the Tamil original, but Father Lebeau, S. J., a missionary, resident for many years in Southern India, and a competent Tamil scholar, has very kindly read through Mr. Pillay's manuscript and assures me that the renderings furnished are quite correct. Father Lebeau also is acquainted personally with the Bishop and several of the clergy referred to in the narrative. For Mr. Pillay, who presumably had never heard anything of poltergeist phenomena, the annoyances to which he was subjected could only be explained as the

[1] *The Month,* September and October 1929

work of the devils. The hatred manifested of all religious emblems, and the obvious effort to bring them into contempt, naturally supported such a conclusion, and it is quite possible that the view was justified. It can only be said that the whole matter is very perplexing. One may regret that Mr. Pillay does not furnish more information regarding the members of which his household consisted. There was probably, as almost always happens in such cases, some child or young person round whom the manifestations centred, but the narrative as it stands does not suggest anything of the sort. Possibly the daughter mentioned in the opening paragraph may have been an unconscious medium, but it is clear that there were also other children. There can be no doubt about the fact that these occurrences attracted attention locally and that they were commented upon by certain Hindu journals published in Tamil. I quote Mr. Pillay's title as well as his narrative.

DETAILS OF THE SUFFERINGS BY DEVIL'S ACTION FROM 3RD TO 19TH MARCH, 1920, AND ULTIMATE VICTORY OVER DEVIL ON THE 19TH MARCH.

March 3rd, 1920, at 5 p.m. The clothes in the upstairs which were left in[1] the " rope " took fire and the clothes were burning. Females became aware of the fire as soon as the child lying in the cradle upstairs having been terrified on seeing the fire, cried out. The fire was extinguished by water and the wet half-burnt clothes placed on the chair. Half an hour after when the females went to upstairs, again the wet clothes and the chair were burning. Thinking that the fire was due to some carelessness of my daughter who had an occasion to light a chimney in the upstairs, she was given a good beating.

March 4th. I went to office at 8 a.m. At 8.30 a.m. a silk female cloth which was left tied in the nails fixed in the wall for being dried in the same upstairs took fire. My people went upstairs, noticed this and put out the fire. The sack curtain in the cooking apartment took fire in two different places. It was this which created a suspicion that it was the act of devil. A peon came to me and informed me of the occurrence. I made haste to the house and suspended pictures of the Sacred Heart, Blessed Virgin and other saints in the upstairs and downstairs and put chalk crosses in the walls and doors and also in the garden doorway entrances and

[1] As already hinted, the writer's English is not flawless. For example, he constantly uses the preposition " in " for " on." When he speaks a little lower down of " lighting a chimney," he presumably means kindling a fire in the grate.

doors and frames. All the pictures were burnt, cross marks were found rubbed out by cow dung[1] and a big picture of St. Margaret Mary with a glass frame was found thrown down and the glass broken to pieces, though the knot which tied it in the nail in the wall was intact. I took the picture with frame and placed it standing on the wall in the cooking room and recited prayers. After finishing the prayers we went inside the 1st compartment. After an hour my people went to the cooking room and found the picture of St. Margaret Mary torn to pieces and the torn pieces placed over the frame. I at once sent a special man to the parish priest of Mannargudi with a request to come to Nidamangalam in order to bless the house. The chalk crosses which were rubbed out were renewed, and the next hour we saw them again rubbed out by means of ashes and cow dung. Cow dung in big quantity was placed over the cross marks on doors. The Mannargudi priest and Brother Joseph S. J., manager of St. Joseph's Industrial School and Press, Trichinopoly, who happened to be at Mannargudi, went to my house at 6 p.m. I explained to them everything and showed them the ashes of the pictures burnt and remnants of the burnt clothes.

[So far we have nothing which might not quite conceivably have been the work of some mischievous child or practical joker. The witnesses appealed to saw nothing that was evidential, though there is extraneous proof that they credited the account, believing Mr. Pillay to be a trustworthy person. The house was blessed and a medal hung up, but the medal almost immediately disappeared and the disturbances were only intensified. Next day, however, we get something more inexplicable, assuming the statement to be reliable.]

Seeing the devilish troubles I took a standing crucifix made of black wood stand and placed it in the raised place [mantle-piece] by the side of the hearth. I myself sat about three feet to the north and was reciting the Apostles' Creed over and over. Within a second the crucifix was missing. To my great grief and extreme sorrow I found the crucifix in the fire and the wood was burning. None else was there except me. I then took an enthronement picture of the Sacred Heart painted in a strong tin plate, and placed it fixed over the hearth wall with two nails in the two holes in

---

[1] This is not quite such an outrage in the eyes of a Hindu as it would seem to a European; for the cow being a sacred animal, everything belonging to it is regarded with a certain amount of respect.

the top. Some time afterwards the tin plate began to roll [to curl up?] We were seeing it. It was made straight by me and two other nails were fixed on the bottom holes. When my daughter was working there the tin plate began to roll again . . . In the noon I placed a standing crucifix made of German silver, and a strong one, also in the upstairs. Sometime afterwards the crucifix was missing . . . The next northern house man came and reported that something fell over his roof. When it was examined the crucifix was found on the roof of that house.

[Next day, 6 March, came a relative, " Mr. David Pillay, sub-assistant surgeon, Nidamangalam, and a Catholic," to whom the obliterated crosses, torn pictures, etc., were shown.]

We were just entering the 2nd compartment when we heard the entrance door of the 3rd compartment [the cooking-room] shut with great force and noise. We went there and saw the door bolted inside while none were inside. We forced open the door[1] but could not do it. My servant was then asked to climb over the wall. He went inside by climbing over it and found the door bolted. He removed the bolts and we went inside and saw all the chalk crosses rubbed out with cow dung and sign of Belly god [copied in the MS.] drawn over them by charcoal and a multiplication symbol $\times$ also over the same. How the devil was able to get cow dung and rub all these several crosses within 5 minutes and how the door bolted inside are matters requiring deep consideration.

[Assuming the facts to be as stated, it certainly is a problem. So much trouble had occurred in the " cooking room " that the preparation of the next meal was transferred to the " 2nd compartment," and Mr. Pillay's daughter was given a medal of St. Benedict to hang up there. She went to fetch a nail, but before she got back the medal had disappeared.]

Half an hour after this I was standing in the 2nd compartment with daughter's husband and a catechist from the Trichinopoly cathedral who happened to come to my house. Just then the medal which was kept by my daughter and was missing, came from the roof and fell before us. I with these two persons saw it come from the roof of the house in a slanting direction as if somebody threw it from the roof, while there was none in fact. A few minutes after this a mud vessel [presumably a basin of rough baked clay] with milk inside, was thrown on the ground from the hearth and

---

[1] Obviously the writer means that force was used to open the door but that the effort failed. It is clear that these " compartments " were cubicles separated by partitions which did not reach to the roof or ceiling; hence the servant was able to clamber over.

the milk spilled on the floor and spoiled. We took our noon meals, and my family, female inmates, were taking their meals, when the mud vessel which contained sauce and which they left in front of them was thrown away[1] and upset with the sauce. They all got up and I was standing with them. All on a sudden the mud vessel with cooked rice rose high to the roof of the house and fell down, the pot itself having been broken to pieces, and the contents fell to the ground. Immediately after this, the sauce vessel and butter-milk vessel rose high, fell down and were broken. We became terrified and were advised to shift ourselves to a new residence for the reason that the devil might be confined to one particular house and that in the new house we could have peace of mind. At once arrangements were accordingly made and I sent my articles and family to the new house at 5 p.m. A Hindu Samiyar [priest] who is known to me came to see me and it was he who advised me to go to the new house . . . As soon as I reached the new house I felt a very great peace of mind. I found myself very happy, as the troubles from the 3rd idem gave me great uneasiness and anxiety. We took our meals. I went to the garden and returned. While returning I noticed two broomsticks placed over the cupboard in the northern verandah were burning. Oh! My God! what my troubles would have been on having seen the diabolical acts resumed in the new house also, it was not possible to imagine. I at once put out the fire, when my people also saw this. To the middle hall I went, when the mud vessels which were newly purchased for preparing the night meals were all broken in the same manner as in the noon. The metal crucifix was broken into two and thrown with great force. We were wounded in our minds and become confused, not knowing what to do. We went to sleep.[2]

7 March 1920. As soon as the day dawned the mischief of the devil commenced. Other mischiefs, narrated above, continued as before by the throwing of bronze vessels, cocoanut shells and the like. Three children received blows at one and the same time, and all these three began to weep simultaneously; when I became quite confused. I received a letter from my nephew, Rev. Father

---

[1] As the attentive reader will notice from other instances in the course of this relation, " thrown away " in Mr. Pillay's vocabulary means only wasted or spilt.

[2] From other passages in the narrative it seems clear that when the writer says " went to sleep," he only means " we went to bed." After all, his way of looking at it is the more logical. " Went to sleep " in current English is synonymous with " fell asleep," but strictly, and, as we may suppose, originally, it meant " I went to get my night's rest " (*ibam dormitum*). Whether sleep did, or did not, follow was another matter.

Amandu, S.J., encouraging me and asking me to at once go and explain matters to the Bishop of Mylapore. On the previous day I sent a letter to my brother-in-law at Tanjore [Native Doctor] Mr. Ponnusamy Pillay, who came to Nidamangalam with a specially blessed medal which he got from the Bishop and a picture of Margaret Mary painted in tin. This specially blessed medal was hung up tied to a nail. But I was afraid to fix the tin picture for fear that the devil would be irritated and do us much more mischief. My daughter took it inside and was about to fix it in the wall of the middle hall, when the brass vessel with milk which was placed in the hearth was thrown away with great force. My daughter's husband, without fixing the above picture, brought it outside. On hearing the above details my Deputy-Collector (a native of Malabar) with Circle-Inspector of Police, Mannargudi, and the Police Sub-inspector of both Nidamangalam and Mannargudi, came to see me. He, the Deputy-Collector, said that he would give a temporary cure, and that I should adopt measures to secure who will affect a radical cure and asked me to see the Bishop. He asked me to purchase toddy both morning and evening and place a cocoanut shell of toddy in one of the corners of the house and asked me to have it replaced with new toddy[1] both morning and evening. As soon as I saw the Deputy-Inspector I was very much moved with grief, and he consoled me to a great extent and my thanks are due to him. I got toddy at once and placed it in a copper vessel in one corner of the house and left the balance in another vessel for being kept on reserve for the evening use. The toddy which was reserved for the evening use was thrown away. [The writer presumably means that the malicious agency which was persecuting them upset the receptacle and that the contents were lost.] In the evening fresh toddy was purchased and the same was left poured in a vessel. Our house was without any mud vessel. I got a big brass vessel for preparing meals. We made use of copper vessels for heating milk and preparing sauce. Small vessels, cocoanut shells and small baskets were being thrown throughout the day from one place to another. On the noon after we finished our meals and when meals were served for the females, one of the female inmates took sauce in a copper vessel which was snatched away from her hands by an invisible force and thrown on the ground. My daughter's husband took hold of the rice vessel and there was a regular tug-of-war between him and the devil, the former seizing the vessel very

---

[1] " Toddy " is the fermented juice or sap of certain species of palm. It is alcoholic and intoxicant, and on distillation is more correctly known as " arrack."

strongly and the latter trying with great force to snatch away the vessel with rice inside from the hold of my son-in-law. It was with great haste meals were served and taken. From that moment it was arranged to tie the vessel with cooked rice with strong rope round the neck of the vessel between the two legs of a cot which was in the middle hall.

[At this point Mr. Pillay inserts a sketch plan of what is presumably " the new house," with points of the compass, " compound wall," verandahs, cupboards, doors, etc., carefully indicated. It was apparently a bungalow with a large apartment, called the " middle hall," occupying most of the space; but the details do not seem to have any particular importance in illustrating his narrative It will be readily understood that in the paragraph which follows the phrase " will be " simply indicates reiteration.]

As soon as sauce is prepared it will be brought to the middle hall, placed under the cot and taken hold of until the whole is served. Every day from 5.30 a.m. up to 10 p.m. vessels, with water or without water, cocoanut shells, etc., will be thrown from one place to another. Bricks will be thrown inside from outside. Hence it will be unnecessary to detail them. I may in a word say that once every five minutes we may see some act or other done within the hours specified. While the females would prepare coffee in the hearth in the north verandah, the devil will draw the burning fuel from the hearth and throw it elsewhere. Things which were left inside the cupboard will be thrown upon the females who are working in the hearth. It would not allow them to do their cooking work. Hence I engaged males to prepare meals. When a female was cleaning fish, a fish was snatched away from her hands and thrown about fifty feet off. Hence females were afraid to clean it. when the mother-in-law of my daughter said that she would do it. She accordingly washed the fish, when she received a blow by means of a piece of wood. At 4 p.m. a Brahmin professing that he knew something of Hindu mantrams [prayers or spells] was brought to me by one of my office clerks. He wrote a chit and its contents were these. [The spell is given in Tamil, and the translation is as follows.] " Are you subject to God's laws ? If you are not, I will not have anything to do with you. If you are, why do you trouble these people ? " He asked me to place the chit in the northern verandah and cover it with a vessel and said that the devil should give him a reply in half an hour. Three quarters of an hour passed, when the vessel which covered the chit referred to above was thrown about 30 feet off and the chit placed inside it was missing. At

8 p.m. I went inside with a rosary on my neck and a crucifix in my hand, being my only defence in all these troubles, and proceeded to the eastern room, where females and children were sitting with great fear. From 3rd to 19th March I was always armed with these two defensive weapons. I told them to recite the prayers of St. Antony. Before I closed my mouth I received a blow on my back. I turned round and found that I was beaten [struck ?] by means of a piece of oil cake. It caused swelling and gave me pain for about one full hour.

8 March, 1920. The undermentioned writings were found this morning written in one of the walls of the lavatory which form part of the house. [A figure somewhat like the Arabic numeral 2.] Symbol of Hindus = Belly God symbol. [Tamil words then follow.] English—" My name is Rajamadan [chief mischief maker]. I will not leave you," and some illegible characters. As soon as the writings were noticed in the wall, many people went to see the same, of whom my office 3rd clerk was one. Below the writing he [presumably the clerk] wrote thus in English:

Reply sharp. If you don't run away from this house, I would recommend you to my goddess for punishment.

Signed ——

On the same date the undermentioned writings were found written in Tamil in the same wall. [Tamil text follows.] In English:

I will kill the man who wrote these lines. Don't you know that I am the King ? I will not leave this house, whatever the inmates do.

The clerk became terrified and wrote this: " Please excuse me. I beg your pardon."

Other mischiefs narrated continued as before. New toddy was purchased for this day. Before the man with new toddy entered the verandah, the vessel with toddy which was kept in the middle hall was thrown away. New toddy was substituted. That night I went inside for night prayer. As soon as I finished the prayers, a small prayer-book which was left over one of the boxes was thrown over me. Big boxes were seen to move. Big vessels with their contents began to shake with tremendous noise. Rattan covering of a box and a paper plate with paintings were constantly thrown up and down by the devil. The whole day my head will be confused. The whole day my heart will be full of anxieties and cares. The whole day I will be unable to do any kind of work. The whole day I will not take proper meals. I made up my mind to go to the Bishop of Mylapore who happened to halt at Tanjore on his pastoral visit.

9 March, 1920.—The day dawned as well as usual mischiefs. The train service changed from this day, unfortunately for me.[1] Hence there was no noon train to go to Tanjore. I was informed by the station-master of Nidamangalam that a goods train would run at 11 a.m. Without taking my noon meals I went to the station and got a first class ticket as it was a goods train. That train instead of coming at 11.30 a.m. reached Nidamangalam at 1.20 p.m. I got into it and reached Tanjore at 3 p.m. and went to the presbytery direct. The Bishop was very busy with the visitors and petitioners. Very Rev. Father Mederlet and Rev. Father Ignatius were there with the Bishop . . .

As I saw the Bishop I told him that I was the man troubled by devil; as the Bishop had already heard about my troubles from Doctor Ponnusamy Pillay of Tanjore, to whom I had written about my troubles. His Lordship, the Bishop of Mylapore, gave me a seat close to his seat and heard me patiently, putting off all other affairs arranged for the time. The Bishop took a very great interest in my affairs, and gave me sound advice that I should be firm in my faith and that I should not have recourse to Hindu magicians. He quoted the case of Job and of many saints. I told him that I had not got that moral strength and that I would become mad soon if early relief were not given.

The undermentioned writings were found (on the morning of 9 March before I left Nidamangalam to see the Bishop) below the apology of my clerk on the previous day. [Tamil text follows, but is here omitted]. English: " I pardoned you. I will not leave them. Have you got sense? I am instigated by some one. Whatever they may do, I will not leave them." When I was

---

[1] In the passage which follows we get an interesting side-light on the working of the railway system in southern India, which, it would seem, does not always function with the smoothness which in this country we should consider desirable. That Mr. T. P.—he will pardon us we trust an informality which economises space—was evidently much flattered by the attention which His Lordship, Mgr. Theotonius E. Ribeiro Vieira de Castro, paid to his story, is as natural and inevitable as the distress of mind which preceded the interview. In spite of a phrase or two there is not much indication in the narrative that the author was trying to pose as a hero.

talking with the Bishop I mentioned to him of the above correspondence, and he advised me not to have correspondence with the devil and that all the writings should be rubbed out. The Bishop was attentively hearing me without caring for other matters already arranged for the time. He took the squeezed tin and enthronement picture of the Sacred Heart. I requested the Bishop to send me a priest in order to bless my house at Nidamangalam. He readily consented. I wanted to have the Very Rev. Father Mederlet, who has already the interest of my family in view ever since his arrival in Tanjore, and the Bishop gave a ready permission. Very Rev. Father Mederlet promised to go [come] on the 11th idem by 10 a.m. train after saying Mass in Tanjore. I had my weapons, a crucifix which the Bishop specially blessed and gave it to me and my rosary. I returned to Nidamangalam at 6.30 p.m. and went to my house with a heart full of sorrow and grief with equal fear. That night we began to recite prayers and I placed the specially blessed crucifix before us, with two candles burning before it. As we were praying, the crucifix was thrown from its place and it fell on the cloth of my daughter aged about six years who was sitting next to me. I took care after that to hold the crucifix tightly in my hands.

10 March, 1920. I went inside the middle hall, when I found the hall damp with water. I asked my people why it was damp and they replied that from the hearth which was burning in the northern verandah a piece of casuarina wood[1] full with fire was thrown inside the middle hall from which fire spread throughout the hall and that water was therefore poured to clean it. I became irritated and went to the burning place and said thus: " You devil, why do you trouble us like this ? You know very well that we are all the children of God and we have not done anything wrong to you. Why should you then come trouble us like this ? Your proper place is hell, where there would always be burning fire. It would be well and good if you would go back to your place." Having said these words I recited the Apostles' Creed. After finishing it, I went to the middle hall and went towards the eastern room about ten feet off the hearth, with my boy aged two in one of my hands. He was also walking with me. The devil suddenly took another

---

[1] As far back as 1885 one may read in Sir W. W. Hunter's *Imperial Gazatteer of India*, under " Chengalpat " (Vol. III, pp. 381-382), how " the *casuarina* plantations are extending year by year " in the Madras Presidency; and he adds: " The tree yields rapid returns, attaining in favourable localities its full growth in about fifteen years; and as there is a large and increasing demand for firewood in Madras, the enterprise has attained such proportions as to change materially the physical aspect of long stretches of the coast."

big piece of burning fire and threw it with great force between my legs. I at once turned back and saw the whole hall filled with fire.

Oh! my God! I became very much irritated and beat the floor where the casuarina wood piece fell with my shoes five or six times, and so did Dr. Ponnusamy Pillay. The same havoc continued without mitigation. The undermentioned writings were again found in the bathroom. [Tamil given with the following translation]:

Sir, you rogue, are you so very strong-headed. The inmates of this house have done nothing against me. I will not leave them alone unless they become Hindus.

(Signed) R. M. Kurali.

As soon as I saw these writings I was a new man altogether. My faith towards my God become more deeply rooted and I gave expressions to the following words, as from the above incidents it would seem that the devil was always hearing us.

O Devil, You think it easy to convert me to Hinduism by your threatening writings. Beware, I am the child of God; I give you to understand clearly this moment once for all that I am ready to lose my property, wife, children and all that I possess and my life too. But don't think I will ever lose my soul. I am ready to die a martyr for the sake of my Saviour, Lord Jesus Christ.

Dr. Ponnusamy Pillay who heard me replying in the above tone said I did well in having replied to the devil in the manner indicated above. I know that the devil was always in the house, and whatever remarks we passed there was a ready reply.

At about 11 a.m. I went inside, when my people told me that the toddy which was placed in a cocoa-nut shell in one of the corners of the middle hall was thrown away [spilt] after two hours by the devil. I was just then standing in the entrance to the eastern room. Just in front of me in the corner toddy was left in the vessel. Immediately this vessel with toddy was thrown away a few feet off. Then my maternal aunt who was lying inside the eastern room said that it was not right to give the devil toddy, and that I should not repeat if for the evening. Before she closed her mouth she was beaten [struck ?] with a plantain peel, and a handful of sand was thrown on her head, and she received a blow by a mat which was close to

6

her. I then made up my mind not to give toddy any longer. From that moment I stopped it. The mischief continued until we went to bed.

11 March. The day dawned and we were all very happy and merry, full of hopes that the presence of the priest would surely give us relief. In the morning I was supervising the cleaning of the western room with the object that Very Rev. Father Mederlet might stop there for the day. My daughter was sweeping this room and I was standing just near the entrance, when I received a severe blow in my left hand and something fell down. To my great grief I found it to be a metal crucifix made of brass, which was kept inside a box in the eastern room, thrown at me with very great force. Then I said: " O Devil, you used my good crucifix as a weapon to beat me." Before I closed my mouth I observed a shadow high as a human being, covered with black blanket, but no human being visible, throwing with very great force something, and it was a big wooden plate which fell just in front of me in the middle hall. Just at this moment the whole house seemed to be filled with dust.

Afterwards I went to the railway station to receive Very Rev. Father Mederlet. He came with Rao Sahib M. R. Ry [?] S. Arogiasamy Pillay, Retired Huzur Sheristadar of the Tanjore Collectorate and a Catholic. We all went to our house. Very Rev. Father Mederlet blessed the broken crucifix since repaired and the one blessed by the Bishop on the 9th and thrown away [down ?] by the devil that night while we were reciting our prayers. These crucifixes were left inside the eastern room over a small raised seat. These two were thrown out one after the other from the eastern room in [into ?] the middle hall while the Rev. Father and myself were in the western room. I saw the throwing away of the crucifixes and at once pointed it out to Very Rev. Father Mederlet. The Rev. Father took his dinner in the western room. After this, I, Mr. Arogiasamy Pillay and Dr. Ponnusamy Pillay, with Mr. A. P. in the middle were taking our meals. When we were thus taking our meals, two small mangoes fell over my leaf [used for a plate ?] from the roof of the house. At 3 p.m. Very Rev. Father Mederlet with his own hands fixed nails with special medals in all the rooms and pasted picture of the Sacred Heart of Jesus in the eastern room. After this, the consecration ceremony of the family to the Sacred Heart was performed and I was asked by the Rev. Father to fix the enthronement picture to the wall of the eastern room by means of four nails. It was so done. Just below it, the relic of Don Bosco[1] was fixed and nailed. The medal which was placed in the southern wall of the eastern room was immediately missing. Another medal was substituted; it was also missing, and this was not replaced. Very Rev. Father Mederlet and Mr. A. P. strongly advised that I should have a novena in honour of St. Joseph, invoking his special aid to drive away the devil, and that it should commence that very day (11 March) so that it should finish on the 19th *idem*, feast of St. Joseph.

[The novena was faithfully carried through in spite of disturbances and interruptions. Some of these latter were due to the interest taken in the phenomena by neighbours and other wellmeaning persons.]

I would be receiving letters [Mr. T. P. continues] from my Hindu friends, suggesting the names of very clever Hindu and Mohammedan magicians well-versed in the Black Art. I would tell them that I was a Christian and that it would be against my faith if I would have recourse to magicians to drive out devils. My house was a regular prayer-house both day and night. I would be always hearing the muttering of prayers. When the prayers would finish the devil will commence to do us mischief and I will be hearing the noise of the throwing of brick-bats, metal vessels and the like. The one peculiarity I was noticing throughout was a cessation of all troubles as soon as prayers would commence until it would be finished. An Udaiyar Christian of Thachangurietu was sent by Mr. Periyashambi Nadar, a rich and influential Christian resident of Tanjore, in order to recite prayers from *Sathuru Sankaramalai* (Christian prayer book containing prayers to St. Michael and St. Antony for driving out devils). As soon as he entered the middle hall he sat down and said in a loud noise [*sic*, ? voice]: " Well, devil, come before me." Before he closed his mouth a big casuarina wood which was burning in the hearth in the northern verandah was thrown with great force before him. In the course of the same day he sat with my family members to recite prayers. The devil at once threw over him an aluminium vessel used for leaving chunam[2] for betel-leaf, and as a result of such throwing his body was covered with the chunam water.

[1] The relic of Don Bosco was no doubt supplied by Fr. Mederlet, who was a Salesian.

[2] Chunam is a very fine kind of quicklime made from calcined shells and used for chewing with betel. A small piece of the betel nut is wrapped up in a leaf of the betel vine with a pellet of chunam. The mastication causes a copious flow of saliva of brick-red colour which dyes the lips, etc.

On one of these days it [the devil] set fire to the thatched shed in front of the northern verandah, which was at once put out, and without much damage. It set fire to the cloth of the cousin, brother of the Rev. Father Maria Jeganndar, S.J., of the Trichinopoly College, who was helping me all these days. I was filled with very great anxiety and care. How many times I was beaten [struck ?], the children were beaten, the vessels were thrown, sacred pictures torn and sacred medals missing, God only knows. When we began to pray with crucifix or picture, it was immediately thrown away. Hence whenever we recited our prayers I would hold the crucifix in my hand tightly until the prayers are finished. The holy Bible was removed from the box and thrown away several times. Hence I removed the Bible to the Office verandah as well as the crucifix.

[These details seem somewhat inconsistent with the statement made above concerning " the cessation of all troubles as soon as prayers began," but it may be that the disturbance only marked the actual moment of beginning prayers. Possibly when the prayers had once got under weigh the tormenting agency was quiet. It is curious that in several European hauntings of the same kind, some of them two or three centuries old, and even in Lutheran households, the same observation is made that while prayers were going on, the disturbances—moving and breaking of crockery, etc.—were, for the time suspended.]

Another little incident, which happened on the night of the 13th instant and on the morning of the 14th *idem*, may be taken for what it is worth. On this night at 3 a.m. I went out of my room and returned. As I was half asleep I saw a female figure standing at the entrance to the eastern room in which I was sleeping. Though there was a light burning, it appeared to me to be dark. While lying down I asked the figure " Who are you ? " The figure without giving me a reply retraced [*sic*] not turning its back. As it was going I was also watching it closely. As soon as it retracted as far as the wall it stopped. Within two seconds it rushed into the room in which I was lying down, and as soon as I saw it again, I asked " Who are you ? Who are you ? " The figure replied [Tamil words quoted] " Why, Father! " and so replying, without standing a minute, it went inside the room. I at once revealed this to the unfortunate wife, who is much reduced on account of these troubles, and [to] my maternal aunt whom God has sent for my help.

We went to sleep again. After day dawned at 9 a.m. my wife

was narrating this to my eldest daughter who is here with her husband. She appears to have said in reply that she prayed the previous night before going to bed in the western room to the unfortunate deceased sister, Achi Ammal, saying, [Tamil again]: " Father is much troubled without help," and requesting her to come for help. Just at this time I went inside the particular room where my wife, my daughter and aunt were sitting discussing about the vision and dream, when my wife told me about my eldest daughter's prayer, and said that the vision I saw in the might must be that of our beloved daughter Achi Ammal, alias Lourdes Mary Ammal (deceased). I was considering over it, and went to the next bath-room within a minute after this, where in the wall these writings were found. [Tamil given as before]. In English: " My beloved Mamma. I am in the dark place. If I had been in heaven would I have left you in this condition ? (signed) Lourdes Mary." The writing [of] each letter resembles that of my deceased daughter. As soon as I saw this, I shed tears and called my wife to come and see the writings. She was in the next adjoining room. She and all the children and maternal aunt, came and saw these writings. All began to weep; it was a weeping house for one full hour or more.

The Sub-Registrar of Nidamangalam, a Hindu, is a pious and God-fearing man and he is an obliging officer. Having heard of my troubles he came to see me on the night of the 4th instant when the parish priest of Mannargudi was in my house. He took his seat in a bench in the front verandah of the old house. After the priest left he wanted to see the several places where the havoc was committed. I took him to the upstairs and showed him the several places where clothes were burnt and pictures pasted in the walls were burnt, and also to the downstairs cooking room where cross marks were rubbed out by means of cow dung. He closely noted all these and asked me to send a piece of silk on the next morning. He added that he would send something rolled in the silk and that I might leave it in a place where there would be no access to children and others. I sent a piece of silk and the Sub-Registrar was kind enough to send a packet. I accordingly left it in the upstairs in a niche. When crucifixes, pictures and other holy things were either destroyed, thrown away or burnt, this silk packet alone was left untouched. As stated above, I left the old house on the night of the 6th instant. The distance from the old house to the new house will be more than a furlong. On 11 March when Very Rev. Father Mederlet came for the first time, after he blessed the new house I took him to the old house, where I noticed this silk packet in the niche I left it. Two or three days after this that silk packet was found in one of the windows of the new house . . .

[We are not told anything of the contents of the packet, but when its mysterious transference from one house to the other was being discussed, one of the " females " of the household remarked: " would it not be equally possible for the devil to bring back the medal of the Madonna," which after sundry disappearances and reappearances had finally been lost in the old house ? Whereupon, as Mr. T. P. assures us, before she had finished speaking this medal fell from the roof into the middle of the group. The disturbances did not cease, or apparently grow less, with the continuance of the novena. In particular the diary states that the Enthronement picture, the Agnus Dei, and the relic containing the blood of Don Bosco, all of which had been fixed in their places securely by Father Mederlet on the occasion of his visit on 11 March, were torn to pieces. The Bishop of Mylapore accordingly authorised the same Very Rev. Father to say Mass in the house, and the news of this reached Mr. T. P. on the 17th.]

How happy I was when I got these happy tidings, God only knows. Next morning the Very Rev. Father arrived and went straight to my house. His whole care was to give me relief. Though it was 10 a.m. when his train arrived, he did not care for his coffee. [The writer's views as to the obligation of fasting communion would seem, it must be admitted, to be a little vague]. We all confessed. There was the solemn Mass, we received holy communion and the Mass finished. After taking the poor and untimely coffee given to Rev. Father Mederlet, S.C., he sat in the entrance to the eastern room, having the middle hall and westen room in his view, and said thus '' I would see what the devil would do." Nothing serious happened. Everything seemed to be quiet and calm. He left Nidamangalam for Tanjore by the evening 6.30 p.m. train and said that I would be all right on the next day, being the last day of the novena and the day of the festival of St. Joseph.

I told the Very Rev. Father that I have strong hopes in St. Joseph that he would give me complete relief from the next day, and added that if I could get such relief I would arrange to say High Mass [presumably he means—have High Mass said] for the souls of the dead in my family on a Wednesday after Easter, that I would feed not less than 100 poor persons, that a procession would be had on the evening of the same day in honour of St. Joseph, that I would publish this great favour done to my family both in Christian and

Hindu newspapers, and that this would be also announced in the church on the rejoicing day. I related the same thing to my Hindu friends and magicians who were constantly visiting me and watching the result.

19 March, 1920. The day dawned and my heart was full of anxiety as to what would happen. At 6.30 a.m. an iron frying-pan which was in the northern verandah fell suddenly with a loud noise just very close to my head when I was lying down in the eastern room. I immediately got up saying: " Oh, you devil, you have not left me yet " and recited Apostle's Creed. Half an hour hence my upper cloth which was kept in an open box, was taken out of it, kept [sic] on the floor and burnt. We were all anxiously waiting how the day would pass. To our great joy and surprise we saw writings in the bath-room that the devil had left us, that it would never appear, and that it was proceeding to trouble the person who instigated it to trouble us. How happy a day it was! Thanks to St. Joseph! He gave us complete relief. From that moment till this date, viz., 21 April, 1920, we are enjoying complete peace of mind. How grateful we are to our patron saint, we cannot express in word of mouth. 28 April has been fixed for the day to render our heart-felt homage to our patron saint and benefactor St. Joseph. As promised by me I had the happy news published in the Hindu papers [Tamil titles quoted] "the Friend of the Hindu" and " The Truth-Teller," dated 16 Panguni Siddherti, equivalent to 28 March, 1920.

A. S. THANGAPRAGASAM PILLAY.

This is certainly a very curious narrative and the first impulse of the reader, especially if he has never looked into the evidence cited in similar cases of poltergeist phenomena, will be to dismiss the whole as a cock-and-bull story, or a pious fraud, and at any rate as a fresh argument justifying the mistrust of native Christians entertained by the average Englishman in India.

On the other hand, the story has at least this confirmation, that a summary of it was published in the neighbourhood when the events were still recent. I have before me, the *Morning Star* for July, 1920, a Catholic journal edited at Trichinopoly. The *Morning Star*, as we may learn from its wrapper, was " printed by Rev. Brother Joseph, S.J., Superintendent of St. Joseph's Industrial School Press, Trichinopoly." This is the same Brother Joseph, who, as stated in the earlier portion of this account, visited Mr. T. P.'s house on 4 March, the day after the manifestations began, and saw the damaged pictures with the remnants of the burnt clothes. But lest anyone should suspect that the Jesuits at Trichinopoly were simply parties to an imposture organised in the interest of Catholic propaganda, it may be pointed out that the *Morning Star* calls attention to the references made to the case in " several Hindu papers," and in particular quotes and translates from the Tamil a paragraph which appeared in the newspaper called the *Hindu Nesan* (" The Hindu Friend "). It runs as follows:

Some time ago we heard that someone had through a magician induced the devil to do havoc in the house of Mr. Thangapragasams Pillay, the Sub-Magistrate of Nidamangalam, and that all attempts to drive away the devil had been fruitless. It is a fact that from 3 March, 1920 to the 19th, Mr. T. P. himself and his family suffered a great deal from the devil's persecution, as was already published in our last week's issue. Mr. T. P. being a Catholic made a *Novena*, which we call *Virutham* (prayer and penance), to a certain Catholic Saint, requesting that he might be delivered from the devilish persecution on Friday 19 March. His prayer was heard, and we are very glad to learn that all the troubles stopped on Friday the 19th.

Again, however much we may be inclined to suspect exaggeration, there can be no doubt as to the fact that Mr. T. P. quitted his first house and took another. The *Morning Star* mentions this migration made under stress of the continuous annoyance of the spook and it must have been well known throughout the neighbourhood. Even under Oriental conditions such a step is not suddenly taken by a large family without serious cause.

Another remark made by the *Morning Star* seems worthy of special notice.

Such cases of haunted houses are not infrequent in these parts, especially among Hindus. One often hears that stones or worse things are falling in the house of Mr. So-and-So. The ordinary— one might almost say the classical—way of removing the cause of the mischief is to call in a professional magician, and offer him a decent remuneration for his trouble and a sum of money for a sacrifice to the evil one. The magician comes, performs the sacrifice, recites *mantras*, and the mischief ceases. Mr. T. P. in refusing the *hundreds of offers of service by magicians*, went against the ordinary way of doing.

It seems likely that such incidents are more familiar in pagan India than in Christian Europe, but as we have seen, they occur not rarely in every part of the world. No mal-observation, or expectant attention, or nerves, or lapse of memory can lead a man to state in good faith, only a few weeks after the event: " We all got up and were standing amazed, when of a sudden the vessel containing cooked rice rose to the roof of the house and crashed down to the floor in pieces. Immediately the sauce and the butter-milk vessels followed suit, rose to the roof, fell down and were broken." Either this did happen, or the narrator is consciously lying; and lying in such a way that all his family and neighbours, who undoubtedly will have read the *Morning Star*, must know that he is lying.

Further it seems extremely improbable that anyone who was simply bent on courting favour with Catholic ecclesiastical authorities, or magnifying the efficacy of saintly intercessions, would invent a story in which blessed pictures, medals, crucifixes, relics, holy-water and exorcisms play such a very inglorious part. In spite of Mr. T. P.'s faith in them, they appear in his diary to have been quite powerless to keep in check the evil agencies against which they are commonly employed.

Finally, reference may be made to a circumstance of which I was quite unaware when the first part of the foregoing narrative was published in 1929. The Very Rev. Fr. Mederlet, the Salesian missionary and parish priest at Tanjore, so frequently referred to above, has since then been appointed Archbishop of Madras. His Grace came to England for the Emancipation centenary, and he remembered perfectly the visits he paid to Mr. T. P.'s house at Nidamangalam, as I heard from himself. Though, as the diary shows, Archbishop Mederlet was not himself an eye-witness of any of the manifestations, he is able to testify to the real excitement and consternation of the whole family and the impression made in the locality by these doings.

CHAPTER VII

POLTERGEISTS BEFORE THE LAW COURTS[1]

SPEAKING generally, it rarely happens that spiritistic phenomena are subjected to any such test of their authenticity as is supplied by the taking of oaths and cross-examination of witnesses before a legal tribunal. But this does occasionally occur, especially as a result of the damage to property or the disturbances to peace of mind caused by the alleged poltergeists. It has struck me, then, that it might be of interest to bring together such scanty records as are accessible of this kind of official inquiry, though I may confess from the outset that the efforts of bench and bar to arrive at the truth seem to have proved just as inconclusive as the investigations of private individuals.

The earliest case which I have come upon—excluding prosecutions for witchcraft—dates from 1575. A certain M. Gilles Bolacre had rented a house at Tours, but when he came to take possession he found that it was haunted and that his nights were seriously disturbed by turbulent spirits. He accordingly made application before the local tribunals to obtain a declaration that the lease was null and void. This was granted, but the lessor lodged an appeal before a higher Court in Paris, and Pierre Le Loyer in his book *Quatre Livres des Spectres* (1586) prints at full length what purport to be the pleadings of Counsel in the hearing of the case. The gentlemen of the long robe, it appears, did things in great style in those days. The speech of Maître René Chopin for the appellant contains numerous quotations from ancient Greek authors including Aeschylus, Marcus Aurelius, Euripides, Philo, Alexius Comnenus, Epictetus and Lucian, together with extracts from such everyday Latin authorities as Tertullian, Seneca, Quintilian and the British historian, Gildas. His theme was, of course, the sacred character of a contract which had been signed, sealed and delivered, but he also urged that a belief in ghosts was a superstition of the common people, and that the decision of the judge in the lower Court was deplorable and scandalous, seeing that it served no better purpose

---

[1] *The Month*, April and May 1934

than to encourage vulgar credulity.   So far as I can make out, the evidence of witnesses was not tendered in the appeal.   The facts were apparently accepted from the records of the lower tribunal.

Maître Vau, the opposing Counsel, in his reply, did not allow himself to be outdone in the matter of quotations from the classics. His point was that infestation by ghosts had always been recognised as a fact of common experience.   He cited texts to that effect from Jamblichus, Origen, Gregory of Nyssa, Cyprian, Seneca, Livy, Philo, Cicero, Plutarch, Lucan, Athenodorus, Pliny the younger, Suetonius, and Dion Chrysostom, etc., etc.   Whether the judges were asked to verify each quotation is not recorded.   It would have needed rather a large library.   The Court seems to have reserved judgment so far as regards any pronouncement on the question of principle, but it decided that the annulment of the lease in the lower tribunal could not be upheld, owing to an informality. The judge had no power to invalidate the lease unless " lettres royaux " were obtained, and this had not been done.   The lease, therefore, held good, Le Loyer, however, states that the necessary " lettres royaux " were subsequently procured and that the lease was, accordingly, voided.[1]

Further, Le Loyer, who was himself a jurisconsult, quotes Alphonsus on the Digests, and amongst later authorities Arnault Ferrou of Bordeaux as well as the Spanish jurist Didacus Covarrubias on the question of haunted houses.   The Spaniard last named had in particular stated that the question had more than once been debated before the Courts of Granada, and that it was always laid down that a tenant who found himself disturbed by ghosts was justified in refusing to pay the rent.   Anyway one would think that an invasion of poltergeister was almost as unpleasant as an invasion of cockroaches, and we know that the last named has of late been definitely recognised as ground for rescinding a contract.

But let us turn to something more modern.   The Cideville case is interesting because we possess a copy, or at least, a summary, of the proceedings in Court; for Mr. Andrew Lang, through an influential friend, was able to obtain a transcript from the Court archives. The incidents which became the subject of inquiry occurred in 1850-51.[2]

Before M. Foloppe, Juge de Paix at Yerville (Seine Inférieure)

---

[1] Le Loyer, " Discours " (ed. 1608), pp. 662-670.

[2] See the *Proceedings of the Society for Psychical Research*, Vol. XVIII (1904), pp. 454-463.

one Thorel, a shepherd, summoned M. l'Abbé Tinel, the Curé of Cideville, for defamation of character and for an assault, the prosecutor alleging that he had been beaten with a stick " to the effusion of blood." The Curé's answer to the charge was that, so far as concerned the assault, he had struck the man in self-defence, and that the defamation amounted to no more than the statement that he (Thorel) pretended to be a sorcerer and claimed to be able to make things uncomfortable for those who offended him. The case had arisen in this wise. In November, 1850, strange poltergeist disturbances had begun to occur at the presbytery of Cideville in connection with two boys aged fourteen and twelve who were the Curé's pupils. Weird noises, knockings and hammerings were heard at intervals. These, as time went on, increased in violence. On some occasions the uproar was deafening, so that it was impossible to stay in the room. Furthermore, tables and chairs and fire-irons began to move of themselves. The children were frightened and naturally the disturbances became a topic of conversation throughout the neighbourhood. The shepherd, Thorel, seems clearly to have let it be understood that he knew more about these doings than he chose to say. He posed as one possessing occult powers. The younger boy also declared himself to be haunted by a spectre wearing a blouse, and later on gave evidence in Court to that effect. Moreover, on one occasion (when in company with the Curé) he met Thorel and identified him as the man in the blouse who haunted him. The Curé, who by this time had been almost driven out of his wits by the noises and the general upset, seems to have believed that there was something diabolical going on, and that Thorel was the cause of it. He scolded the shepherd in violent terms, until the man actually knelt down and begged the boy's pardon. The Curé afterwards spoke of the matter to the shepherd's employer who dismissed him from his service. Then the man Thorel, meeting the priest again, threatened physical violence and the Curé struck him with his stick. A summons followed, and the case, after an adjournment, came before the Juge de Paix on 28 January, 1851.

Though the poltergeist disturbances were only indirectly connected with the charge against the priest, a great deal of evidence concerning them was given by the witnesses, who were presumably on oath. The two boys corroborated each other in their accounts of what had occurred. They seem, also, from certain private letters which have been preserved, to have made a good impression when they were transferred elsewhere after the trial and the phenomena had ceased. Still, the boys and the Curé may be regarded as deeply interested parties. The evidence of the neighbours and visitors is less open to suspicion. Cheval, a farmer, described as the " *Maire*" of Cideville, declares that he saw the tongs and shovel at the house of M. Tinel " leave the hearth and travel to the middle of the room." They were replaced, but at once flew out again. " My eyes," he said, " were fixed on them to see what moved them, but I saw nothing at all." He had lain in bed with the children on one occasion, his hands in their hands and his feet on their feet, and in these circumstances he " saw the coverlet whisked off the bed."

M. Leroux, the Curé of a neighbouring village, swore that he saw a hammer, moved by some invisible force, " leave the shelf where it lay and fall in the middle of the room without making more noise than if a hand had gently laid it down."

Madame de Saint-Victor, a lady of good social position, living at a Château in the neighbourhood, states in her evidence: " Yesterday, again, I saw a candlestick leave the chimney-piece in the kitchen and hit my *femme de chambre* in the back, while a key, lying on the table, flew off and struck the child's ear. I must admit that I cannot say precisely where the key was, as I did not see it start on its flight, but only saw it as it landed."

Her son, Robert de Saint-Victor, aged twenty-three, gave this testimony:

A week ago I went to the presbytery again, and was alone with the children and the old servant-maid; I set one of the children in each of the windows of the room upstairs, I being outside, but so placed that I could watch all their movements. Besides, they could not have stirred without risk of falling; and I then heard raps struck in the room, similar to those caused by a mallet. I went up to the room and I saw one of the children's desks advancing towards me with no visible force to push it; however, I did not notice it at the moment of its starting. I am convinced that the children had nothing to do with it, since they were still standing in the windows. Being, one day, at the presbytery with the mayor, I heard loud blows such as the children could not have produced.

Another witness, a man named Bouffay, gave very material evidence regarding the Curé's first remonstrance to Thorel.

Being [he stated] at the presbytery, I saw M. Tinel put his hand lightly on Thorel's shoulder saying, " You have spoken very impudently; I should not be surprised if you knew something about what is happening at the presbytery "; and the child then said, " I know this man to be the one who has been following me about for a fortnight." M. Tinel told Thorel to go on his knees and ask the child's pardon. Thorel fell on his knees and begged pardon, adding, " but I don't know what for."

The same witness declared that he had been several times at the presbytery when the noises were going on. The first time the racket was continual, but it occurred only in places where the children were, both in the church and at the presbytery. On this first visit the noise showed intelligence and responded to suggestions. . . . " It was sometimes so loud that when I was lying in the same room with the children I thought the ceiling would fall in." He declared further that both upstairs and downstairs he saw a perfectly isolated table shift its position without any perceptible cause.

Several other witnesses spoke in terms which imputed intelligence to the agency producing the knockings. If asked to drum a particular tune it drummed in such a way that the tune was quite clearly indicated, though the ghostly repertoire was not extensive. It gave a highly satisfactory rendering of " Au clair de la lune," and of the " Cujus animam " of Rossini's " Stabat Mater," and we are told of other pieces, e.g., " J'ai du bon tabac " and " Maître corbeau." The spirit seems, however, to have failed when asked to favour the company with the waltz from " William Tell," but when somebody hummed the tune, it was heard practising this new piece during the day.

The most impressive witness, however, was the Marquis de Mirville. He was interested in such phenomena, and came forty-two miles—one has to bear in mind that there were no automobiles and few railways in those days—to be present at the presbytery as soon as he heard of the disturbances. He slept there, and when the Curé went off to say Mass, he conducted a little private séance with the two boys all by himself. He was an absolute stranger to the children, and, supposing his testimony reliable, the evidence is certainly curious. I quote Mr. Andrew Lang's summary.

Last Wednesday I went to the presbytery of Cideville and said to the Agency, " When you wish to reply affirmatively knock once; if negatively, knock twice." Immediately a single rap was heard. " Then you will be able to tell me how many letters there are in my name ? " Eight raps were heard, the last more emphatic than the rest, apparently to indicate that it was the last! After similarly obtaining a correct answer for his Christian names, he asked about his children. First the eldest. Five raps—quite correct, she is called *Aline*. Then the youngest. Nine raps. A mistake, but immediately rectified, for seven raps were struck. She is called *Blanche*. " Now let us pass to my age, strike as many raps as I have years." Instantly the raps succeeded each other with such rapidity that I was obliged to stop their flow in order to count them. On their being repeated more slowly, forty-eight raps were given very distinctly, the forty-eighth being accentuated. " That is not all; how many months do you reckon between the first of January this year and the day I shall be forty-nine ? " Three loud raps and a faint one followed. Correct, and by further questioning the exact day was indicated.

" How many letters are there in the name of the village where I live. Be careful not to make the usual mistake." Ten raps were given. Now I live at Gomerville, a name often written incorrectly with two m's, but the mistake was here avoided.

The witness was questioned by the defence as to the possibility that the Curé had produced the phenomena himself. He answered: " I should be much surprised if anyone within these walls could seriously believe that. I cannot think it possible to produce such disturbances by natural means. The cause must be supernatural." On behalf of the plaintiff he was asked whether he believed the phenomena could be produced by a poor shepherd unable to read or write. To which he replied: " I do not think he could produce them by himself, but he might with the assistance of an occult and supernatural cause." He was further asked whether the Curé had called upon him at Gomerville, because the priest had apparently been seen in the neighbourhood! He replied that he had never set eyes on the Curé before last Wednesday, and he had not previously even known that such a place as Cideville existed.

This is, after all, only a specimen of the evidence. We hear of window panes which were broken and which had to be boarded up. Also a man named Dufour, a land agent, when at the presbytery, saw a table advance into the room without anyone touching it. The witness put it back in its place. It moved forward a second time and came about ten feet into the room, the children not touching it. As the witness was going downstairs, he stopped on the first flight to look round at the table, and saw it come forward to the edge of the stairway impelled by an invisible force. The witness also remarked that the table had no castors. This occurred in the absence of the Curé from the presbytery.

It must be admitted that the procedure seems very confused, and that the witnesses were allowed to ramble on and to give hearsay evidence with a freedom which would not be tolerated in an English Court, but, after thirty-four witnesses in all had been heard, judgment was delivered on 4 February. The case was decided in the Curé's favour and against the plaintiff. No conclusion was arrived at as to the cause of the phenomena. It was held that though the Curé had undoubtedly stated that Thorel was mixed up in the disturbances in his house, still the evidence of at least five witnesses proved that the plaintiff had himself spoken in terms which suggested this, and that he had also boasted that he was able to exercise necromantic powers! Consequently he had only himself to thank for his dismissal. The alleged assault was a trifling matter, and had been provoked by his own conduct. Thorel had claimed 1,200 francs damages, but he was non-suited, and the Court ordered him to pay 150 francs by way of costs.

It is somewhat regrettable, from the point of view of the psychic researcher, that the disquietudes caused by alleged poltergeists have not more frequently led to litigation. One would, for example, very much like to be able to refer to a judicial investigation of the Worksop disturbances of 1883. They are described by Mr. Andrew Lang at some length in his admirable article on " Poltergeists " in the eleventh edition (Cambridge, 1911) of the *Encyclopædia Britannica*, and again in his book *The Making of Religion*. It would have been interesting to learn the behaviour under cross-examination of such witnesses as the doctor, Lloyd, and the policeman, Higgs, who, in their signed statements, described how they watched objects securely at rest like basins and china ornaments, jump up into the air and break on the floor, or saw a glass jar fly out of a cupboard and, following a curved line through the open door, dash itself to pieces in the yard. There is often a good deal of exaggeration and failure of memory among the humbler folk who narrate such happenings, and there have been, beyond doubt, many naughty little girls and mischievous urchins who enjoyed the disturbance their pranks had caused and grew extremely skilful in escaping detection. I was present at a meeting of the Society for Psychical Research when an account was given of certain investigations undertaken in connection with a Battersea poltergeist which created a considerable sensation in the London newspapers during January, 1928. More than one sober and intelligent member of the household concerned was convinced of the supernatural character of the phenomena, but skilful inquiry elicited a number of suspicious incidents which pointed to a different conclusion. The fact seemed to be that a spell of skylarking on the part of people outside the house who threw coals and other missiles over the garden wall had caused a panic among some of the inmates and had thoroughly frightened an elderly invalid whose continued presence in the house was not desired by all his younger relatives. This put an idea into the heads of these malcontents that a prolongation of the disturbances might result in a clearance (as in fact it did) which would be to their advantage, and there seems good reason to believe that the later developments were cunningly organised by a couple of them acting in collusion but without the knowledge of the rest.

I should be quite prepared to find that the majority of the reported poltergeist phenomena, especially nowadays when the activity of newspaper editors in search of sensation has made such stories universally familiar, would resolve themselves, under judicial investigation, into cases of trickery in which hysteria, malice, cunning and mere high spirits were all apt to play a part, but there would probably also be found a residuum very difficult to explain. In such a contingency it is more than likely that the presiding magistrate would in practice rule out the evidence for any supernatural event as incredible and inadmissible, or at best would be ingenious enough to find grounds for deciding the case before him upon some other issue.

Shortly after these disturbances at Cideville, a poltergeist outbreak occurred in Russia, which owing, as Dr. Walter Leaf pointed out, " to the happy accident that it resulted in damage to Government property, became the subject of an official inquiry of an obviously unprejudiced character." It will be convenient here to follow rather closely the summary of the case, which Dr. Leaf, having before him the Russian text of the documents printed by Aksakoff, furnished for the *Proceedings* of the Society for Psychical Research in 1897.[1]

In January, 1853, a small cavalry post at the hamlet of Liptsy, in the district of Kharkoff, was commanded by a Captain Jandachenko—the German translation of Aksakoff's volume transliterates the name Shandatschenko—who, with his wife, lived in a fourroomed house, which had been taken by the village community for his official residence. On 4 January, 1853, this house, which previously had been free from any suspicion of ghostly antics, was

[1] See Vol. XII, pp. 319 seq.

7

taken over by the Captain and his wife. They had a bedroom and a sitting-room on one side of the passage, while on the other side were the store-room and the kitchen in which the servants slept at night. There were two maids and three soldiers who, between them, did the work of the house. The probable medium seems to have been the maid Ephimia, but the information available does not enable us to speak with confidence.

After the servants had put out the light but before they had gone to sleep—such is the account which they give in their depositions, without any variation—sundry small objects, such as cups and wooden platters standing on the stove, were thrown about the room. A light was struck, but the throwing continued when no one was looking, and no cause could be found for it. Next day, the 5th, Captain Jandachenko mentioned this to his parish priest, Victor Selyezneff, who came with his church officers on the 6th, the Epiphany, after the ceremony of blessing the water in the river. " Entering the house," says the priest, " I saw a brazier fall in the passage; a basin full of dumplings landed at my feet in the midst of the attendants who were carrying the icons, and I heard repeated knocks." Captain Jandachenko adds that after the house had been sprinkled with holy water—the object of the priest's visit—" an axe was thrown from the loft in the passage against the doors with remarkable velocity and noise." Another priest, whose curiosity had been aroused by what he had been told during the blessing of the river, was also present with several other official visitors who had come to call on the Captain. They went into the kitchen, when " in sight of all of us there was smashed against the door in the passage, where no human being was, a bottle of varnish which had been standing in the sitting-room cupboard under lock and key."

Undaunted, says Dr. Leaf, by the small success of the aspersion, the good priests brought the heavy artillery of the Church into play next day. With the assistance of a third Father, of the church officials, and the icons, a solemn service was read. Hardly had they begun when a stone was thrown in the kitchen, which was empty, and smashed a window in the sight of all. Then a piece of wood, followed by a pail of water, flew out of the kitchen into the midst of the assembly, the pail upsetting in the process. The culminating horror was the fall of a stone into the basin of holy water itself. The house was again thoroughly sprinkled, and the holy objects carried back to the church; but, as the phenomena still continued, the Captain begged two of the priests to return and read the formal prayers for the exorcism of evil spirits. This seems to have had little more effect than the previous services. The phenomena continued in the presence of several fresh witnesses, and on the 8th took a new turn. The bed in the room of the Captain and his wife caught fire in the presence of both; they put it out, but it immediately blazed out in a fresh place, and had to be again extinguished.[1] At the same time two blows were struck on the window by a brick and four panes of glass broken. Captain Jandachenko was at last driven to change his quarters, but moved back after a few days. At the same time, he again had recourse to the services of a priest, which, for the time were successful, as the phenomena were reduced to nothing worse than some " human groaning " of a most doleful description heard by the servants in the kitchen.

But after a few days it all began again; and on 22 January the Captain brought some friends in to witness what was going on. On this occasion his Orderly was slightly wounded in the head by a knife thrown by the evil agency. Things grew worse and worse, and a number of peasants were brought into the house to watch, but, in spite of all care, next afternoon (the 23rd) the roof of the house caught fire and was burnt off, the efforts of the firemen being much hindered by a peculiarly thick and malodorous smoke blown in their faces. This led to an inquiry by the local " ispravnik " (head of the district police) which took place on February 4th and 5th.

In this inquiry nothing was found to direct suspicion against any individual; on the other hand, for no very obvious reason, the manifestations ceased for some months. Captain Jandachenko had, in the meantime, taken another house, and here, on 23 July, the old games began once more. In one room the pillows were thrown off the beds, and in another, jars of water were upset. The Captain made an official application for help, and a guard of peasants were set all round the house as before. In spite of this the phenomena became more violent throughout the next day, and on 25 July a crisis was reached. At eight o'clock the thatched roof was suddenly found to be on fire. It was extinguished before the fire-engine came, but for precaution's sake engine and firemen were kept on the spot. At three o'clock in the afternoon thick smoke was seen coming from a shed in a wing of the house. A soldier crawled in on hands and knees, and dragged out a hay mattress full of smouldering fire, which was put out. Finally, at five o'clock,

---

[1] Compare the similar manifestations of the Indian poltergeist near Tanjore, p. 70 above.

a sudden gust of wind arose, and with it the whole roof of the wing burst into flames. The fire spread so rapidly that the men not only could not start the engine, but had great difficulty in dragging it into a place of safety, and, with the Captain's house, four neighbouring cottages were completely burned to the ground.

This serious damage led to a second official investiagtion, and in the course of this, most of the inhabitants of the village as well as the inmates of the house were examined. The inquiry lasted five days, and no conclusion having been arrived at, the matter was transferred to the civil court at Kharkoff, where, as Dr. Leaf remarks, it was duly pigeon-holed. It was not till many reminders had come from headquarters that a final inquiry was held in July, 1856, three years after the event. The evidence previously given was repeated and the only conclusion reached was that there was no ground of suspicion against any of the people connected with the case. In 1895, Mr. Alexander Aksakoff unearthed the records of the court and printed the depositions *in extenso*, in a work written in Russian. In reviewing this Dr. Walter Leaf published the summary from which I have borrowed most of the above. Since then Aksakoff's book has been translated into German under the title *Vorläufer des Spiritismus*.

It would occupy too much space to reproduce any of these depositions in full, but one may read them in Aksakoff's volume printed without abridgment. There we learn from the Russian Popes how a stone came straight towards them, narrowly missing their heads, and then shattered a pane of glass in the window, and how a small stone grazed the chasuble of one of them, and then fell plump into the vessel of holy water, etc., etc.[1] A plan of the rooms in the first house and a picture of a stove in the kitchen is also furnished in the same book.

The next two prosecutions I propose to touch upon in some detail both occurred in Germany. The first belongs to the year 1888-1889, and the scene of the disturbance was a little hamlet called Resau not far from Berlin. The propinquity to the capital contributed largely to the publicity given to the proceedings. From the

---

[1] A. Aksakoff, *Vorläufer des Spiritismus*, Leipzig, 1898, pp. 51-56 and pp. 163-165. Aksakoff himself was a wealthy man and a distinguished scholar. He belonged to a family of high standing in Russian Court circles. He has reproduced the depositions, even in the German translation, exactly as they stand, with all their wearisome formalities. Much, however, of the evidence, both of the more educated witnesses and of the serfs, leaves an impression of sincerity. The smashing of crockery in an unoccupied room, outside the open door of which the servants were standing (as recounted, for example, in document 33, pp. 77-78), is not easily explained.

point of view of the believer in psychic phenomena it seems to have been a case of a poltergeist, manifesting, as usual, in the vicinity of some child or young person who was an unconscious medium. There were knockings and bangings and the movement of furniture, while stones and other light objects were flung about. Some of the stones broke the windows in an adjoining house. The neighbour prosecuted a boy as the author of the damage. I follow roughly an account of the trial as printed in the *National Zeitung*, but I have also some other sources of information supplied by a booklet issued shortly after,[1] and by the *Psychische Studien* for 1889.

The case was one for the Schöffengericht, *i.e.*, a police court, in which the proceedings are heard by a petty judge and two assessors. The judge in this instance was a certain Dr. Meyer and the jurors or assessors were Herr Brauereibesitzer (Brewery proprietor) Hildebrandt, and Herr Tischlermeister (Master-joiner) Kluge. The Spiritualists of Berlin retained a certain Herr Bieber, a barrister, to defend the accused. The charge was that this lad of fifteen named Karl Wolter, had broken by stones and other missiles six panes of glass, of the value of from ten to twelve marks, in the house of one Neumann; and further that he had been guilty of a grave mis-demeanour in counterfeiting the activities of a so-called " Spuk," whereby great disturbance had been created in the village and the surrounding district.

The accused declared that he knew absolutely nothing of the offences charged against him, that he had never thrown any stones, had never knocked on the shutters and had never made clogs dance about. Fourteen witnesses were called in the case.

The first was the farmer, Karl Böttcher (sixty-four) a relation of the boy. It was in Böttcher's house, where the lad was living as a help, that the manifestations had occurred. Böttcher stated in a voice trembling with emotion that the Spuk had first manifested in November in this way. Every night it happened that his pigs were let out of the pigsty by some unknown hand which unfastened the door. This went on until they locked the sty. Then disturbances began in their own house, and particularly in the recess where they all slept. It began by knocking loudly and suddenly on the wall, though there was nothing to be seen when one lit a lantern. Böttcher had gone out with the boy and looked up and down out-side the house, and, while so engaged a stone broke one of the windows. As the racket continued, Böttcher sent the boy to

[1] *Der Spuk von Resau*, Berlin, 1888.

summon his neighbour Neumann who lived next door. The lad was absent some time and the noise meanwhile increased, but ceased with Neumann's entrance. Later, however, it began again and utensils of all kinds began to move about. Next evening things were worse. Wolter's clogs, which stood beside his bed, flew across to the stove, and his coat which had been placed on a stool was whisked on to the bed of the old wife. When the accused thereupon started up, the Spuk began throwing potatoes and turnips. They were all frightened, " hid their heads under the bedclothes and began praying and singing hymns." The next day they sent for the Lutheran pastor, Dr. Müller, from Bliesensdorf, and he, after convincing himself of the reality of the Spuk, had said to them: " In this house you cannot stay." A little later, while the accused was hewing wood one day in the yard, several stones were thrown against the wall, and on the same day Neumann, his neighbour, had his window panes broken. Stones and cowdung were thrown about freely. The old wife had the bedclothes pulled over her head, and so had the accused. The witness was convinced that Wolter was not the cause of the disturbances though he admitted that he was always close by when they happened. The accused had nothing to gain by producing them.

By far the most important witness was the Pastor, Dr. Müller. He described how, as he entered the house, he saw the milk splash up in the milk pan as a potato fell into it, and how a moment after there was a thundering blow, the reverberations of which lasted three or four seconds. A number of potatoes flew at his head, and as he sat down some object lightly grazed the back of his neck. It was a baking-dish which had sailed horizontally from the stove, and then stopped and fell at his feet. Then a tin funnel came drifting across the room as if it was a leaf blown about by a high wind. Before he left, more potatoes flew at his head and a hambone with meat on it floated towards him out of the open door of a cupboard.

Several other witnesses gave evidence that they had seen stones, etc., flying which no one apparently had thrown, though this always happened in the neighbourhood of Wolter. The court was satisfied that considerable alarm and disturbance had been caused in the district, so much so that thefts which had been committed were put down to the Spuk.

The prosecutor Neumann himself believed in the Spuk at first, but he became convinced as time went on that his windows were broken by no one but the accused. Wolter had seemed to be much amused when he told him that the Spuk was playing pranks in their house; he laughed outright at the recollection of the ham-bone flying at the Minister's head.

The Presiding Magistrate directed attention to the fact that from the moment when the lad had been taken into custody the disturbances had ceased.

A forest-keeper, Forner, described how he had tried to catch Wolter throwing stones. He saw a fragment of tile come flying along and it started from the quarter where Wolter was working in the yard. Two other witnesses told how they came to Böttcher's house to find out what was happening. They also had potatoes flung in their faces. They taxed the accused with doing it and he admitted the charge. Then one of them by stealth threw a potato himself at the old man Böttcher. It struck him in the eye, and he cried out in distress: " My God! my God! here is another already." The master of the school who had had Wolter as a pupil gave evidence to the effect that he was very sly, and an expert ball thrower. With very little apparent movement he nearly always hit his mark.[1]

For the damage to property the prosecution (*Amtsanwalt*) demanded a penalty of fourteen days' imprisonment, and for the sundry misdemeanours of the accused four weeks' detention in custody (*Haft*). Counsel for the defence pleaded for an acquittal and sought to attribute what had occurred to invisible forces of Nature which science had not yet sufficiently investigated. The Court, so the President declared, must take its stand wholly and entirely on the ground of enlightened science, and absolutely refuse to entertain the idea that a magnetic or any other force can play the part of a Spuk. The full penalty demanded was imposed when sentence was given, but an appeal was allowed to a higher court.

When this came on, some fresh evidence was produced regarding the movement of objects in the one big room in which the Böttchers lived, but the sentence of the lower court was upheld by the tribunal which heard the appeal. Fuller detail is impossible here, but the most interesting feature in the case was the evidence given by Dr. Müller in both trials, and by others, concerning the weird path followed by the potatoes, turnips and other missiles. They not only flew round corners and seemed sometimes to move with leisurely deliberation, but they were apt to come to a dead stop suddenly, just as if an invisible hand had checked them in their flight. If this description is veracious, it is absolutely impossible

[1] *National Zeitung*, 11 January, 1889.

that the movement of these objects can have been normally produced. Wolter certainly cannot have thrown them. But if, on
the other hand, the account was an invention, how very curious
that these simple people, who certainly knew nothing about psychic
research or spiritualism, should have hit upon just those precise
characteristics which occur repeatedly in the description of the
stone-throwing phenomena attributed to poltergeists! Mr. Andrew
Lang records several such cases, quoting among other things the
statement of police constable Higgs of Worksop: " then suddenly a
basin, which stood near the end of the bin, near the door, got up
into the air, turning over and over as it went. It went up not very
quickly, not as quickly as if it had been thrown. When it reached
the ceiling it fell plump and smashed." So also at Swanland, near
Hull, in a carpenter's shop, three workmen were pelted by odds and
ends of wood. " Each blamed the others, until this explanation
became untenable. The bits of wood mentioned danced about the
floor, more commonly sailed quickly along, or moved as if borne
by gentle heaving waves." One of the workmen described a piece
of wood coming towards him from a distant corner of the workshop
describing a corkscrew path of about eighteen inches diameter.
" If these were thrown," remarks Mr. Lang, " the thrower must
certainly have had a native genius for pitching at baseball."[1]

No doubt Wolter did throw some missiles when people came
fussing round at a time when nothing particular was happening.
But what boy would refrain from joining in when a piece of fun
like that was going on, or what boy could fail to be highly amused
when a ham-bone flew out of the cupboard and went straight for
the parson? It would have been a joke to last him a lifetime.
On the other hand, in the circumstances, his schoolmaster would be
sure to remember that the culprit, now in trouble, was always
throwing things and hitting the target he aimed at.

The latest, in point of time, of the cases I have to record, came
before the Schöffengericht at Vieselbach, near Weimar, in February,
1921. A young man, Otto Sauerbrey, aged twenty-one, was
charged with contributing to the death of his stepmother by dangerous practices, using mesmeric passes and other treatments which
had the effect of exciting and alarming her. He came to visit her
at Hopfgarten, where she lived with her husband, and he stayed
there from 10 February to 12 February, 1921. He was known to
be addicted to spiritualistic and occult practices. The stepmother

---

[1] Andrew Lang, *The Making of Religion*, 1898, pp. 354-360.

was an invalid confined to her bed. From the time of his visit, during which he used what purported to be hypnotic treatments, all sorts of strange noises were heard and objects in the rooms moved unaccountably. The police were called in to discover the the source of the noises, etc., but found nothing to explain them. Frau Sauerbrey died on 27 March. The case came on before the Schöffengericht on 19 April, 1921. After much evidence had been heard, the accused was acquitted. The official report of the case has been printed, and the abnormal occurrences therein recounted are interesting because it is difficult to see that anyone could have had any motive in inventing or exaggerating them. The husband declares that unaccountable knockings began on 12 February and lasted all night, resounding from the table and from the doors. His wife, who had been bedridden for many months, was physically incapable of making them, and in this her doctor (though he gave medical evidence which exonerated the stepson from having contributed to her death) fully agreed. A stool on which stood a coffee cup, moved of itself, the cup fell and was broken. A table changed its position, so also a bucket and a hand-basin. The next day eight police constables came from Weimar. In the presence of several of these, objects in the room moved without anyone touching them.

The daughter of the deceased, Frieda Pappe, confirmed all this, and declared that the police made experiments, putting the stool, etc., quite beyond the sick woman's reach, but still the things moved, and moved in a direction away from the invalid. A chair and a bucket which were near each other clashed loudly together.

Walter Degenkolbe also swore that he heard the noises and saw the movements of table and stool. The knockings were heard only at night for the most part. Dr. Mahle, a nerve specialist who was called to the case, was of opinion that the noises were caused by the invalid herself. They always ceased when the light was turned up.[1]

The police, unfortunately, were not called upon to give evidence in the case, but by the report of the police-sergeant Pfeil, they were convinced of the movement of the table, buckets, hand-basins, etc., and equally certain that this movement could not have been produced by the invalid.

[1] I take all these details from a paper read at the Copenhagen meeting of the International Congress for Psychical Research (1921), by Dr. Freiherr von Schrenck-Notzing, of Munich. The paper, which is entitled *Der Spuk in Hopfgarten*, is printed in the Official Report of the Congress, pp. 187-221. It quotes in full the minutes of the Schöffengericht and supplies a plan of the room in which the disturbances took place.

CHAPTER VIII

A CITY OF LONDON POLTERGEIST[1]

THE following curious narrative giving an account of disturbances occurring in 1901 upon certain business premises in the heart of the city of London seems worthy of permanent record. The writer was Mr. Lister Drummond, who at that date was practising as a barrister, but who in 1913 became a Metropolitan Police Magistrate. He died in 1916, but his memory was long an inspiration to many of his contemporaries, for his character was one which by its geniality, integrity and devotion to every charitable cause, impressed itself upon all who came into contact with him. A convert to the Catholic Church in 1875 at the age of nineteen, he was conspicuous for his earnest and practical piety, a piety, however, which pre-eminently spelt good works and had nothing in it of emotional extravagance. A short sketch of the life of this model Catholic has been written by His Honour Mr. Robert Noble, till recently Acting Chief Justice of the Leeward Islands, and is published as a pamphlet, now in its second edition, by the Catholic Truth Society.

As the character of the witness is of vital importance in all questions of evidence, it may be well to borrow from Mr. Noble's brief account an appreciation or two penned by Drummond's non-Catholic friends. Mr. Walter Sichel, the author, whose well-known biographies of Bolingbroke and Sheridan leave the impression of a rather cynical outlook upon humanity at large, after Drummond's death wrote of him as follows:

I think that of all men that I have ever met, Lister Drummond most recommended goodness, for he made it lovely and lovable . . . You came away from him not only better, but happier. There was a natural shrewdness in all his simplicity. Twice I had the pleasure of sitting next to him in his court, and his conduct of the varied cases before him was wonderful, so quick, so inseeing, so firm, yet so merciful . . . Hypocrisy was his abhorrence, and he had

[1] *The Month*, June 1932

an instinct for the class of character before him, and an intuition into motive or situation. He was the right man in the right place, doing not only justice, but good, and bringing unusual gifts to assist and relieve his functions.

Not less warmly sympathetic was the tribute paid to his former colleague by Sir Chartres Biron, famous among London Police Magistrates.

For all Drummond's friends [he writes] something of the sunshine of life seemed to go with him. After a full and varied life, which meant so much to many, to be missed by all may be a better record than many a one of more material triumph . . . At one time I shared a room with him. It was a wonderful tonic to have, as it were on tap, this radiant ally, always cheerful, always sympathetic.[1]

Other friends tell of his simplicity of heart, of his frankness of speech, of " his wisdom that was never cynical, and a deep experience of life where disillusionment caused no despondency "; while Mr. Theobald Mathew, the able and witty counsel who shared his legal chambers, informs us how " he certainly communicated to others both his holiness and his joy." It can hardly be too much to say of such a man that deception was impossible to him. His word must be trusted as an absolutely faithful witness to his thought, neither is it easy to suppose that a man of his legal experience could readily be imposed upon by clumsy trickery. And in any case his own character was in some degree a guarantee of the character of those whom he called his friends. This much premised for the benefit of those who may not have enjoyed the privilege of Lister Drummond's personal acquaintance, I leave his narrative to speak for itself.

ACCOUNT OF CERTAIN PHENOMENA WITNESSED BY ME AT THE
OFFICES OF THE[2] . . .

27 *Jan.* 1901. After luncheon at the Mathews' I was on my way

---

[1] Of course these appreciations of Lister Drummond's high character which have been printed in Justice Noble's pamphlet do not connect the writers in any way with the story which follows, or suggest that they had any knowledge of it.

[2] The name of the business firm in question is given in the manuscript before me, but readers will readily understand that I have no right to make it public without permission. I am indebted for the communication of the manuscript to the kindness of the late Father Charles Beauclerk, S.J., who had this copy in his possession for many years. An endorsement, " By me, Lister Drummond, 27 June, 1901," may, or may not, indicate the date at which the narrative was drawn up. It possibly refers only to the making of a copy.

to Vespers at the Oratory, when I was accosted by a gentleman who said he wanted to speak to me on an important matter which would perhaps take too long to explain there. He suggested that he should come and see me. I said that I had a quarter of an hour then and perhaps he could give me an outline of what he wished to say. He then told me that he had heard I had some experience in investigating supernatural phenomena (a mistake on his part) and he wanted my assistance in elucidating certain extraordinary occurrences which for the past eighteen months had greatly disturbed him in the Office of the . . . ., where he was employed as Registrar. He had been in the employment of the Company for a considerable number of years and had been fifteen years a Catholic.

He complained that at intervals, which had latterly become more frequent, articles of office furniture, such as the tops of ink bottles, rulers, blotting pads, etc., had been thrown violently about the office, apparently through no human agency, in the day time and in his presence and in that of his fellow clerks. Chairs had been overthrown, coal and asbestos scattered about and the fender in the outer office had been dragged out at an angle of forty-five degrees. On the previous Friday a bottle of oil, used for the copying press, with a narrow neck down which a sixpence could not be dropped, was found to contain a French (Empire) penny.[1] It was seen by all the clerks and placed in a cupboard under the counter and locked up. On one of the clerks, who had been out when the discovery was made, expressing a wish to see the bottle, Steward unlocked the cupboard and took out the bottle. The penny had disappeared. While he was in the room occupied by Stoer, the accountant, who was examining the bottle with him, small missiles— pieces of plaster, etc.— were thrown at them from the ceiling in the corner of the room. He also stated that at a recent date an old iron screw was flung at them in the office, and just before leaving he and two other clerks placed it upon the mantlepiece in the outer office. They then left, locking the office doors behind them. Just as they were descending the stone public staircase, something was thrown after them: it was the screw.

He also complained of the swing door, leading from the outer to the inner office, being on several occasions violently opened and swung backwards and forwards.

He stated that Stoer had seen the glass door of the Secretary's

---

[1] Mr. G. Elliot Anstruther pointed out to Fr. Thurston that this was a well-known conjuring trick, for which French pennies were necessary. English ones were not suitable, as being too hard.—J.H.C.

room, softly open and close when he (Stoer) was the only person in the office. I promised to call and see him at the office on the following day.

28 *Jan.* Went with Keane at about 5 p.m. to the . . . . . Offices; was introduced to Stoer[1] (accountant), Sharpe, Knapp, Coulson and Wedrell. They corroborated what Steward had told me on previous day. They produced a tray full of odds and ends, such as pieces of sealing wax, silver-paper pellets, part of a metal lizard that formerly was on a marble ball used as a letter weight belonging to Steward, and which has been mysteriously smashed to pieces and the ball broken in half some time before. They asserted that these were articles, from time to time thrown at them or about the room, by some unknown agency. They all professed to be entirely ignorant of the cause of the phenomena. On all the clerks, except Steward, leaving the office, Keane and I made a careful examination of the office and cupboard under the counter, but could find nothing abnormal in any way whatever. After the clerks left we placed the tray with the various articles which had been shown to us by the clerks, a bottle of oil, and some other things including the two halves of the marble letter weight, which we called for short the " discs," in the cupboard, and sealed it with red tape in such a way that the cupboard could be opened wide enough for anyone to see what was in it, but not wide enough for it to be possible to take anything out of it. Steward then locked the cupboard and we left the office.

30 *Jan.* Came to the office early, in response to a postcard from Steward. He stated that on the previous day, early in the afternoon one of the " discs " we had placed in the cupboard, had come down in front of his desk, apparently from the ceiling. On this happening, he and the other clerks looked into the cupboard which was still sealed. They saw that all the articles, which had been in the tray when the cupboard was sealed, were out of the tray and scattered about the cupboard shelf. The bottle of oil, which had been placed by me in a standing position, was lying on its side, filled with apparently some inky substance, and both " discs " were gone. The cupboard was left sealed up and remained so till I arrived. In the afternoon, in the company of Keane, I broke the seals. The cupboard was entirely empty, tray, the articles it originally contained, bottle of oil and " discs " had disappeared. After the

---

[1] Miss Monica Drummond, sister of the diarist, wrote to Fr. Thurston (10 June, 1932) to say that the names were Storr and Kupp, not Stoer and Knapp. Otherwise she confirmed her brother's account.—J.H.C.

departure of all the clerks except Steward, he and Keane and I collected various articles with a view to sealing them up in the cupboard again. We placed in the cupboard, amongst other things, the top of an ink bottle and a quarter pound tin of snuff. On proposing to place the latter in the cupboard, Steward opened the tin, and had considerable difficulty in doing so owing to the top being so tightly fixed. On opening it and seeing that it contained snuff, Steward put the top firmly on the tin again, and placed the tin in the cupboard. We then endeavoured to find a bottle of oil or other liquid to place in the cupboard.

While we were searching for such an article, the cupboard door being wide open, we heard a sharp ring of something falling, and on looking into the cupboard we found the top of the tin of snuff lying by the side of the tin. We replaced the top, locked the cupboard and sealed it closely, it being impossible to open the door in the slightest degree without breaking the seals.

31 *Jan.* While at the Seamen's Home, 16 Wellclose Square, in the evening, Steward and Keane came and told me that at mid-day the sealed cupboard burst open and at the same time one of the " discs " fell in front of it.

1 *Feb.* Keane and Steward again sealed up the cupboard, which then contained some half dozen copies of the *Royalist*, the tin of snuff, the letter weight, bottle of gum, a broken model of a steam engine and one of the " discs." The cupboard was sealed by Keane, with a medal he got in Rome with the heads of SS. Peter and Paul engraved on it.

4 *Feb.* I received the following letter from Steward:

Queen's Hotel, Brighton.
3 Feb. 1901.

My dear Sir,

You will have received from me by post at the Temple, half the " disc " and a variety of odds and ends that descended on us on the morning of Friday. As I informed you on the card, the seal of the cupboard door was then intact and remained so till 6.20 p.m. that day. For your satisfaction I may say I watched it every hour that afternoon, realizing the importance in such matters, of absolute certainty as to facts. It must have been about three o'clock or just a little after, when the two or three who go out to lunch last had but recently returned, that something descended from the ceiling, or to speak more strictly, from the top of the cupboard in the outer office, to the right of the fireplace, on which, you may remember, there

are four large boxes labelled No. 1, 2, 3, and 4, and struck the floor
with terrific violence. This proved to be the other half of the
" disc," or rather, the greater portion of it. Keane at once got a
ladder to see the place from which it had come, and while mounting,
the lid of one of the boxes suddenly flew open. He only saved it
coming down on his head by putting up his hand. At that moment
our " Jack in the Box " Secretary came out and he descended, but
on his disappearance again into his room, reascended and called
out to me to come and look on what he had discovered on the top
of the said boxes within a few inches of the ceiling. I did so and
found to my surprise the tray containing the articles he had put
into the cupboard on a previous occasion. It had also a plentiful
supply of pins on it, and looked in every respect just as he had left
it in the cupboard. I brought it down and locked it up in my
private drawer of the large Milner safe which has a Chubb's patent
lock. A succession of missiles was then showered on us from the
top of the safe; portions of gaspipes, nuts and screws, and I began
to have serious apprehension that the spook was going slowly to
tear the safe to pieces. He, however, turned his attention to the
other end of the office and Stoer's room, and now began a perfect
fusillade of missiles.

The Secretary happened to leave at this time but at the moment
of his going through the passage did not notice anything. Then
in Stoer's room occurred a strange phenomenon, a perfect shower
of articles descended from the ceiling—stones and pieces of quartz,
copper coins, old nails, etc. The situation was not without a
certain sense of humour, and Stoer ran to the corner of the room
for his umbrella, which he put up, devoutly wishing you and Keane
would put in an appearance. My hands were simply full of these
missiles, many of which are now at my rooms at Brompton Square.

Two friends of Stoer's looked in at this moment, and witnessed
what was going on.

In the outer office things were even worse. I saw a few moments
later Stoer and Coulson dancing from side to side to escape the
heavy letter weights which were being thrown about. Coulson's
curved blotting pad was thrown right across the office; a chair
near the screen by which he was standing was thrown bodily across
the office, in the direction of the fireplace with comparatively little
noise and no injury. The doors of the safe then slammed violently
and a high stool close by fell straight over. This kind of thing went
on till about 6.20 p.m. Then Stoer suddenly shouted out " Great
God, look! " I alone got up from my desk and rushed forward to

find the doors of the counter cupboard had been flung violently open, but there was no vestige of the seal or the red wax on the cupboard that formed its groundwork. We all searched the floor all round and could not find a particle of it. At this moment, from my desk at the other end of the office where not a soul was standing (everybody being near the counter) there fell upon the floor in front of the fireplace a *Pearson's Magazine* which had been thrown out of the cupboard of my desk only a few days before, in a rather mysterious manner. On the present occasion it fell, as I was saying, in the middle of the floor in front of the fireplace. The leaves were then slowly turned over until they at length remained open at a certain page. The book was not open wide, if you can understand, but drawn together at the lower end, as if held together by someone's finger and thumb; and in this strange position it remained for several seconds, so that we could all see the picture on the open page. It was a horrible one, representing a Spirit trying to hurl a man with a gun over a precipice, and it was an illustration of a series of " Real Ghost Stories," published in that Magazine about two years ago. The magazines were removed to the office on my leaving my rooms at Osnaburgh Street about that time, for want of space. As everyone saw this picture and everyone seemed to recognize the significance of its meaning even before I did myself, I snatched up the magazine and went to my desk. On it was an open ledger and on the open page was the unbroken seal of SS. Peter and Paul, perfectly intact, so much so that I recognized most distinctly the features of the Apostle Peter.

I locked up the seal in my safe drawer together with the magazine and tray.

A perfect silence and intense feeling of relief then followed. Everyone felt it, and Stoer said " I am as certain as I am of my existence that the thing is gone and will never trouble us." We all remained in the Office till 9.30 and not a sound again disturbed us nor was there the slightest further manifestation.

Yours very sincerely,
F. Villiers Steward.

8 *Feb.* Went to the office in the afternoon. Empty tobacco tins were flying about and a 1 lb. weight was thrown down in the passage leading from the clerks' room to board-room.

I watched carefully, but could detect no sign of any of the clerks, who were all present, having anything to do with the disturbance.

12 *Feb.* Went to the office in the afternoon, found Keane with

an umbrella up to ward off the missiles that were flying about the office. All was in confusion and work, they said, was impossible. The clerks showed me an old boot, which they said had been flung about the office all the afternoon. Steward and Stoer asserted that a few minutes before I came into the office, Steward had, in Stoer's presence, locked the boot up in Stoer's iron safe in his room. Steward having locked the safe turned away to cross the room, when he was struck in the back by the boot. They opened the safe and the boot was gone. I replaced the boot with some other articles in the safe, but did not lock it. Shortly after the boot appeared on the counter in the outer office. No one had been near the safe between the time I placed the boot in it, and its appearance on the counter.

Keane came in while I was at the office and witnessed most of the phenomena that afternoon.

Note, 8 Feb. On this occasion I saw a tin kettle, used by the clerks for boiling water for their tea, go across the room. It could hardly be said to be thrown, as I could see its passage through the air. It described the following figure [here, in the manuscript, a curved line is drawn].

At this point the narrative abruptly ends.

Mr. W. M. Keane retained a clear recollection of the incidents recounted above when I questioned him in 1932. He was kind enough to allow me to discuss the matter with him, and I heard from his own lips the confirmation of what his friend Drummond had set down. Moreover, though these two, having little direct interest in psychic research, made no attempt to push their experiences further, he informs me that, as he heard from Steward, the manifestations continued for some time afterwards, and were marked by notable developments. In particular the spook began to communicate orally or by raps with the clerks whose names are mentioned above. They asked questions and received answers which were often characterised by an inexplicable knowledge of matters beyond the cognizance of anyone present. For example, they inquired one day where was the Mr. Keane whose acquaintance they had made on the occasion described above. The reply was given that he was at Lourdes, which was quite correct; but Mr. Keane assures me that he had slipped off there without announcing his intention to anyone, even his own mother being ignorant of it. It also appears that many of the communications received through the poltergeist were of a very unpleasant character, obscenities often predominating. Another point of interest is that one evening, after the staff of clerks had gone home, the three Catholics fetched a priest—it was Father Nicholas Power of St. Mary's, Moorfields—to bless the premises with holy water. Some temporary cessation of the disturbances seems to have resulted, but soon afterwards things were worse than ever. It is curious to note that in a description which Giraldus Cambrensis has left of a mud-throwing poltergeist in Wales at the end of the twelfth century it is stated that the exorcisms of the Church were similarly ineffective. The priests coming in procession with cross and holy water were themselves made a target, and Giraldus concludes that the sacramentals are meant to protect mankind against serious injury, not against mere mischief and illusion.[1]

Perhaps the most interesting detail in Mr. Drummond's statement is the reference made at its conclusion to the path of a kettle which " could hardly be said to be thrown, as I could see its passage through the air. It described the following figure," and then he draws a curved line. The sentence is not very happily worded, but he obviously means that the path the kettle followed was such as could not have resulted from a man's throwing it. Now this is exactly what Mr. Andrew Lang, Sir William Barrett and others have noticed as characteristic in a great number of poltergeist disturbances. When the same curious feature of a curved path, in which stones and other objects travel round corners, is recorded at first hand by witness after witness, all of whom obviously have no acquaintance with psychic literature, there is ground for the conclusion that this phenomenon which has independently been noticed by so many observers must be real and super-normal. Mr. Lang, in his *Making of Religion*, cites the statement of Police Constable Higgs in the Worksop case (1883):

White had hardly shut the cupboard doors when they flew open and a large glass jar came out past me, and pitched in the yard outside, smashing itself. I didn't see the jar leave the cupboard or fly through the air; it went too quick. But I am quite sure that it wasn't thrown by White or anyone else. White couldn't have done it without my seeing him. The jar couldn't go in a straight line from the cupboard out of the door; but it certainly did go.[2]

[1] See p. 8 above. The Indian Poltergeist, spoken of in Chapter vi, seems to have shown an equal indifference to the protective influence of exorcisms, relics and objects of piety.

[2] *Making of Religion*, p. 354.

As Mr. Lang observes of the supposed human agent in another case when the missiles followed a curved path, if they were thrown, " the thrower must certainly have had a native genius for ' pitching ' at base ball." An extreme example of projectiles behaving in a manner absolutely irreconcilable with the received laws of motion is that previously recorded in these pages (see page 29) of the " stones " at Münchhof, which flew out from under the settle and broke window panes which stood higher up on the same side of the room. As I there explained, " they must have doubled back in a semi-circular course against the window, precisely as an imprisoned bird might have done."

CHAPTER IX

A POLTERGEIST IN WESTMORLAND [1]

MOST of the readers who frequent the library of the British Museum are aware that, owing to the immense bulk of the printed matter which annually flows into its presses, it was found necessary some years since to build another repository at Colindale, near Hendon, in order to house the stacks of bound newspapers of every class which tend to accumulate so rapidly. In these new premises it is possible to consult not only files of the great dailies, or literary and technical journals, etc., printed since A.D. 1800 in the metropolis, but also to inspect obscure provincial weeklies wherein is often preserved detailed information regarding sensations of local interest quite beneath the notice of our more dignified London editors. Some time ago my attention was drawn to a curious case of poltergeist disturbances reported in Westmorland as far back as 1849. The only account I had seen was that published by the well-known William Howitt (author of *A History of the Supernatural* and many other works), which professed to be taken from the *Westmorland Gazette* of that date. There were unusual features in the case, and I was anxious to see whether Mr. Howitt's statement could be corroborated by other contemporary notices from the same part of the country. I betook myself to Colindale, and there was able to search at my leisure not only the journal named by Mr. Howitt, but also two other newspapers, the *Kendal Mercury* and the *Carlisle Journal*, which suggested the prospect of some further illumination. But, first of all, it will be desirable to quote at some length the narrative I had already seen. It runs as follows:

The *Westmorland Gazette* of that time relates the following extraordinary occurrences. Near the little town of Orlon [*sic*, a misprint for Orton] stood an old country house with its walls, gardens and fishpond, the property of Mr. Robert Gibson, who would appear to have been an old bachelor, as his nephew, William Gibson, lived with him. The old man was found, to the astonishment of the whole neighbourhood, drowned either in the fish-pond or in a ditch connected with it. A year after this his nephew, who inherited the property, married a daughter of Mr. John Bland of Bybeck and took her to this house. The whole inhabitants of the house were the married couple, two little children, and a maid-servant; no man, besides Gibson himself, slept in it. Suddenly on 17 April, 1849, the whole neighbourhood was startled by the report that the house was haunted in a very extraordinary manner. There were knock-ings on the walls and doors; articles that stood on shelves and con-soles flew off to the ground, one thing after another. The next day it began again half an hour before noon. Two childs' chairs that were placed in a cradle began to move; the cradle rocked itself, the chairs flew out of it together with the baby-linen, and then flew under the fire-grate. The old-fashioned chairs of the room began to dance with incredible swiftness; one only stood stock still, and this had been lately purchased at an auction, the rest belonged of old to the house. The churn was capsized out of the door, the churn-dish and cover flew here and there to the amazement of the maid who daily used them. They flew against the door and bounced back. The maid shrieked fearfully at the sight. But then the table with dishes and plates rose up from the ground and pitched about madly. Knives, forks, spoons, the cruet stand, etc., and different vessels, rattled on the walls or shelves as if they would leap off and take part in a general witch dance. The tablecloth blew itself out as a sail. Most extraordinary was it to see the salt and pepper spring out of their receptacles and cross each other in the air, whirling about like a swarm of bees, and then return unmixed, each to their own place. The butter-slice circled round the table like the moon round the earth, till it fell all at once on the table and on the dish where it had before lain.

Let me interrupt Mr. Howitt's narrative to say that while the *Westmorland Gazette* for 28 April, 1849, undoubtedly does print a description of the disturbances at Orton—the house was called '' Cowper's farm ''—the account is very far from agreeing textually with that just quoted. In particular, there is not a word said about the salt and the pepper or about the evolutions of the butter-slice. Mr. Howitt was an honest man, and I take it that his version of the incident must have been derived from some third, unnamed, source which perhaps made reference to the *Westmorland Gazette* as an authority, but did not confine itself to what was there stated. The phenomena mentioned in that journal accord pretty well with the earlier part of the story, but do not include the sensational incidents which centred round the dinner table.   But to continue:

William Gibson and his wife hastened with the maid and the little children to Mr. Robert Bousfield, a neighbour, to seek his advice.   At first he laughed at the whole thing, but going back with them after tea, was soon satisfied of the truth; and retreating rom the house in alarm, invited the inhabitants to go along with him.   This they did, but on the 19 April returning, they received a visit from Mr. Bland, from Bybeck, brother of Mrs. Gibson, and as they sat at tea Mr. Thomas Bland's hat was raised from the table where it stood, and flung under the fireplace.   Then everything on hooks and nails on the wall began to swing to and fro.   Coats and cloaks were all alive, gowns puffed themselves out in balloon-like and in the hoop-petticoat style.   An old riding coat of the late Robert Gibson was agitated in an astonishing way, stretching the right and then the left arm out, and a pair of old riding boots issued from a lumber room and came walking down stairs.   At this sight the young Gibson, who had so far laughed at the whole of it, became struck with fear.   He rose up pale and declared that they had better go altogether to Bybeck for a while.   This they did, quitting the house and leaving it to the ghost.   And two weeks later, when this account appeared, they still remained there.

On the 21 April a number of persons from Orton went to and through the house, but all was still.   On the 24th a party of gentlemen, the surgeon Torbuck, and Messrs. Elwood, Wilson, Robertson, Atkinson, and Bland of Bybeck, made a fresh examination and finding all quiet, advised the family to return.   They did so, but no sooner were they in the house, than all the old commotion commenced.   It was observed that when the children entered the house the disturbance was always the worst.   The family were compelled to abandon the house, and the people of the neighbourhood shook their heads and whispered that the old Gibson could not have come fairly to his end.[1]

Whatever may have been the real source of this information, the whole story is very puzzling, and at the same time instructive. Howitt leads the reader to suppose that the facts narrated by him

[1] Howitt, *Throwing of Stones and other Substances by Spirits*, 1865, (seemingly reprinted from the *Spiritual Magazine*), pp. 22-24.

were vouched for by the *Westmorland Gazette*, but anyone who studies the successive issues of that paper will discover that the first rather hesitating description of the phenomena, which appeared on 28 April, 1849, at once provoked sceptical protests. The announcement which next meets us in the same journal runs as follows:

We are informed that the ghost has been laid by a policeman, Mr. Slee. The said officer from Penrith elicited from the maid that she, with the connivance of the " missus," had been the contriver of all the " dobbie " work, their motive being a dislike to the house, which is at present very old and ramshackle. The stories of the internal parts of the churn flying through the air are, of course, gross fictions.

There seems no doubt that the " servant maid," who, one discovers, was a mere child, thirteen years old, did, when taken apart and interrogated by two police officers, make some sort of confession. But, so far as I can learn, the only definite act to which she pleaded guilty was that of knocking on the wall in a way which led people to suppose that the spook was doing it. The girl afterwards maintained that she was intimidated by the exhibition of a pair of handcuffs and a two-bladed jack knife. It is likely enough that she lied about it. The policemen, on their part, indignantly asserted that they had been as gentle as possible with her. But in the midst of the conflict of evidence it seems pretty clear that the ghost alleged to have been laid by the prompt action of the police did quite definitely manifest on one or two occasions subsequently. And there were other difficulties. In a letter printed by the *Westmorland Gazette* on 12 May, and emanating from a resident at Orton, we are told that—

" Dobbie," though scornfully treated, is not yet intimidated; he has reappeared and on Saturday last [5 May] performed some wonderful tricks. Whatever may be the opinion of the shrewd Kendalians [the *Gazette* was published at Kendal] or any other persons, there is still something connected with this mysterious affair which is quite unaccountable. Many respectable witnesses have corroborated the fact that with their own eyes they beheld chairs, tables and other articles move in the house without any apparent cause. If it were a hoax to get the house rebuilt why did dobbie accompany the family to Bybeck and carry on its freaks there for two successive days?

I do not doubt that to critics of the temper of the late Mr. Frank Podmore, any admission of trickery by a child concerned in the case will seem sufficient to render all further inquiry superfluous. Such people conclude at once that the whole proceeding from beginning to end can be nothing but a fraud. But for my part I submit that once we allow that such weird happenings as those here described may possibly be real, it is almost inevitable that any mischievous child who was in the centre of all the excitement and who had found that there was nothing to be particularly afraid of, would seize the opportunity of keeping the fun going, and would probably lie if questioned afterwards. For an adult a chair moving of itself is a serious problem inspiring a certain element of fear, but for a thought-less little girl it is simply a lark, once she has got used to the strange-ness of it. On the other hand, the evidence adduced in behalf of poltergeist phenomena by such competent observers as Sir William Barrett, Professor Lombroso, Baron von Schrenck Notzing, Alexan-der Aksakoff, and many other others is, in my judgment, quite irresistible. There *are* cases when stones are hurled from empty space, heavy tables and bedsteads are moved without human contact, and chimney ornaments fly about in eccentric paths. The doubt whether we are or are not in contact with such a genuine case is not settled by a child's confession that she has herself slyly hammered on a wall or thrown a few pebbles when nobody was looking. Neither, may I add, is the spurious nature of the pheno-mena proved because we can show that there has been gross exag-geration on the part of some of the witnesses. The more really astonished and bewildered the rustic is, the more prone he is to embellish the account he subsequently gives of what he believes he saw. There cannot, I think, be any question that the excitement caused in the neighbourhood by the report of these happenings was considerable; though that perhaps proves little. The newspaper I have so far been quoting states that on Sunday, 29 April, " not less than five hundred persons visited the spot." They do not appear to have seen much of Mr. Gibson, but all the talking, we are told, was done by the mistress and a " mischievous-looking servant lass." The fact, however, that this girl was only thirteen years old does not seem to have been disputed.

Besides the *Westmorland Gazette*, there was another weekly paper, the *Kendal Mercury*, which was likewise published at Kendal. Seeing that Orton is only fifteen miles distant, it was inevitable that the *Mercury* also should take an interest in the case. I have looked through the issues for April, May and June in the year we are concerned with, but I have not discovered any new facts of notable importance.[1] In the *Mercury*, as in the *Gazette*, opinions seemed to be very much divided. On 26 May, when the interest was beginning to die down, the former journal printed a long letter signed " An Unbelieving Jew," which ridiculed the whole history. On 2 June, however, an equally long reply from " A Believing Christian " seems to have been the final contribution admitted by the *Mercury* on this subject. It impresses me as a document of great good sense, and I hope to be pardoned for making two or three quotations. Taking the indictment framed by his opponent, paragraph by paragraph, we find the believer stoutly contending:

I must also object to his next argument which is that the state-ments in the newspapers were made from hearsay. The statement which first appeared in your paper was authenticated by the names of five individuals who were eye-witnesses of the doings there related . . . Again he seems unwilling to accept of those who, as he terms it, are " tainted with hereditary superstition." As I do not know how he defines such a disease, I am unable to determine whether I am myself afflicted with it or not; but this I know, that before I had been to the place I was even more incredulous than the " Jew " himself, as I regarded all ghosts, apparitions, etc., as superstitious fancies; and it was not until I had seen things done which no human power could do that I would believe.[2]

The writer, whose choice of words shows him to have been a man of education, goes on to propound a very serious difficulty to the contention of the police that the disturbances were caused by Mrs. Gibson and the maid. He declares very positively—and the same statement was made elsewhere—that other phenomena occurred at Bybeck when " none of Gibson's family were there except the children, the eldest of whom is but three years old. How is it possible," he asks, " that Mrs. Gibson or the servant could cause disturbances at Bybeck, while they were at ' Cowper House,' distant more than a mile ? " As against the allegation that the police, by visiting the farm and putting the fear of the Lord into

---

[1] The account printed in the *Mercury* for 28 April does, however, add some few particulars in the description it gives of the general racket. It tells us, for example, that the milk from the churn " was dashed about like spray "; and it mentions that on 19 April, Mr. Bland, Gibson's brother-in-law, having " offered up a prayer, a knife was thrown at him which struck against his side."

[2] " A Believing Christian," in the *Kendal Mercury*, 2 June, 1849.

the maid, had laid the ghost, which thereafter " lost courage,"
" A Christian Believer " replies:

The ghost could not have " lost courage " entirely *after* the visit
of the Penrith constables, for it had nearly ceased before, *and* it was
in motion, more or less, for a day or two afterwards.   It then was
perfectly quiet for several days, after which it recommenced with
greater violence than ever.   This your correspondent seems to
doubt, but I have good proof of it, as a very near relative of mine
was there, and witnessed some of its movements after it had resumed
operations.

Finally, with regard to the maid, whom he describes as " a mere
child," he remarks:
Now I know that, at first, she was excessively frightened and
cried very much; but when she saw so many people visiting the
place, numbers of whom were inclined to regard it in the light of an
amusement, is it surprising that, with the natural versatility of
childhood, she should begin to look upon it in the same way?
I do not say that such would have been the case had there been any
apparition, far from it; but as it was, there was nothing very frightful about it.   The tapping at the window [this was admitted by the
girl] was merely done as a practical joke upon a good-natured
neighbour in the house.

It cannot, I think, be pretended that in the discussions concerning
the Orton spook which then went on in Cumberland and Westmorland the sceptical side achieved any notable victory.   It must be
sufficient to cite one extract from the *Carlisle Journal*, then the leading
newspaper of that remote part of England, which says in the course
of an editorial on the subject:

Whether the girl was frightened into confession or not does not
matter much, for the dobbie has since been at work when both
mistress and servant girl were out of the house, and many parties,
who have seen the strange performance, declare that it was impossible any human hand, gifted with only human powers, could have
played the tricks they witnessed . . . The truth is yet enveloped in
much mystery.

Shortly after Mr. Howitt had sent to the *Spiritual Magazine* the account printed at the beginning of this article, a supplementary note appeared in the same journal (July, 1865) in the following form. The writer was speaking from his recollection of an incident sixteen years old. It is not, then, surprising if, in some unimportant details, his memory was inexact. The police, for example, seem to have come from Penrith, and not from Kendal. The letter runs thus:

Liverpool, 8th February, 1865

SIR.—It was my intention to send you some account of the " riotous haunting " in Westmorland, had I not seen that in your last number Mr. Howitt gives a fuller narrative than it was in my power to give. I may yet, however, add a few items which may be interesting.

The haunted house stood on a dreary upland moor called Orton Fell (not Orlon), about two miles from Teebay Station, on the Lancaster and Carlisle Railway. At the time the disturbances took place—about sixteen years ago—I had frequent occasion to travel on that line, was well acquainted with the enginemen and others employed upon it, and heard a deal about the " Orton Boggart," as it was called. At first I received the rumours as a hoax; but they became so numerous, and were given with such circumstantial minuteness, by people I knew to be entirely trustworthy, that I, along with a friend, was induced to pay a visit to the place. But when we got to Teebay station, we were told not to go any farther, as the disturbances had ceased. We went, however, to see the house, and when there we got from the inmates a somewhat similar account to the one Mr. Howitt extracts from the Westmorland paper. In addition to that, we were told that the police had come from Kendal to investigate the case, that suspicions had fallen on the servant girl, whom they had handled rather roughly and taken with them to Kendal, and that during her absence there were no manifestations. This seemed to give some colour to the suspicions of the police that the whole affair was a trick of the girl's, and this, indeed, was the conclusion most people, without thinking, jumped to. But that a young girl of about fifteen years of age could have done the things both seen and heard, is too preposterous to bear a thought; and if they really did not take place unless when she was present, the only reasonable conclusion is that she was the necessary *medium*.

We were somewhat disappointed at not seeing or hearing something direct from the *Boggart* itself; but the people of the house spoke so seriously about it (always alluding to it as IT), that we could have no doubt of their truthfulness; and if the *effects* of the noisy proceedings could add to our belief, we saw abundance of these in the shape of broken dishes.

Some most curious incidents we got from the engineman, who with his engine was then stationed at Loup's Fell, and whose duty it was to assist goods trains up the steep incline to Shap. He told us that one Sunday morning he and his fireman determined to visit the *Boggart House.* They had better than two miles to walk and, passing a small farm-steading, the fireman robbed a hen's nest of two or three eggs, wherewith they had rum and eggs at a public house about half way. On entering the haunted house the engineman respectfully took off his cap and sat down, but the fireman rather rudely took a seat, leaving his cap on, when immediately it was snatched off by an invisible hand and slapped in his face, and right upon the back of this an egg was thrown across the room and hit him in the breast. They had scarcely time to feel amazed at all this, when other phenomena attracted their attention. The child's cradle was rocked without anyone touching it, the clothes were thrown out of it, and, when replaced, were immediately tossed out again ; the chain that hangs on the crook in the chimney was violently shaken; spoons came from the plate, rack, and like birds flew across the room; and, more remarkable still, the lid of a pot rose on its edge, trundled across the floor, turned a corner, rolled along the passage, then rounded another corner, and lay down at the outer door.

These incidents were told us with a degree of seriousness that made them the more amusing. We declared to the engineman that he wanted to make merry with us (strange enough, his name was Peter Merry), and tried to laugh him into confessing as much, but he stuck to his statement, and solemnly averred that every word he had told us was strictly true. His fireman did the same, and it may be worth remarking that the egg incident seemed to give his mind a serious turn. Certain it is, that he was afterwards afraid to tamper with hen's nests that did not belong to him, lest other eyes than his own might be upon him. I forget the fireman's name, but I knew both him and Peter Merry intimately.

Yours truly,
ROBERT LEIGHTON.

What lends additional weight to this statement is the fact that the writer, Robert Leighton, was a man of some literary standing who has a place in the Dictionary of National Biography. The short notice there devoted to him identifies him completely, for it lets us know that in later life he resided in Liverpool, and that for several years after 1845 he had been in the service of the London and North Western Railway, making Preston, at that time, his headquarters. Leighton, who had been born in Dundee, was chiefly famous for the verses he wrote in his native dialect and was described as " the Scottish poet." He was known outside of England, and we are told that Emerson paid a high compliment to Leighton's " purity and manliness of thought and the deep moral tone which dictated every verse." Leighton's brother William, to whom this was written, was a shipowner in Dundee.

In view of the fact that none of the sceptics seem actually to have been present at the Cowper farm when the phenomena were in progress, their objections, based fundamentally upon antipathy to all that smacked of superstition, carry no great weight. On the one occasion when the constables visited the spot, the disturbances had already been in abeyance for two or three days previously. They themselves did not claim to have witnessed any trick or attempt at imposture. Further, we must remember that in April, 1849, Spiritualism had not yet been heard of in England. Even in America the rapping manifestations had hardly begun to take hold. In these circumstances the respectful hearing which the " dobbie " of Orton managed to secure for itself constitutes in my judgment a fairly strong presumption of its genuineness.

CHAPTER X

SOME EARLY AMERICAN POLTERGEISTS[1]

IN case it might be thought that the racketing spirit has been confined to the old world of Europe, it might be worth while to recall the story of three early American examples which seem to rest upon fairly satisfactory evidence. As they occurred so many years ago, it would be practically hopeless now to obtain more reliable data. But their mere remoteness in time and the fact that they happened a long way from England does not prejudice the truth of these incidents. Professor William James, the psychologist of Harvard, made no difficulty in confessing that he had been immensely impressed by certain occurrences of this sort which had been reported to him. One of these was the famous " Amherst Mystery " in which the girl, Esther Cox at Amherst, Nova Scotia, was tormented by spirits, believed by her and others to be demons. In this outbreak incredible ferocity seems to have been shown from which severe physical injuries resulted. This is an extremely unusual feature in such cases. None the less, it is plain from the terms in which Professor James touched upon the matter in his Presidential Address delivered before the English Society for Psychical Research in 1894, that he took it very seriously. Also a letter of his has been published in the *Proceedings* of the American S.P.R., Vol. VII (1913) p. 205, which makes it clear that he was very far from attributing the startling details recorded in connection with some of these visitations either to trickery or mal-observation. The Amherst story has been too often told in comparatively recent times for me to repeat it here. Neither do I wish to recall certain other sensational occurrences of this type which are fairly well known to those who take an interest in such matters. The three which I propose to recount are, perhaps, tame in comparison, but one often learns most from incidents which, while exciting enough to those who took part in them, have not afterwards become the subject of acrimonious discussion.

[1] *The Month,* December 1934

A fairly representative example of manifestations reported from time to time at different places in the United States, may be borrowed from the *Philadelphia Inquirer* of Monday, 5 February, 1866. A house in South Fifth Street, Philadelphia, had been occupied for ten years by a family consisting of father, mother and three " young ladies," their daughters. We also hear of a servant in their employ. There is no mention of any previous disturbance during the tenancy, but suddenly on the night of 1 February, 1866, the three girls who occupied one bedroom, were awakened by a clatter, caused, as they found, by their brushes, combs and other toilet appliances having been thrown on to the floor. Much bewildered, they replaced them, but after an interval the same thing happened a second time; moreover, a looking-glass which hung against the wall " jumped " from the nail into a corner and was there shattered to pieces. They fetched their father from his bed, but he was unable to discover anything which would account for the phenomenon. Of the next morning nothing much is recorded, save that a saucer flew off the breakfast table and was broken. But in the evening a perfect stampede set in among the chimney ornaments, with the most disastrous results. Not only were there many breakages of vases and small articles, but pictures and mirrors began to be involved in the disturbance, so that the family thought it wise to take them down hurriedly and lay them upon the floor in the hope of preventing further damage. No great success, however, attended this manoeuvre. One large looking-glass, " taking a zig-zag flight across the room," struck the opposite wall and was smashed to atoms. In the end, the victims of this visitation removed such breakable possessions as they most prized to a neighbouring house, where they seem to have remained in security.

The evidence upon which we are asked to believe this story is rather characteristic of what so often happens in such cases. When the matter began to excite attention in the city, Press reporters flocked to the spot, but on their arrival the more violent manifestations were suspended or had already ceased. Speaking of the Sunday afternoon (4 February), the newspaper from which I am here quoting remarks : " Our reporters visited the house, they heard the strange, unaccountable rumbling noises, but saw nothing in transition through the air. Broken dishes, shattered mirrors, damaged books and the absence of all ornamental furniture, were ample evidence of the strange annoyance to which the dwelling had been subjected." The editor, or whoever was responsible for the article in the *Inquirer*, is careful not to commit himself to any belief in the operation of a supernatural agency. He suspects " some trickery," while at the same time admitting that nothing of the sort had so far been detected. He jeers at the Spiritualists, and in a later notice remarks that " there are unbelieving heathens who unhesitatingly assert that the Spiritualists are at the bottom of the entire affair, and that they got the exhibition up for the purpose of making spiritualistic capital." At the same time, he is, perforce, constrained to add: " the family, however, all solemnly aver that they are not Spiritualists themselves, and have not the slightest belief in such nonsense." That this was, in fact, the case seems to be conclusively proved by the statements of the *Inquirer's* own reporters. Evidentially speaking, the most satisfactory piece of testimony in the whole account is contained in the following passage:

The master and mother of the family being communicants of the Baptist Church, imparted the circumstances of this strange visitation to their pastor, and on Saturday evening that gentleman, accompanied by another clergyman, went to the haunted dwelling to pass the night. With one of these clerical gentlemen, we had a protracted interview. He is a very clear-minded scholar who has received a collegiate training ... He assures us that he entered the house with the belief that the inmates were the dupes of trickery and that he left it yesterday morning perplexed in the extreme.

Soon after he entered the parlour a hymn book was projected from a table and thrown with violence against the door. With his own hands he picked up the book and replaced it. Before his eyes the volume was seized by an invisible force and for a second time thrown across the room, and a Testament sent to keep it company. Again the books were replaced, and again sent whirling around the room, at times making the entire circuit of the apartment; then they would fly off at a tangent and come to a full stop violently against the walls. Bibles, Testaments and hymn books, were endowed with strange powers of volition [*sic*] during Saturday night. Both the clergymen present did their best to discover some trick by which the inanimate objects were made to circumnavigate rooms in so mysterious a manner, but in vain, they could discover no clue to these unaccountable movements.

For the other phenomena we have no better authority than the statements made to the reporters by members of the family; but the incidents related, if untrue, do credit to the liveliness of their imagination. One of the daughters, we are told, on her return from church on the Sunday, had her Bible snatched from her hand with such force as to tear the covers utterly off. " The keys flew out of the locks of the doors; the few remaining dishes threw violent somersaults from shelves to floor." It was impossible to lay the table for Sunday dinner; the plates jumped off the table, and the hapless family had to eat their meal from their laps. As the servant was washing up some of the few unbroken remnants of the crockery, a tumbler flew up out of the water and struck her forehead with such force that her face was cut as well as bruised. Even the bread seemed endowed with life and went spinning in eccentric paths over the dining-room table. We are told finally that the inmates of the house were driven to distraction by the crowds of would-be visitors who besieged them, that a posse of police had to be stationed before the door to keep them out, also that it was found necessary to remove two or three of the ladies to other quarters, " their nervous system having been utterly shattered by the excitements of the last few days."

Extravagant as are the incidents recorded above, one finds it difficult to suggest any plausible explanation for the concoction of such a narrative. It is incredible that the whole story can be a joke. The street in Philadelphia is named, even if the number of the house, " at the urgent request of the family," was suppressed in the communications first published regarding it. The fact that pictures and other more fragile property were removed elsewhere and that some of the occupants were forced in the end to quit the scene of turmoil can hardly be an invention. But such drastic measures are not usually resorted to by a middle-class family—they kept a " small dry-goods store "—without grave cause. There do not seem to have been any mischievous children concerned in this case and no motive can well be imagined for seeking notoriety at the expense of much inconvenience and a considerable destruction of property. Lastly, the inmates, being pious Protestants and strongly opposed to Spiritualism, are not in the least likely to have been familiar with poltergeist phenomena. In fact, before 1866, very little had been printed on the subject. Nevertheless, the manifestations they describe are in striking accord with those which have since been recorded by a multitude of other witnesses in every part of the world.

Another remarkable American case is that detailed in the *Religio-Philosophical Journal* of Chicago for 29 August, 1874. This is a Spiritualist newspaper, but the account given is no more than

9

a copy of articles which appeared in the *Milwaukee Sentinel*, Milwaukee itself, which is a city about 200 miles distant from Chicago, having been the scene of the manifestations in question. One is naturally indisposed to put confidence in newspaper stories, in which sensation is too often the main object, but, in this instance, the reporter seems to have been at considerable pains to verify his facts. Many witnesses, men of some local standing, are cited by name, and one realises that this cannot safely be done in a journal printed in the town in which they live without entailing unpleasant consequences if the misrepresentations are serious.

The centre of the disturbances which occurred at Milwaukee was a Polish girl named Mary Spiegel who was employed as a servant in the house of a Mr. and Mrs. Giddings. She was certainly a neurasthenic, as well as a somnambulist, and she appears to have been so brutally treated by her father that she lived in a perpetual state of nervous apprehension. In the presence of this girl of fourteen, and never apart from her presence, the most astonishing movements of inanimate objects are reported to have taken place. The racket, which affected fire-irons, pails, crockery and other kitchen furniture, was of the usual kind, and rather destructive, but there were some features of special interest. Mrs. Giddings, while fully acquitting the girl Mary of having any physical share in these performances, complained that an egg " came at her [Mrs. Giddings] out of the pantry." It could not, from the position in which she was sitting, have travelled as missiles usually travel, but came " shying across the corner " in a curved line. Again, we are told that " some sausages took a journey round the room, several dishes skated out of the pantry, and a stove-cover lifter struck Mr. G. W. Allen on the leg, when certainly there was nobody near to project it."

Now this Mr. Allen, we learn, was one of the partners in " the Wisconsin Leather Company " in whose behalf the house was run by Mr. and Mrs. Giddings as a hostel for the employees of the firm. There were three Messrs. Allen who formed the Company; all three had come to visit the scene and had been present when the disturbances were in progress. Mr. William Allen, together with a Dr. Meacham and a Dr. N. A. Gray, was still there when the reporter was making his inquiries. By him and by the two other gentlemen the reporter was assured that " they had personally satisfied themselves that no human agency was possible in what had taken place under their own observation."

One incident (we are told) particularly impressed Dr. Meacham, who was watching the developments with a calm, unimpassioned interest. He was sharply scrutinizing the actions of the excited girl, who had been set by Mrs. Giddings to sweep up the debris off the floor, and he commanded a full view of the pantry and the girl. As he was looking on, a little china dish " came sailing out on an even keel," filled with small tickets of some sort or another. He dodged it, and it slid on the floor, spilled the cards, but was not broken.

A number of other eye-witnesses made statements to the reporter, and recounted similar incidents. He had a talk with the girl herself who complained of having been frightened by people who charged her with having done these things. She denied all knowledge of how they happened and seemed in a pitiable state of terror. Her mother, who was there, never stopped scolding her, and finally, when the Giddingses, in view of the destruction of property which occurred in her neighbourhood, decided that she was " too expensive to keep " :—

The girl cried and entreated, and finally hid herself in the woodshed, where her father found her, and by way of mending matters began to beat the unfortunate child. The next thing heard of her was that a man brought a poor, dripping, shivering creature up to the house, who turned out to be Mary. She had jumped into the river and tried to commit suicide. On being asked to-day her reason for doing this, she said she was hunted and hounded by everybody, and could not endure her life.

Though the Giddingses again sent her back to her parents, she was given a dish of odds and ends of food to take home with her. Mary afterwards returned with the empty dish, but no sooner had she entered the kitchen and laid the dish upon the table, than the kettle which had been singing peacefully on the hob, sailed off and, crashing on to the floor, was damaged beyond repair. Even this, if we may trust the reporter, was not the last of the disturbances witnessed at the Giddingses' house in Mary's presence. A day or two later she was taken back there by a Dr. C. C. Robinson to make inquiries. Dinner was then in progress, and in the presence of the doctor, the family and the boarders, knives and forks flew off the table and other similar manifestations occurred.

No record is accessible to me by which I can learn anything of the later career of Mary Spiegel, but the *Milwaukee Sentinel* apparently informed its readers, then or shortly afterwards, that the Polish girl " has just been taken into the family of one of our well-known Seventh Ward physicians, and some scientific men are now investigating the phenomena."

A third American case in the past century, which, though it happened in Virginia, attracted attention in the New York dailies, is connected with the name of a Baptist Minister, a Mr. G. C. Thrasher. This clergyman lived at Buchanan, Botetourt Co., about twenty miles from Lexington. The disturbances began in November, 1870, by the removal of a sack of corn from the place where it was kept under padlock, but not apparently with any felonious purpose, for the whole contents of the sack were poured out upon the ground only twenty paces off. This was followed by other annoyances of a more familiar type. Windows barred on the inside were opened unaccountably, knockings were heard, doors were locked and unlocked, furniture was moved from its place, kitchen utensils flew about hither and thither. Mr. Thrasher had three little boys, the eldest of whom was under twelve years of age. It was natural that some suspicion should rest upon them as the possible authors of the mischief, but it seems clear that many of the manifestations were beyond their physical strength, and further, that they often occurred when the children were in another room or under close observation. There was also a young servant, one Anna Pring, who might, it was thought, with the aid of outside confederates, have engineered most of the troubles. But from the descriptions left us, there seem to be insuperable difficulties to such a solution, and it is certain that her master and mistress, after watching her closely, entirely exonerated her. Also a certain Major Paxton who, with a number of other residents in the locality, had maintained continuous observation, both inside and outside the house, declared himself fully satisfied that Anna had nothing to do with it. He said in particular that one night while he was there and a number of young men were on guard, the knocking at the door being very violent and frequent, they resorted to every stratagem and made every effort to detect the cause, but in vain. This same Major Paxton furthermore bore witness to the fact that chips flew about the house in a way that was utterly inexplicable. A Lexington paper, the *Gazette*, summarized as follows the contents of a letter received from Mr. Thrasher himself:

For five days during the past week the manifestations were frequent, varied and violent. Brickbats, old bones, billets of wood, ears of corn, stones, etc., were thrown about the house in the most unaccountable manner and again and again everything would be turned topsy-turvy in the parlour and the chambers without their being able to detect the agent. One day, two young ladies being at the house, they determined to use every effort to ferret out the mystery. Accordingly, they arranged the parlour, locked all the doors, sent Anna Pring to the kitchen with Mr. Thrasher's little boy to watch her, and carried all the keys to Mrs. Thrasher's room. They waited but a few minutes, and returned to find that the doors had been opened, the books from the centre table scattered over the floor, the lamps from the mantlepiece put on the ground, and things disarranged generally; and, to increase the mystery, they found a strange key that would neither unlock nor lock any door in the house, sticking in the keyhole of the parlour door. One day Mr. Thrasher himself left the dining-room, carefully locked the door, and went upstairs to his wife's chamber. Just as he was about to enter he heard a noise downstairs and returned immediately not having been absent from the room more than three minutes. He found the door open, the furniture disarranged, and all the dishes from the press distributed over the ground.

We also learn from the same newspaper that when a visitor at the house was sleeping in one of the rooms the coverlet of his bed was pulled so violently that he awoke, but on jumping up he could neither see nor hear anything.

I borrow this account partly from the London *Spiritual Magazine* (April, 1871), which prints a communication from a correspondent in Virginia, partly fron Dr. Eugene Crowell's book *Primitive Christianity and Modern Spiritualism*, Vol. I, pp, 183—186. One point of interest is the fact that Dr. Crowell cites two letters addressed to himself by the Rev. Mr. Thrasher in answer to inquiries. These confirm the general accuracy of the newspaper reports, and we learn from the latter of the two letters, dated 6 May, 1871, that in consequence of this unendurable visitation Mr Thrasher has been compelled to leave his house in Virginia and had taken up his abode in Tennessee. He writes:

The manifestations continued at my house in Virginia for four months, and only ceased about one week before I moved to this place. I have not been able to make any discovery as to the cause; it is still wrapped in profound mystery.

No one, of course, will maintain that this evidence coming to us from such a distance and incapable of verification, is conclusive; but there can be no reasonable doubt that for some weeks together the neighbourhood of Buchanan was in a state of excitement over these reported happenings. On the other hand, there seems to have been a complete absence of motive for the production of such disturbances. The Baptist Minister himself would be very unlikely to welcome the publicity earned by phenomena which were being exploited in the interest of the Spiritualists and which eventually forced him to find a home elsewhere.

CHAPTER XI

A NEW ENGLAND POLTERGEIST[1]

LITHOBOLIA is a word which means stone-throwing. The term was chosen—not altogether inappropriately—for the title of a pamphlet printed in London in 1698 to give an account of certain astounding disturbances which had taken place some years before in New Hampshire on the other side of the Atlantic. The author does not disclose his name, but his initials and a multitude of other details leave no doubt that he was a Mr. Richard Chamberlain, the same of whom we read in the " Acts of the English Privy Council " that, on 15 September, 1680, " the Earl of Sunderland was directed to prepare a warrant constituting Richard Chamberlain Esq. to be Secretary of the Province of New Hampshire. "[2] As for the pamphlet, of which there are two copies in the British Museum, the title-page is so curious that it deserves to reproduced entire. Here it is:

LITHOBOLIA, or the Stone-throwing Devil. Being an Exact and True account (by way of Journal) of the various actions of infernal Spirits or (Devils Incarnate) Witches or both: and the great Disturbance and Amazement they gave to George Walton's Family at a place called Great Island in the Province of New Hampshire in New England, chiefly in throwing about (by an Invisible hand) Stones, Bricks and Brick-Bats of all Sizes, with several other things, as Hammers, Mauls, Iron-Crows, Spits and other domestic Utensils, as came into their Hellish Minds, and this for the space of a Quarter of a Year.

By R.C. Esq., who was a sojourner in the same Family the whole Time and an Ocular Witness of these Diabolick Inventions. The Contents hereof being manifestly known to the Inhabitants of that

---

[1] *The Month*, May 1937

[2] *Acts of the Privy Council*, Colonial Series, Vol. II, 1680-1720, p. 11. This volume of records was printed in 1910.

Province and persons of other Provinces, and is upon record in his Majestie's Council-Court held for that Province.

Printed and are to be sold by E. Whitlock, near Stationers-Hall, 1698.

A chapbook story of diabolic manifestations, supposed to have occured 4,000 miles away beyond seas, is bound to awaken many misgivings as to the reliability of the facts narrated. But although R.C.'s description is the most circumstantial and detailed, it does not stand alone. Much earlier than 1698 we have another account of the same occurences which was printed in New England itself when the incidents were still fresh in the memory of those who had been present. This narrative was given to the world at the end of 1683 by Increase Mather in his book *An essay for the recording of Illustrious Providences*. I shall have something to say later upon the question of Mather's trustworthiness, but for the moment it will be sufficient to copy what he has written. He does not name his authority, but he tells us that he received the account "from a worthy hand." It may be noted that " the Secretary, " who is several times referred to therein, is undoubtedly Richard Chamberlain. This was his official title in New Hampshire.

On 11 June, 1682, being the Lord's Day, at night showers of stones were thrown both against the sides and roof of the house of George Walton. Some of the people went abroad, found the gate at some distance from the house wrung off the hinges, and stones came thick about them, sometimes falling down by them, sometimes touching them without any hurt done to them; though they seemed to come with great force, yet did no more but softly touch them; stones flying about the room, the doors being shut; the glass windows shattered to pieces by stones that seemed to come not from without but within, the lead of the glass casements, window-bars, etc., being driven forcibly outwards and so standing bent.

While the Secretary was walking in the room, a great hammer came brushing along against the chamber floor that was over his head and fell down by him. A candlestick [was] beaten off the table. They took up nine of the stones and marked them, and laid them on the table, some of them being as hot as if they came out of the fire; but some of those marked stones were found flying about again. In this manner things continued about four hours' space that night. The Secretary then went to bed, but a stone came and broke up his chamber door, being put to, not locked; a brick was sent upon the like errand. The aforesaid stone the Secretary locked up in his chamber, but it was fetched out, and carried with great noise into the next chamber.

The spit was carried up the chimney, and came down with the point forward, and stuck in the back-log, and being removed by one of the company to one side of the chimney was by an unseen hand thrown out at window.

This trade was driven on the next day, and so from day to day; now and then there would be some intermission and then to it again. The stones were most frequent where the master of the house was, whether in the field or barn, etc. A black cat was seen once when the stones came, and was shot at, but she was too nimble for them. Some of the family say that they once saw the appearance of a hand put forth at the hall window, throwing stones towards the entry, though there was nobody in the hall the while; sometimes a dismal hollow whistling would be heard, sometimes the noise of the trotting of a horse and snorting, but nothing seen.

The man went up the great bay in his boat to a farm he had there, and while haling wood or timber to the boat, he was disturbed by the stones as before at home. He carried a stirrup-iron from the house down to the boat, and there left it; but while he was going up to the house, the iron came jingling after him through the woods, and returned to the house, and so again, and at last went away, and was heard of no more. Their anchor leapt overboard several times as they were going home and stopped the boat. A cheese hath been taken out of the press and crumbled all over the floor. A piece of iron with which they weighed up the cheese-press, stuck into the wall and a kettle hung thereon. Several cocks of English hay, mowed near the house, were taken and hung upon trees; and some made into small whisps, and put all up and down the kitchen, *cum multis aliis*, etc.

After this manner have they been treated ever since at times. It were needless to particularize. Of late they thought the bitterness of death had been past; being quiet for sundry days and nights; but last week were sundry returnings again; and this week (2 August, 1682) as bad or worse than ever. The man is sorely hurt by some of the stones that came on him, and like to feel the effects of them for many days.

"Thus far in that relation," says Mather, adding, "I am, moreover, informed that the demon was quiet all the last winter [this was the winter of 1682–1683] but in the spring he began to play some ludicrous tricks, carrying away some axes that were locked up safe.   This last summer he has not made such disturbance as formerly; but of this no more at present."[1]

Unfortunately, the names of Increase Mather and his son Cotton are so associated in the popular mind with the Salem witch prosecutions that it will at once be assumed that any marvellous story retailed by either of them is likely to be as illusory as the fantastical powers attributed to the hags who rode to the Sabbat on broomsticks.   It is only of recent years that justice has been done to the Mathers by certain American scholars of distinction.   Increase Mather was President of Harvard from 1685 to 1701, and it is perhaps natural that the modern representatives of that University should be anxious to clear away some of the load of obloquy which has, in a large measure undeservedly, rested upon him.   Dr. K. B. Murdock's biography, published in 1925, has been generally received as authoritative.   Undoubtedly the two Mathers, like all professing Christians of that age, believed in a personal devil and attributed to him infinite malice and the power of interfering even physically with the affairs of men.   But Increase, like Robert Boyle and the founders of the English Royal Society, was not indefinitely credulous and was alive to the possibility of a natural explanation of marvels which at first seemed baffling.

Speaking of the work from which I have been quoting, Dr. Murdock says " the book was written as a scientific and historical recording of phenomena observed in New England," though he adds that " its significance as one of the first scientific writings in America is for the most part neglected."   Of another book of Increase Mather's, *i.e.*, *Cases of Conscience concerning Evil Spirits* (1693), the same biographer declares that it was " the most outspoken and almost certainly the earliest, public utterance issued in New England in opposition to the practice of the [Witch] Court."   Finally, we are told that Increase Mather " deserves a place, not with superstitious divines, but on the same plane with Glanville and Dr. Henry More, who were serious students in ' psychical research ' and seekers for empirical proof of what had hitherto been forced upon men's minds by authority alone."[2]

Similarly Mr. T. J. Holmes, who has devoted the most painstaking research to the Mather bibliography, remarks: " Increase Mather's attitude to the witch episode, was very clearly the exact opposite

---

[1] I have not troubled to reproduce the spelling and the eccentric capitals of the original, but I have used the reprint published in London in 1856, pp. 114-116. The original edition of the *Illustrious Providences* appeared at Boston in 1684.   I have consulted it and satisfied myself that the reprint is accurate.

[2] See Murdock, *Increase Mather*, pp. 167-171.

of that which many popular historians have hitherto represented it to have been "; and with particular reference to the book quoted above, he says: " If this work had been widely read and thoroughly heeded, the witch panic, that broke out eight years after its publication would never have occurred."[1]

When Increase Mather, or his informant, lays stress upon the fact that the stones at George Walton's house for the most part " though they seemed to come with great force, yet did no more but softly touch them, without any hurt done to them," he is all unconsciously calling attention to one of the most familiar characteristics of poltergeist phenomena. Many such examples have been previously noted in these pages, but I will appeal here only to a case which I came upon recently for the first time. It was described at some length by Dr. Pietro Gatti in the *Annali dello Spiritismo in Italia* for 1865. A little girl of thirteen, by name Maddalena Rimassa, a child at Genoa, was the constant butt of projectiles, thrown at her apparently from outside the house, which often broke windows before they landed in the interior. Dr. Gatti states: " It was noticed that when the child crossed in front of the window, there was at once a shower of missiles which struck her more particularly on the head, but without producing any sort of wound or bruise, or leaving any feeling of pain behind. It was also observed that a big piece of brick [*mattone*] hit her violently on the forehead but did not hurt her in the least. Its only trace was a smear of dirt in the place where she was struck. I was also told that it was quite impossible to determine where the missiles came from, because they never became visible before they crossed the window sill."[2]

But it is time to turn to Mr. Richard Chamberlain's own narrative. One must confess that he is a somewhat irritating writer. The parentheses and brackets, already sufficiently conspicuous in his title page, are multiplied in almost every sentence of the text. The type of this seventeenth-century pamphlet is also trying to the eyes, and though I have inspected the original, I have found it convenient to avail myself of a reprint which appeared in *The Historical Magazine*, New York, 1861. In not a few passages Mr. Chamberlain is almost incoherent, and the first printed text does not help us. He would seem to have sent to the press, practically without revision, certain rough notes taken at the time. The pamphlet begins with the statement that this " lithobolia " was supposed by the neighbours to have " happened by witchcraft,"

[1] T. J. Holmes, *The Mather Literature* (1927), pp. 40 and 45.
[2] *Annali dello Spiritismo in Italia*, Vol. II (1865), pp. 313 and 287.

and to have been maliciously instigated by an elderly woman who declared that Mr. George Walton had annexed and retained a certain strip of land which rightfully belonged to her.[1] Mr. Secretary Chamberlain would seem previously to have been sceptical in this matter of witchcraft; but his experiences at Great Island had clearly produced a considerable impression. The incident, as he tells us, " has confirmed myself and others in the opinion that there are such things as witches and the effects of witchcraft, or at least the mischievous actions of evil spirits, which some of us do little give credit to, as in the case of witches, utterly rejecting both their operations and their beings." It would be tedious to reproduce the whole of his account and I must confine myself to a few specimens; anyway the narrative portion of his pamphlet begins thus:

Some time ago being in America (in his then Majesty's service) I was lodged in the said George Walton's house, a planter there, and on a Sunday night, about 10 o'clock, many stones were heard by myself and the rest of the family, to be thrown and (with noise) hit against the top and all sides of the house, after he, the said Walton, had been at his fence-gate, which was between him and his neighbour, one John Amazeen, an Italian, to view it; for it was again, as formerly it had been (the manner how being unknown) wrung off the hinges, and cast upon the ground: and in his being there, and return home, with several persons of (and frequenting) his family and house, about a slight shot distance from the gate, they were all assaulted with a peal of stones (taken, we conceive, from the rocks hard by the house) and this by unseen hands or agents. For by this time I was come down to them, having risen out of my bed at this strange alarm of all that were in the house, and do know that they all looked out as narrowly as I did, or any person could (it being a bright moonlight night) but could make no discovery.

Thereupon because there came many stones, and those pretty great ones, some as big as my fist, into the entry or porch of the house, we withdrew into the next room to the porch, no person having received any hurt (Praised be Almighty Providence, for certainly the infernal agent, constant enemy to mankind, had he not been overruled, intended no less than death or maim) save only that

---

[1] This explanation is also given by Cotton Mather, the son of Increase, who tells the story of the hauntings at Great Island in much the same words as those used in his father's earlier book. He lets us know, however, that George Walton was a Quaker. See Cotton Mather's *Magnalia Christi Americana* (1702), Bk. VI, ch. 7, n. 5.

two youths were hit, one on the leg the other on the thigh, not-
withstanding the stones came so thick and so forcibly against the
sides of so narrow a room.   Whilst we stood amazed at this accident,
one of the maidens imagined she saw them come from the hall
next to that we were in.   Where searching (and in the cellar down
out of the hall) and finding nobody, another and myself observed
two little stones in a short space successively to fall on the floor,
coming as from the ceiling close by us, and we concluded it must
necessarily be done by means extraordinary and preternatural.

There can be no doubt that whatever took place, starting from
the very first evening, was witnessed by a considerable number of
people.   Mr. Walton's house seems to have served as a sort of
unofficial lodging for Government administrators, and neighbours
also congregated from outside.   For example, under date 2 August
we are told: " At night as I, with others, were in the kitchen, many
more [stones] came in, and one great stone that lay on a spinning
wheel to keep it steady, was thrown to the other side of the room.
Several neighbours then present were ready to testify to the matter."
So again Chamberlain records on another occasion:

Some persons of note being then in the field (whose names are
here under-written) to visit Mr. Walton there, are substantial
witnesses of the same stonery, both in the field, and afterward in the
house that night, viz., one Mr. Hussey, son of a Counsellor there.
He took up one that having first alighted on the ground, with
rebound from thence hit him on the heel, and he keeps it to show.
And Captain Barefoot, mentioned above, has that which (among
other stones) flew into the hall a little before supper; which myself
also saw as it first came in at the upper part of the door, into the
middle of the room; and then (though a good flat stone) yet was seen
to roll over and over, as if trundled, under a bed in the same room.
In short, these persons, being wondrously affected by the strangeness
of these passages, offered themselves (desiring me to take them) as
testimonies.   I did so and made a memorandum by way of Record,
thereof, to this effect, viz.:

" These persons under-written do hereby attest the truth of their
being eye-witnesses of at least half a score stones that evening thrown
invisibly into the field, and in the entry of the house, hall and one of
the chambers of George Walton's "—viz.

Samuel Jennings, Esq., Governor of West Jersey.

Walter Clark, Esq., Deputy-Governor of Rhode Island.
Mr. Arthur Cook.
Mr. Matt. Borden of Rhode Island.
Mr. Oliver Hooton of Barbadoes, Merchant.
Mr. T. Maul, of Salem in New England, Merchant.
Captain Walter Barefoot.
Mr. John Hussey, and the wife of the said Mr. Hussey.

Now these are not imaginary names. The majority have been identified by a local antiquary in New England[1]; and I myself have found several in the published *Calender of State Papers*; *Colonial*, 1681—1685 issued by the Record Office. For instance, Chamberlain speaks of " one Mr. Hussey, son of a counsellor there, " but in the *Calendar* referred to (p. 43) we have under date 16 March, 1681, a list of the Council, meeting at Portsmouth, New Hampshire, and in it occurs the name of Christopher Hussey. He was still Counsellor in 1684 (*ibid.*, p. 741). Similarly the name of Captain Walter Barefoot recurs again and again in the same record. He was deputy-collector under Randolph (an official also mentioned in the pamphlet as visiting Mr. Walton) and subsequently Barefoot became Captain of the Fort, a Judge, and President of the Council.

Moreover, in the same *Calendar* (p. 409) we find mention not only of a "letter of attorney from Walter Barefoot to Edward Randolph to prosecute his appeal "; but this is immediately followed by another entry beginning thus: " The case and title of George Walton to his land in New Hampshire. Robert Mason on 22 April, 1681 confirmed to George Walton a parcel of land on Great Island formerly granted by his agents. Jeremy Walford and John Amazeen[2] pretended a town grant of the year 1658 for some of the land, though never improved. The jury, being all of them possessed of lands by virtue of town grants derived from the authority of Massachusetts, found against Walton, who appeals to the King in Council. Signed Richard Chamberlain. Authenticated by the hand of Governor Cranfield and the public seal. " The date of all this is 23 March, 1683. By this and a number of other entries in official documents still preserved in our Record Office, it is at least made clear that Chamberlain at the time spoken of was in close personal contact with the people whom he names.

[1] See a note by the Rev. Mr. Alden of Newcastle (N.H.) in *The Historical Magazine* for 1862.

[2] We learn from Chamberlain's pamphlet that the estate of Amazeen, " the Italian," immediately adjoined Walton's. There were Amazeens still living in the locality when Mr. Alden wrote in 1862.

There is no very great variety in the phenomena observed, and some of the incidents mentioned by Mather are not to be found in Chamberlain's narrative. We hear of such objects as candlesticks or pewter pots being swept to the ground by a stone, or again of their suddenly disappearing the moment those present turned their backs to observe something which was happening elsewhere. But I must content myself with one final quotation.

On Saturday, June 24,[1] one of the family at the usual hour at night, observed some few (not above half a dozen) of these natural (or rather unnatural) weapons to fly into the kitchen, as formerly; but some of them in an unusual manner, lighting gently on him, or coming towards him so easily, as that he took them before they fell to the ground. I think there was not anything more that night remarkable. But as if the malicious demon had laid up for Sunday and Monday, then it was that he began (more furiously than formerly) with a great stone in the kitchen, and so continued with throwing down the pewter dishes, etc. A great part of it all at once came clattering down, without the stroke of a stone, little or great, to move it.

Then about midnight this impious operation not ceasing, but trespassing with a *continuando*, two very great stones weighing about 30 pound apiece (that used to lie in the kitchen, in or near the chimney) were, in the former wonted rebounding manner, let fly against my desk and wall in the ante-chamber, but with some little distance of time. This thundering noise must needs bring up the men from below, as before (I need not say to wake me) to tell me the effect, which was the beating down several pictures, and displacing abundance of things about my chamber. But the repetition of this cannon-play by these great rumbling engines, now ready at hand for the purpose, and the like additional disturbance by four bricks that lay in the outer room chimney (one of which having been so employed the first Sunday night, as has been said) made me despair of taking rest and so forced me to rise from my bed.

Then finding my door burst open, I also found many stones, and great pieces of bricks to fly in, breaking the glass windows and a paper light, sometimes inwards, sometimes outwards; so hitting the

[1] " July 24 " is what stands in the original pamphlet; but this is clearly an oversight or a misprint. 24 July, 1682, was not a Saturday but a Monday. On the other hand 24 June was a Saturday, and the incidents recorded clearly preceded what occurred on " Monday night, 26 June," which is mentioned a little further on.

door of my chamber, as I came through the ante-chamber, lighting very near me as I was fetching the candlestick, and afterwards, the candle being struck out, as I was going to light it again. So, a little after, coming up for another candle, and being at the stair-foot door, a wooden mortar with a great noise struck against the floor and was just at my feet, only not touching me, moving from the other end of the kitchen where it used to lie. . .

Now for Monday night, June 26, one of the severest. The disturbance began in the kitchen with stones; then as I was at supper above in the ante-chamber, the window near which I sat at table was broken in two or three parts of it inwards, and one of the stones that broke it flew in, and I took it up at the further end of the room. The manner is observable; for one of the squares was broken into nine or ten small square pieces, as if it had been regularly marked out into such even squares by a workman, to the end some of these little pieces might fly in my face (as they did) and give me a surprise, but without any hurt.

In the meantime it went on in the kitchen, whither I went down for company, all or most of the family and a neighbour being there; where many stones (some great ones) came thick and three-fold among us, and an old hoeing-iron from a room hard by where such utensils lay. Then, as if I had been the designed object for that time, most of the stones that came (the smaller I mean) hit me (sometimes pretty hard) to the number of above twenty—near thirty as I remember—and whether I removed, sat or walked, I had them, and great ones sometimes, lighting gently on me, and in hand and lap as I sat, and falling to the ground and sometimes thumping against the wall, as near as could be to me, without touching me. There was a room over the kitchen infested, that had not been so before, and many stones greater than usual lumbering there over our heads, not only to ours, but to the great disturbance and affrightment of some children that lay there. And for variety there were sometimes three great distinct knocks, sometimes five such rounds, as with a great maul, reiterated divers times.

In the portion omitted Chamberlain gives many dates besides those mentioned above, specifying in each case the day of the week. After checking them all and finding the correspondence correct, I am inclined to attach a good deal of importance to this accuracy. It seems to me to show that he was writing from diary notes and not from memory. Few men would take the trouble in a chapbook like this to insert correctly the days of the week for incidents which had happened sixteen years earlier. Finally, I may quote a few quaint lines from a copy of verses prefixed and signed R.C.

To tell strange feats of Dæmons here I am;
Strange but most true they are, ev'n to a dram,
Tho' Sadduceans cry, 'tis all a Sham.
Here's Stony Arguments of persuasive Dint;
They'll not believe it, told, nor yet in Print;
What should the Reason be ?   The Devil's in't.

If this remarkable story stood alone, one would probably make little account of it, but it is impossible to shut one's eyes to the fact that for more than a thousand years similar happenings have been recorded by seemingly credible witnesses in almost every region of the habitable globe.[1]

---

[1] Fr. Thurston had obtained from the *Académie Delphinale* of Grenoble in Feb. 1938 the following account of a stone-throwing case which he never discussed in print but which seems to present the phenomena in a very simplified, and therefore instructive, form.

The *Courrier de l'Isère* of Tuesday, 3 January, 1843, relates that two girls of fourteen years, Marie Genevoix and Marguerite Pinel, living in the hamlet of les Clavaux near Livet, experienced a shower of stones as they went along the road together. Other people who were with them were also hit. M. Micha-Bonnardon, *maire* of Vizille at the time left a written account of the happening which was witnessed by the priest, the doctor, the schoolmaster, two legal officials and many others.   It cannot be that all these men with local knowledge were duped by a party of mischievous small boys.   J.H.C.

10

CHAPTER XII

A WEST INDIAN POLTERGEIST[1]

IN the summer of 1937 I received a kind letter from Father Aldhelm Bowring, O.P., telling me that he had read some of my poltergeist tales and that he thought I might be interested to hear of a poltergeist disturbance which had taken place two or three years before in the island of Grenada, B.W.I. The Dominican Fathers have a mission there, as they have in Trinidad, and Father Bowring was resident in Grenada at the time of the occurrence. What lent exceptional interest to the manifestation was the fact that it culminated in the burning down of the house in which the trouble had occurred, and that an official inquiry into the cause of the fire had consequently been held before the local magistrate. The occurrence, I was further told, was fully reported in the Grenada newspaper, *The West Indian*, which, if not quite a daily, is published several times in the week.

Father Bowring on returning to England had not, of course, brought with him copies of the journal in question, but it was afterwards suggested to me by a friend that such newspapers were likely to be sent to the Colonial Office, and on inquiring there I was courteously informed that files, after accumulating for a year or two, were passed on to the British Museum.

The earliest notice I could meet with of the poltergeist disturbances occured in *The West Indian* for Sunday, 23 September, 1934. It was preceded by the usual large type heading

MYSTERIOUS NOISES MOLEST LOWTHER LANE COTTAGE DWELLERS.

STONES RAIN ON ROOF EACH NIGHT OF PAST WEEK.
ELEVEN YEAR OLD GIRL SEES GHOST.

In the account which follows it is stated that " mysterious noises occurring between the hours of 7 o'clock and midnight each night since Monday last [*i.e.*, September 17th] at a cottage at the Botanic

[1] *The Month*, August 1937

Station end of Lowther's Lane, baffling the most zealous police and voluntary watchers, have attracted hundreds to the scene all the past week, " We are further told that the many persons who searched the house and the surrounding area, including " police and detectives "—one is inclined to wonder a little what type of individual exercises the functions of policeman and detective in Grenada, B.W.I.—" are satisfied that the occurrence is no hoax. " More definitely the account continues:

Police have climbed to the roof from the windows and seen the stones dropping on the roof. Another puzzling feature of the stone-throwing is that the missiles fall as if dropped from the skies and yet remain stationary where they fall. The stones up to the present have injured no one, though crowds press thickly round the cottage each night. They vary in weight between two ounces and a pound.

There were, however, other circumstances which pointed to the intervention of human agency working out a malicious purpose. There was an anonymous letter, or letters, containing threats and warnings against a certain young woman who at the time was living in the house. There was also a strange parcel of dirty odds and ends left upon the roof which was suggestive of Obeah practices, and there was a child, really much older than she looked, who professed to see a man dressed in white, apparently, in her belief, the agent of these disorders, but in any case a figure which no one else could see. In view of these complications, an editorial in *The West Indian* two days later showed a sane and cautious reserve in pronouncing upon the nature of the happenings reported. There seemed to be no explanation of the missiles, but the very fact of the presence of crowds of spectators must have hindered anything like accurate observation.

The stone-throwing seems to have continued persistently for a month or two, until the occupants, losing heart, left the house altogether. Eventually, on the night of 14 January, 1935, the cottage mysteriously took fire and was burned to the ground. Thereupon in the same newspaper for 16 January, we find a revival of interest in the subject. It published a recapitulation of what has already been described and went on to state that when the phenommena first began in September the house was occupied by the proprietress, who bore the curious name of Mrs. Excelia Mark and was apparently a woman of colour. With her were her two daughters and a grandchild, this last the daughter of an absent son.   It was upon this grandchild and upon her aunt Dolly that attention was specially concentrated.   The report, after giving the name of the mother, goes on to speak of—

Dolly Woodroffe, 20, her daughter, who since her return to the colony from Trinidad on 9 September from a holiday visit, rumour had it, was the butt of the mysterious attacks on the dwelling.   The stones would fall on the roof over her bedroom, and she would find notes addressed to her by supposedly strange media.

Ivy is the 11 year old granddaughter of Excelia Mark, to whom the letters also made reference.

Several weeks ago, however, the house was deserted.   At later times foul-looking paper packets were mingled with the stones.   These would contain greasy matter, garlic, coarse salt, bits of broken glass, and a variety of other material properly associated with the Obeah cult.

In *The West Indian* for 24 January, 1935, it is stated that " on Wednesday, 23rd, an investigation into the origin of the fire which destroyed the ' haunted ' house in Lowther's Lane was held before His Worship C. H. Lucas, Acting-Magistrate of the Western District."   Excelia Mark, giving evidence, stated that Ivy was her son's daughter and was aged fifteen; her son, Ivy's father, was in Cuba.   She further narrated how she " made a sacrifice " in November; with regard to which occurrence the report summarizes a part of her statement thus:

Some African people made prayers for three days.   No stones fell during those three days.   They left about 10 o'clock one Saturday, and about 12 o'clock stones began to fall on the house again.   No fire was lit in the house from the time the " sacrifice " ended.   She also said: " I noticed that whenever Ivy was present more stones would fall, but when she was not there everything was quiet.   Besides stones such things as salt, various powders, matches and letters were picked up on the roof of the house."

In *The West Indian* for 29 January we have a report of the continuation of the inquiry.   Several of the witnesses spoke only of the fire and of the impossibility of explaining how it originated.   Dolly Woodroffe confirmed the account given by her mother and niece of the evening in September when the disturbances began, but she stated that after two or three such experiences she had left the house and had gone to stay with a friend in the town. With regard to the phenomena, interest centres in the depositions of Ivy, the grand-daughter, who, in agreement with her grandmother, describes herself as fifteen, not eleven, years of age, and of the " Detective " Bernadine who long before the fire had been deputed to investigate the mysterious stone-throwings. Ivy is reported as saying:

One night in September last I was inside the house with my grandmother and my two aunts Gertrude and Dolly and I heard something fall on the house. My grandmother told me to look out and see if there was anyone in the road. I looked out and saw a white man in the road about 12 feet away. He ran down the road and through the gate of the Botanical Gardens. He then stood up. I tried to show him to my grandmother but she could not see him . . .

That same night several stones fell on the house before I went to bed. While the stones were falling the man was there, but I did not see him throwing any. The stones continued falling for more than a month, day and night. Sometimes stones would fall inside the house even when it was closed. Every time the stones were falling I used to see the man. I used to see the man inside the house sometimes; sometimes sitting on the bed. After a while I saw not only one man but two men and a woman standing by the Botanical Gardens. One of the persons I saw was white, but the other two were not so fair. The other man and the woman were both dressed in white.

I pointed the one man out to several persons, including the police, but they all said they did not see anything.

In confirmation of this it may be interesting to recur to the grandmother's fuller statement which the journal I am quoting from reported more in detail in a later issue. It is difficult to see any very obvious motive which the woman could have had for concocting such a story. She apparently stuck to the house for some weeks even after the " sacrifice " had failed to relieve her of the annoyance; but in the end she could endure the disturbances no longer, and though she visited it in the daytime she ceased to sleep there. According to her account:

The stoning began on Monday, 17 September [1934] at 7 o'clock. I reported the matter to the police the day after. I was at home and heard the stones falling on the roof. Gertrude and Ivy were with me at home. I told Ivy to look out and see if anyone was throwing the stones. She said she saw a man dressed in white running to the garden gate. She tried to show the person to me but I could see no one. The stoning continued till 11 p.m. and stopped.

Every night afterwards the house was pelted. Sometimes, gravel, dust and green limes fell inside the house even when all around was closed. This continued until about eight days before the fire occurred . . .

Furniture, tables, chairs, irons pitched all over the house without being moved or touched by anyone. Ivy always said she saw unnatural persons in and around the house but I never saw anything. The matter was reported early to the police. They came night and day and would try to locate who was throwing the stones, but found no one. Some nights the house would be closed up and yet stones were heard falling inside. We would see them in the morning. Besides the police, crowds of people used to visit the scene, and while they were there the stones continued to fall. The crowd was so great the police had to control them at times.

It must be admitted that the deposition of the " detective," Bernadine, is in close accord with the statements previously made. There is nothing to show that he was subjected to any cross-examination, but he could hardly have asserted in open court that from the very beginning of the disturbances, long before the fire, he had been deputed to investigate the stone-throwing, if this was not the case. The account given of his evidence runs thus:

I remember on 17 September last a report was made to the Detective Department of mysterious stone-throwings on a house in Lowther's Lane belonging to Mrs. Excelia Mark. In consequence I went to the house with some other detectives about 8 o'clock on the night of the 16th [sic. presumably it should be 18th] September. We went with the purpose of trying to discover who were throwing the stones. We separated and hid in the surroundings. I heard the stones falling on the house but saw nobody. These duties were continued day and night up to November. No one was seen and no arrests made. I remember on one occasion the little girl, Ivy, pointed to the Botanic Gardens gate and said there was a man standing there. Mr. Knight and I went to the place pointed out by her but saw no one.

I remember one morning I went to the house and removed stones and bottles from the roof. Ivy went on to the roof and said she saw a man sitting with a parcel in his hand. I had just cleared off stones and bottles from the top of the house. I returned to the roof and I saw a paper parcel containing a sort of powder and a scrip threatening Ivy, warning her to leave the place by 7 o'clock or else she would be dead. I took these things, a bottle with some liquid, the scrip and the paper with the powder, and handed them over to the Chief of Police. The house stands from 6 to 8 feet from the ground on one side, and on the road side about 3 feet. No one went on the roof of the house during the time I was there.[1]

When stones fell on the roof they remained there and did not fall to the ground. I remember one morning I was inside the house and the doors and windows were all closed. I heard a sound on the galvanized roof and a stone fell in front of me without making or leaving any hole.

Except for certain witnesses who had been spectators of the conflagration, which, of course, was the main subject of inquiry and at which the detective Bernadine had also been present, the above appears to be a pretty complete summary of the case as presented in court. The whole affair seems to have been very mysterious, and we can hardly be surprised that after a two days' hearing, " His Worship C. H. Lucas, Acting-Magistrate, found that there was no evidence whatever as to the cause or origin of the fire."

Two characters in the drama above described particularly arrest the attention. The first is the granddaughter, Ivy, who in the early accounts is described as eleven years old, and whom the detective, after presumably having heard her own and her grandmother's statement that she was fifteen, still refers to as " the little girl.".. Poltergeist phenomena are generally supposed by the sceptical to be the work of artful and mischievous children, and I should not dream of disputing that naughty little girls have at times been extraordinarily clever in carrying out some trick which has imposed upon their elders, sometimes even upon medical men of wide experience. But in many cases which seem to have been carefully observed and reported the physical effects are of a nature quite incompatible with child agency. A child may produce

[1] How does this agree with the same witness's statement above that " Ivy went on to the roof " ?

strange noises or throw an occasional stone, but the movement of heavy furniture, or the flinging of missiles which enter a room from outside when the child is in the room and actually under observation cannot be explained in that way. Even if I confine myself only to cases which have been discussed here in previous articles, it seems to me that over and over again the hypothesis of a mischievous urchin playing pranks completely breaks down.

The curious fact that Ivy, who certainly is a suspicious character professed to see ghostly shapes which no one else could see, must at once arouse misgivings. But this possible sensitiveness of a psychically endowed child or young person whose mediumistic faculty seems to be the starting-point of the disturbance, has many parallels. In fact, it is a commonplace among spiritualists to hold that this is likely to happen. In what I take to be the well-attested accordion phenomena of D. D. Home, there were several instances in which onlookers of credit professed to observe a phantom hand depressing the keys, while other witnesses at the same moment could only see the keys moving without any perceptible agency. On the other hand, the lively imagination of children under the acute stimulus of strange occurrences may conjure up a mental picture of which their more staid elders are quite incapable. Some of the recent alleged visions of Our Lady may perhaps be accounted for in this way without our imputing conscious deception. In any case, it is unquestionable that in many descriptions of poltergeist phenomena it often happens that children profess to see shapes invisible to the rest of the world.

It would also appear that the aunt, Dolly Woodroffe, was looked at askance by some of those concerned in the case. The mysterious writings were addressed to her. She also seemingly was the intended victim of some Obeah magic, while Ivy was solemnly warned that if she respected her good name she should withdraw herself entirely from Dolly's influence. From a later notice in *The West Indian* we learn that among some of the residents Dolly had acquired the nickname of " Dracula," derived from the film presentment of Mr. Bram Stoker's weird story which had been shown in the island a short time previously. This was used in a way which led to an action for defamation of character, and it is so far to the credit of Mrs. or Miss Dolly Woodroffe that a verdict was given by the Court in her favour and she was awarded the munificent sum of ten shillings damages.

That the atmosphere of Voodoo and Obeah which is prevalent

in greater or less measure in all the West Indian islands is a fruitful soil for the ready acceptance of stories of " duppies " and their stone-throwing propensities may readily be conceded.[1] The stories of such cases are numerous, but unfortunately they come, for the most part, at second or third hand. Father Williams speaks of a Jesuit Father whom he knew well (the Rev. A. J. Emerick) who told or wrote down for him the following account of an experience in Jamaica.

I was on my way [he said] to Alva mission, situated at a lonesome spot on a hill in the Dry Harbour Mountains. I was met by a crowd about a mile away from the mission. They got around me and warned me in an excited way against going up to the mission. They said the duppies were up there at night throwing stones; that the duppies had stoned the teacher away from the Alva school. It seems that the stone-throwing had been going on for a week or more before my arrival. For several nights crowds went up to the old Alva school, not far from the church . . . The teacher of the school, a certain Mr. D., lived in two rooms that overlooked a ravine. Every night the crowd was there, stones were thrown from various directions but most of them seemed to come from the bush-covered ravine. What mystified the people most and made them believe and say, as did the teacher and the most intelligent storekeeper in the district, that the stones were thrown not by human hands but by spirits, was that those who were hit by the stones were not injured, and that some of the stones which came from the bushy declivity, after smashing through the window turned at a right angle and broke the teacher's clock, glasses, etc., on a sideboard. In spite of the dreadful stone-throwing duppies, I went up to the hill followed by a crowd. I found the school building littered with stones broken windows and a generally smashed-up, sure-enough ghost-haunted place.[2]

The story may be true enough, but the evidence is hardly satisfactory—

Sir, he made a chimney in my father's house, and the bricks are alive at this day to testify it; therefore deny it not. (2 Henry VI, iv, 2).

[1] See, for example, the books of Father J. J. Williams, S.J., *Psychic Phenomena in Jamaica*, New York, 1934; and *Voodoos and Obeahs*, New York, 1932.

[2] Williams, *Psychic Phenomena of Jamaica*, p. 7.

One piece of first-hand evidence, however, of a somewhat similar stone-throwing phenomenon I can quote. I owe it to the great kindness of Father John L. Lucchesi, S.J., for many years missionary in Alaska. The setting and the wording add so much to the value of the testimony that I make no apology for quoting the letter exactly as I received it.

Holy Cross Mission—Alaska
18 January, 1937
Reverend, Dear Father Thurston,   P.C.

Your Reverence must perhaps be surprised in receiving a letter from the far-off frozen Alaska. This is the reason.

Last September, I being now in my 79th year of age, of which nearly forty lived in Alaska, was called from the wilder mission of Akulurak to this, more progressive and less hard, I suppose, *ad curandam valetudinem vel senectutem* [*i.e.*, to husband out my health or old age] and with pleasure I found here *The Month*, with your interesting articles. I thought that perhaps one or two of my personal experiences in the preternatural would not be useless.

One happened just before my starting for the Missions in 1896. I was then Minister [this is the Superior who has charge of the household arrangements and discipline in a college] in our residence in Bastia, Corsica. Very near us there was a large Academy for girls, under the care of the Sisters of St. Joseph, from Lyons, France. All was going on well, when without any apparent reason, a strange event caused them great surprise. In the yard, about 40 or 50 yards long, connecting the house with the laundry, began to fall little stones or pebbles, without, however, striking or hurting anybody. Nobody could see where they were coming from, though all were watching and trying to find out the point of departure. This went on for days. The Superior, not knowing what to do, sent for us. Our Superior, Father P., a very venerable old man but very timid, declined to go and sent me in his place. I went and saw with my own eyes the rain of pebbles, that were falling pretty thickly all around me, nor could I find any cause or explanation of the phenomenon. I don't remember exactly what I did, but I am pretty sure I got and said some blessing or prayer from the Ritual, with copious aspersions of holy water. So far as I can still remember after so many years, the phenomenon did not stop at once, but after a while, viz., one or two days, and for ever.

Father Lucchesi's second story has nothing directly to do with our present subject, but it is curious, and I trust that I may be excused for quoting his letter to the end, if only as a further illustration of the writer's attitude, so obviously free from any desire to exaggerate or improve the occasion.

Another strange queer thing went on for years in a convent of Capuchin friars in Genoa, Italy, my birthplace. The convent St. Barnaba, is apart on a hill; it is in great esteem and veneration by the people, on account of the strict observance and holiness of the generally old and selected monks who dwell in it, and their flourishing novitiate. However, a room, the guest room I think, was for many years haunted so that nobody could live or even sleep in it. Invisible beings were blowing out the light, pulling away the blankets, etc., etc., many or such annoying tricks without ever any real harm or injury. All blessings, exorcisms, etc., proved useless. All the community and many others knew that. The probity and truthfulness of the Capuchins was above all suspicion. The people say that it is the work of the "*folletti.*" *Folletti* according to their theology are a kind of spirits, himps [*sic*], harmless but mischievous, who seem to be permitted or ordered to do such things for some reason or other. So were things when I left, and since, I have had no more news, but I am writing and asking more information and details, as I was always a familiar friend of those Capuchins. If there will be anything interesting I will let you know.

Excuse my intruding on your precious time with these bagatelles. Asking the charity of your good prayers for the grace of a good death, Yours fraternally in Xt.,

John L. Lucchesi, S.J.[1]

Although the last section of this letter has nothing to do with stone-throwing, still it does illustrate and confirm one of the most commonly recognized features of poltergeist disturbances, *i.e.*, the pulling off of bed-coverings. Sir William Barrett, some years ago, described in detail such a case occurring at Enniscorthy in 1910, see above, page 4, and we have other similar instances recorded in the seventeenth century. So again it is always a source of wonder to me how witnesses in all parts of the world, who certainly had no connection with each other, should be so generally agreed in affirming that these poltergeist assaults in spite of their seeming violence were hardly ever attended with injury to life or limb.

---

[1] The letter I need hardly say was written in English. I have only corrected one or two slips made by Father Lucchesi in typing it.

CHAPTER XIII

THE POONA POLTERGEIST[1]

ON 31 March, 1934, a letter appeared in the well-known London weekly journal *The Spectator*, the substance of which runs as follows:—

I carefully investigated a remarkable case here in Poona a few years ago. My friend Dr. S. V. Ketkar and his German wife, both persons of culture (the doctor is the famous Marathi historian and encyclopedist), suffered terribly for many years, both in name, in estate, in all their affairs . . . loss of their servants and of their general health. Briefly I may say that when I first visited the house that was " afflicted, " the testimony of various witnesses convinced me that it was impossible to attribute all the amazing disturbances to their son, a lad of eight, around whom these activities seemed to gather. When I entered, I asked all those present to leave the room. I placed the lad (stark naked) on a small bed, felt his pulse, and told him to " lie down quietly ". I then closed the door and windows and sat down on a chair in a corner of the room. I looked at my watch; it was exactly 1.30 p.m. I put a sheet over him. In about fifteen minutes I saw the bedclothes pulled off the bed on which the lad was lying, the bed was pulled into the middle of the room, and the lad actually lifted off the bed and deposited gently on the floor. The lad could feel the arm of an unseen person at work. A bottle of ink that was on the table by the window was flung towards me, and so was a glass paper-weight which narrowly missed my head. The lad's toys were violently flung about from a corner of the room. I was astounded, and told the parents that I found that mal-observation, illusion, etc., could not (as I had previously suggested) account for all this.

Let me interrupt this account to explain that the writer, Mr. J. D. Jenkins, was apparently a medical man who had been invited

[1] *Studies*, March 1935

146

professionally to give his opinion of the case. The boy, whose proper name was Damodar Bapat, had only been adopted by the Ketkars. His father a, Brahmin like Dr. Ketkar himself, had died shortly after the child's birth; the mother, who seems to have been troubled by strange visions or delusions, had committed suicide. Whether Mr. Jenkins was at the time acquainted with these facts is not clear, but at any rate his letter continues:—

The next day I called again accompanied by some friends, a police officer and an irascible old Major (who had settled the whole problem by the simple process of calling me a liar when I related to him the happenings of the day before). On this day even more remarkable and unaccountable phenomena occurred. Here I can only mention one incident. It was broad daylight (2 p.m.); a small table, apparently untouched by anyone, came hobbling across the room to the verandah where we were all sitting and talking. It came directly towards my friend the Major, imprisoning him in the armchair in which he was sitting. That evening we were all invited to dinner at the house. All went well until half way through the meal. My friend's glass fell down. The salt-cellar began to do "the Charleston," so to speak, before our eyes. The whole contents of the table were cleared by unseen hands. My friend the Major promptly got up and said "good night" and left. The police officer also very suddenly remembered that he had another urgent case to investigate of a more terrestrial nature. All this and many thousands of other instances are recorded in a day-to-day diary of events which I kept from June 1928 to January 1930. Most of them were published in *The Times of India* and in *The Statesman*.[1] After infinite havoc had been wrought, they slowly subsided and the family has been enjoying comparative peace and rest ever since.

Mr. Jenkins's diary of these events was not the only record which had been kept. While the phenomena were still in full eruption, *i.e.*, in the early months of 1929, I had chanced in a curious way to receive a letter from Dr. Ketkar's sister-in law, Miss H. Kohn, who was residing with him and his wife at Poona. Though a German by birth, she was a graduate of London University and held an official post as Teacher of European Languages for the Deccan College, Poona, in connection with the University of Bombay. Miss Kohn is not a Catholic, but her work brought her into contact with one of our Jesuit Fathers engaged like herself in the higher

[1] I have seen cuttings of some of these communications.

education of the native races. When the disturbances in the Ketkar household, above referred to, began to be talked about, Miss Kohn, who took no interest in Spiritualism and knew nothing of poltergeists, chanced to speak of the matter to her Jesuit acquaintance, and he lent her one or two of the articles I had contributed on this subject to *The Month* or to *Studies*. Conceiving the very mistaken idea that I might possibly have some remedy to suggest—for the distress caused in the family by these occurrences was acute— Miss Kohn wrote to me and forwarded a typed copy of the notes she had taken of the case. For the greater part of the time she had been present in the house and had been an eye-witness of almost all that had happened. The account was very full. If printed at length, it would occupy forty pages of this work, but I have every reason to believe the statement made in her accompanying letter: " I took especial care, " she says, " to avoid the slightest exaggeration or inaccuracy, and the events were always recorded immediately after their occurrence. " The narrative covers a period of over eleven months. Shortly after writing this, Miss Kohn took advantage of the leave then due to her to pay a long visit to Europe, part of which she spent in London. She came to see me more than once, and she impressed me, as she did others to whom she was introduced, as an exceptionally intelligent and level-headed observer. Her narrative was printed a little later, together with some introductory remarks by Mr. Harry Price, in *Psychic Research* (March to May, 1930).

The character and intelligence of the witnesses is so important a matter in any record of astounding phenomena, that it does not seem out of place to point out that Miss Kohn's sister, Mrs. Ketkar, is, like her husband, a scholar, and the translator of a work of high authority on the early literature of Hindustan. The author, Professor Winternitz, says in his preface to the English edition:—

When I came to Poona in 1922 to visit the Bhandarkar Oriental Research Institute, I was introduced to Dr. S. V. Ketkar, the learned editor of the Marathi Encyclopedia, and to my great surprise he showed me two big volumes, containing a type-written English translation of the first two volumes of my *History of Indian Literature*. The translation, I understood, was the work of Mrs. Ketkar, who had made it for the use of her husband, not for publication. Mrs. Ketkar, being German by her mother tongue, English by education, and Indian by marriage, seemed to me as if predestined for the work, and she agreed to revise and rewrite her translation for the purpose of publication.

The bringing out of this work was undertaken by the University of Calcutta, and the first volume was printed at the Calcutta University Press in 1927.

While Miss Kohn does not disguise the fact that the adopted son Damodar was suspected by many of slyly and mischievously producing the disturbances himself, and though she admits that appearances sometimes pointed in that direction, she also suggests as a result of her close observation of the case that the supernormal agency, whatever its nature may have been, purposely so contrived things on certain occasions as to make the boy appear responsible although he was really quite innocent. This, of course, is a view which the sceptic will receive with derision and which it would be very difficult to prove. On the other hand, in the case of a great number of the more startling phenomena any guilty participation on the child's part (he was only eight years old) seems absolutely out of the question. For example on Sunday 8 July, 1928, Miss Kohn records:—

A small glass jar containing vegetable extract, which stood among other jars in the closed cupboard in the dining room, was hurled forcibly from that room into my bedroom at the moment when Damodar in my presence was undressing for bed. In order to land where it did the jar must have turned a corner. It broke into many pieces.

So again on the next day:—

At 5 p.m. while we were having tea in the dining-room (in the presence of a friend, Miss H.) Damodar stepped into my bedroom. At the same moment a small screw-top jar, in which my brother-in-law had succeeded in preserving some ink[1] for some days, was hurled from his study in the front of the house, across the dining-room in which we were sitting, into my bedroom where Damodar stood. It broke, spilling the ink.

Similarly on 24 June, we have the note:—

At 9 a.m. a man called to see my brother-in-law. I crossed the

[1] One of the peculiarities of this infestation was that almost every receptacle containing ink was smashed and the contents scattered broadcast over floors and furniture.

room and was in the act of picking up a pad and pencil for him, when an aspirin bottle which had stood on a shelf in the dining-room was suddenly hurled in my direction by " an invisible hand " with such tremendous force that I involuntarily screamed, anticipating a violent crash.   However the bottle fell gently by my feet, without breaking; only the metal stopper was dented.   At the moment when this happened, my nephew (Damodar) was standing quietly near me.

It seems to me impossible to reject the evidence of conscientious witnesses who are both free from any abnormality and highly intelligent. The one purpose of the Ketkar family was, not to advertise these strange happenings, which brought them nothing but trouble and suspicion, but to discover some means of bringing them to an end.   There were times when they could never be sure of finding in the house even materials for the next meal.   Here is Miss Kohn's account of a typical incident:

While our friends were still in the house, my sister observed that the heavy padlock on the cupboard in her room was hanging open, though no one was in that room and she had seen it properly locked a few minutes before.   The reason why she chose that moment to inspect that cupboard was that while she crossed the dining-room (in our presence) an empty round basket was flung at her head from a great height.   This particular basket was the identical one which she had that day locked into the cupboard in her room, and the basket had, when she saw it last, contained forty-one eggs.   We inspected the cupboard and these eggs were entirely missing.   We looked in all the corners of the house, even under the beds, as on previous occasions eggs had been found so concealed.   But we saw nothing of our eggs.   We fully expected them to come crashing one by one from mid-air, as had been experienced on former occasions.   However, no more has been seen of these particular eggs.

These sudden disappearances, which affected not only comestibles but money and all sorts of household requisites, must have been intensely annoying; but there was occasionally a humorous incident. That same morning (22 July 1928,) on which day the forty-one eggs disappeared at a later hour, Miss Kohn had wanted to go out and wished first to polish her shoes.

However [she says] I missed the tin of polish from its usual place on the shelf. I asked every member of the household. All denied having taken my polish. I was irritated at the petty nuisance, and after hunting for five minutes decided to go without. Damodar was standing in my room with me. He was at the table sorting some papers which I had given him, and I saw both his hands busy with the papers at the instant when I took up my hat to put it on. At the same moment I was startled by a very swift thud, and behold the the missing tin of polish came from mid-air from some point beyond Damodar and landed precisely at my feet. It did not roll, but came through the air swiftly; yet the aim taken by the invisible one was so sure that the object stopped dead still the very instant when it reached my foot.

The next morning the tin was again missing, but when Miss Kohn called out " shoe-polish, please, " it came to her gently as before. Very curious also were the many incidents connected with the disappearance of money. Notes were taken from locked receptacles. Sometimes they were never recovered, but sometimes also an equivalent was returned in the form of small change.[1] Miss Kohn writes:—

On several occasions in broad daylight we now saw coins fall among us from above. This was always while the boy was in the house . . . .At first we could not always see the coins in mid-air, but merely saw them fall, being startled by the contact of the coin with the floor. Soon, however, we were able to observe more closely, and actually saw the money appear in the air. Generally the coins were one-pice or two-annas. In some cases these seemed to be coins which were missing from our purses; in other cases we could not account for the coins. In every instance it was most obvious that the boy was not himself doing the mischief.[2]

---

[1] On the other hand Miss Kohn reports that on 23 July she inadvertently left her handbag, with purse containing two rupees, in the dining-room. On returning a minute later she found the bag, but the purse was gone. The boy was searched but his pockets were empty. She called out: Purse, please, and thereupon the purse fell at her feet, but it was empty, " not a sign of the two rupees, nor were they returned to me subsequently."—J.H.C.

[2] It is curious that prayer seemed to excite the Poltergeist. Miss Kohn speaks of this with emphasis. " The spirits do show most definite reaction to any serious attempt of an exorcist to interfere with them," she says, recording the fact that on a recrudescence of the trouble in October, a man called to say a *mantra*. At once a cup was smashed into innumerable fragments in the dining-room.—J.H.C.

CHAPTER XIV

DO POLTERGEISTS INVADE THE TOMB ?[1]

ALBEIT I am a firm believer in the reality of poltergeists and in the impossibility of finding any natural explanation of their recorded activities, I must hesitate to return a directly affirmative answer to the question which is here propounded. We need more evidence, and also testimony of a rather better quality than seems to be at present available. The alleged cases of the disturbance of coffins in vaults are rare, and I am compelled in this article to confine myself, practically speaking, to four examples which were already discussed some thirty years ago by the late Mr. Andrew Lang. His paper was read before the Folk-Lore Society and afterwards printed in their Journal.[2] What Andrew Lang himself really thought about these and many kindred phenomena is not easy to say. He unquestionably believed whole-heartedly in the " Voices " of St. Joan of Arc, and anyone who reads his article on " Poltergeists " in the 1911 edition of the *Encyclopædia Britannica* would almost inevitably infer that he regarded these manifestations as proved, but in the Presidential Address which he delivered before the Society for Psychical Research in the same year he told his hearers, while referring to that very subject, that they had a sceptical President. But for the most part Mr. Lang confined himself to aiming mischievous shafts at the out-and-out sceptics and in particular at such adventurous theorists as Sir James George Frazer. It was quite in keeping with the character of his subtle irony that at the outset of his paper on displaced coffins Lang protested:

Though the dead are the sufferers in this affair (and also the actors, according to popular opinion) the sturdy Rationalist need not be nervous: I am not telling a ghost-story; a thing excommunicated (if there be evidence for it) by scientific folklorists. I

[1] *The Month*, March 1938
[2] *Folk-Lore*, Vol. 18 (1907), pp. 376-390.

must confess that a little historical research has been needed, and historical precision is sadly alien to anthropological methods.

The abnormal feature common to the four reported cases cited by Mr. Lang is the displacement of heavy coffins left in a securely-closed vault.   As we should expect, he does not overlook the well-known tendency to revive and renovate old stories by giving them a contemporary date and a familiar locality, but there is little indication that in any one of these instances an ancient saga has been remembered and modernised.   One point which I am able to contribute to the available evidence is the fact that the case at " Staunton "[1] in Suffolk, referred by Lang and others to the year 1815, is really more than half a century older.   It appeared first in a short letter sent by a correspondent who does not sign his name to " the Author [*sic*] of the *London Magazine*" and was there printed in the number for July, 1760.   In the table of contents on the outer page, the occurrence is referred to simply as " a surprising phenomenon."   From *The London Magazine* it was copied into the *Annual Register* for 1760, and many years later the same statement was resuscitated without altering a word, in the *European Magazine* for 1815.   The letter runs as follows:

At Staunton, in Suffolk, is a vault, belonging to the family of the French's.   On opening it some years ago, several leaden coffins, with wooden cases, that had been fixed on biers, were found displaced, to the great astonishment of many of the inhabitants of the village.   It was afterwards properly closed, and the coffins again placed as before; when, about seven years ago, another member of the family dying, they were a second time found displaced; and two years after they were not only found all off the biers, but one coffin, as heavy as to require eight men to raise it, was found on the fourth step that leads to the vault.   Whence arose this operation, in which, it is certain, no one had a hand ?[2]

To this is appended what is presumably an editorial comment in this form:

N.B.   It was occasioned by water, as is imagined, though no

---

[1] " Staunton " is now more commonly spelt Stanton.   There are many villages of this name, but that which is here clearly indicated is Stanton All Saints about nine miles N.E. of Bury St. Edmunds.

[2] *The London Magazine*, July, 1760, p. 371.

signs of it appeared at the different periods of time that the vault was opened.

From this, the earliest, I may pass to the latest of the four specific cases which have attracted attention. This also is English and is equally free from any trace of an effort after sensation. It was communicated to *Notes and Queries* in 1867, by Mr. F. A. Paley, the well-known classical scholar, and incidentally a Catholic, though I am not sure whether he had been received into the Church at that date. The name which he spells Gretford seems now more commonly to appear in gazetteers as Greatford. It is in the extreme south of Lincolnshire, about six miles N.E. of Stamford, and in the Fen country. *Notes and Queries* printed Mr. Paley's letter with this heading:

DISTURBANCE OF COFFINS IN VAULTS

I beg to add an instance which occurred within my own knowledge and recollection some twenty years ago in the parish of Gretford, near Stamford, a small village of which my father was the rector. Twice, if not thrice, the coffins in a vault were found on reopening it to have been disarranged. The matter excited some interest in the village at the time and, of course, was a fertile theme for popular superstition; but I think it was hushed up out of respect to the family to whom the vault belonged.

A leaden coffin is a very heavy thing indeed; some six men can with difficulty carry it. Whether it can float is a question not very difficult to determine. If it will, it seems a natural, indeed the only, explanation of the phenomenon to suppose that the vault had somehow become filled with water.

I enclose an extract from the letter of a lady to whom I wrote, not trusting my own memory as to the details of the case:

Penn, 15 Oct.

I remember very well the Gretford vault being opened when we were there. It was in the church and belonged to the . . . family. The churchwarden came to tell the rector, who went into the vault and saw the coffins all in confusion: one little one on the top of a large one and some tilted on one side against the wall. They were all *lead*, but of course cased in wood. The same vault had been opened once before, and was found in the same state of confusion, and set right by the churchwarden, so that his dismay was great when he found them displaced again.   We had no doubt from the situation and nature of the soil, that it had been full of water during some flood which floated the coffins.[1]

There can be no question, of course, that given an adequate cubic capacity, a watertight lead coffin can float, just as an ironclad can float.   In *The Gentleman's Magazine* for 1751, and in other contemporary journals, a striking case was recorded of a leaden coffin which was picked up at sea after it had been buried in the Goodwin Sands.   And Lieut.-Commander R. T. Gould, who mentions this, also refers us to a more modern example of coffins floating in the vault beneath Edgware parish church.[2]   On the other hand, apart from the movement which might be imparted by something like a current or stream—and this is difficult to imagine in the confined space of a vault—one would expect that a coffin which had been lifted as the water rose would quietly sink back into almost the same position as the flood gradually subsided.   Still, there is nothing very startling or inexplicable in the two English cases just referred to. They are interesting as pointing the way to an easy solution of similar disturbances, and we have no occasion, so far, to invoke a *deus ex machina* in the shape of a poltergeist.

The real difficulties begin with a story which is very well attested, though it is now more than a hundred years old and comes from the island of Barbados on the other side of the Atlantic.   It has been told in many books, sometimes in an unconvincingly melodramatic form and often with inconsistencies as to names and other details.   On the other hand, so shrewd an investigator as Mr. Andrew Lang, after much painstaking research, found himself unable to provide an adequate explanation.

The earliest printed account of the Barbados trouble seems to be that contained in Sir J. E. Alexander's *Transatlantic Sketches*, 1833, which runs as follows:

It is not generally known that in Barbados there is a mysterious vault, in which no one now dares to deposit the dead.   It is in a churchyard near the seaside.   In 1807 the first coffin that was deposited in it was that of a Mrs. Goddard; in 1808 a Miss A. M.

[1] *Notes and Queries*, 3rd Series, Vol. XII, p. 371.   (9 November, 1867.)

[2] See his book entitled *Oddities*, in which the whole question is discussed in detail, and in particular pp. 64-65.

Chase was placed in it; and in 1812 Miss D. Chase. In the end of 1812 the vault was opened for the body of the Hon. T. Chase; but the three first coffins were found in a confused state, having been apparently tossed from their places. Again was the vault opened to receive the body of an infant, and the four coffins, all of lead, were discovered much disturbed. In 1816 a Mr. Brewster's body was placed in the vault, and again great disorder was apparent in the coffins. In 1819 a Mr. [*sic*] Clarke was placed in the vault, and, as before, the coffins were in confusion. Each time that the vault was opened the coffins were replaced in their proper situations, that is, three on the ground, side by side, and the others laid on them. The vault was then regularly closed; the door (and a massive stone which required six or seven men to move) was cemented by masons; and though the floor was of sand, there were no marks of footsteps or water.

The last time the vault was opened was in 1819. Lord Combermere was then present, and the coffins were found confusedly thrown about the vault, some with the heads down and others up. What could have occasioned this phenomenon ? In no other vault in the island has this ever occurred. Was it an earthquake which occasioned it, or the effects of an inundation of the vault ?[1]

This account, in spite of a few slight errors, is substantially correct and so far as regards the dates of the interments there are contemporary documents to confirm it. At the time when Mr. Andrew Lang was investigating the matter he had a brother-in-law, Mr. Foster Alleyne, who was a resident in Barbados. Mr. Alleyne interested himself in the inquiry, and he was eventually able to unearth an autograph report of the final opening of the tomb on 18 April, 1820—Sir J. Alexander wrongly dates it 1819—in the presence and by the direction of the Governor, Lord Combermere. This report was drafted by the Hon. Nathan Lucas, who was present with the Governor on the occasion, and he or another of the party made a sketch of the disorder in the vault. Mr. Lucas's MS., with the sketch, is now preserved in the Public Library of Barbados, and from this a Church of England publication, *The Barbados Diocesan History* (1928) has reproduced, unfortunately on a very small scale, the drawings both of the position of the coffins when the vault was closed after the interment of Thomasina Clarke on 7 July, 1819, and of the confusion in which they were found on 18 April of the following year. It is interesting to note that the Mr. Nathan Lucas

---

[1] Sir J. E. Alexander in *Transatlantic Sketches*, Vol. I, p. 161.

to whom we owe this first-hand information regarding the final opening of the vault was the maternal grandfather of Charles Kingsley, the assailant of Newman and author of *Westward Ho!* Lucas must have been a rather elderly man at the time, for he had been a guest (presumably as an adult) on board the *Formidable* when Sir George Rodney, on 12 April, 1782, fought his victorious action against the French in the Saintes passage.[1]

Whether the exact text of Lucas's memorandum has been anywhere printed I am unable to say, but one can hardly be mistaken in supposing that the account which appears in *The Barbados Diocesan History* and which depends throughout on local records, must have made full use of this manuscript to which it expressly calls attention. Anyway, in that work the editors in their notice of Christ Church refer as follows to the matter with which we are now concerned:

In the churchyard is to be seen the famous vault belonging to the Hon. Thomas Chase. On three occasions when the vault had been opened for the burial of a member of the family it was found that the coffins had been moved from their places. Lord Combermere, the Governor of Barbados, hearing these stories, determined personally to investigate the matter for the satisfaction of his own curiosity as well as to prevent any disturbance among the people. On the next occasion of an interment, that of Thomasina Clarke on 7 July, 1819, Lord Combermere attended the funeral, and on the vault being opened, the coffins for the fourth time were found to be disturbed. The Governor had floor and walls sounded, and after setting the coffins in their place, the floor was covered with white sand. The vault was carefully closed with cement, and the seal of the Governor affixed in several places, while many of those present made their own marks. Various theories were put forth, but the curiosity, instead of abating, grew. After being sealed for nine months and eleven days, permission was given by the Governor to have the vault again opened. In the presence of many thousands on 18 April, 1820, the seal marks and the outside of the tomb were all found intact. The masons had difficulty in getting the slab of the doorway removed, for an immense leaden coffin was resting against it on the inside. It was a leaden coffin which required seven men to lift it, and yet it had been moved into this position and no mark had been made upon the sanded floor. The other coffins to the number of five or six were scattered about.

[1] See *The Barbadian Diary of General Robert Haynes* (1934), p. 51.

During all this period, from 1803 to 1833 to be precise, the rector of Christ Church parish was a certain Thomas Harrison Orderson, D.D. Entries regarding the interments in the vault, each individually signed by him, are apparently still preserved, but besides this he seems to have drawn up a summary account of the disturbances observed in the position of the coffins on all the later occasions when the vault was opened. No original in his own handwriting seems to be in existence, but there are several early copies which do not exactly agree, apparently either because he himself wrote out the list more than once with variations of his own, or because the copies have been carelessly made. There is one example in which his own name appears, we are told, as Anderson. Though the sceptic may fasten on such a detail and find in it justification for rejecting the whole story as a fraud, the mistake is easily explained. In *The Barbadian Diary* of Robert Haynes I find, under date 30 July, 1805, the entry: " Hamlet accompanied my three sons, Richard, Robert and George, under the charge of Mr. Aughterson, to school in England." Aughterson is unquestionably Orderson, though the writer must have known him well, but others may have spelt it Auderson, and to read Auderson as Anderson, is the easiest thing in the world. However this may be, here is the text of one of the copies of what claims to be Dr. Orderson's memorandum.

31 July, 1807. Mrs. Thomasin Goddard was buried in the vault, which, when opened to receive her, was quite empty.

22 February, 1808. Mary Ann Chase [an infant] daughter of the Hon Thomas Chase, was buried in the same vault in a leaden coffin. When the vault was opened for the infant, the coffin of Mrs. Goddard was in its proper place.

6 July, 1812. Dorcas Chase was buried in the same vault, and the two first coffins were in their proper places.

9 August [1812]. The Hon. Thomas Chase was buried in the same vault. Upon its being opened, the two leaden coffins were removed from their situation, particularly that of the infant, which appeared to have been thrown from the corner where it was placed to the opposite angle.

25 September. 1816. Samuel Brewster was removed from the parish of St. Philip, and was buried in the vault, and great confusion was discovered among the leaden coffins.

7 July, 1819. Thomassin Clarke was buried and much confusion among the coffins.

18 April, 1820.   The vault was opened in the presence and at the request of His Excellency Lord Combermere, and the gentlemen of his staff, namely the Hon. N. Lucas, R. B. Clarke, and R. Cotton, Esqrs.

The coffins were in great disorder, some turned upside down. The coffin of one of the children was on the steps which led to the bottom of the vault.

This copy was in the possession of Mrs. De Morgan, the wife of Augustus De Morgan, the mathematician, and mother of William De Morgan, artist, inventor and novelist.   She printed it in *The Spiritual Magazine* for December, 1860, adding comments of her own, from which we learn that the vault was quite a small chamber only 12 feet by 6½ feet, which " had been formed by hewing through the flinty rock."   She adds that " its only approach was by a door or opening, from which steps led down to the bottom."   This information she seems to have obtained from the Orderson manuscript.   On the other hand, she is clearly making a comment of her own when she remarks: " It is a strange coincidence that the disturbance first followed on the interment of Dorcas Chase who is said to have starved herself to death," and she adds that Col. Thomas Chase also died by his own hand, though she expressly mentions that the allegation that these two, father and daughter, committed suicide had been added in the Orderson memorandum in a writing which was not that of the original copy.

So far as I have yet been able to discover, this notice by Mrs De Morgan in 1860 contains the earliest mention of these suicides, but in the notes apparently contributed by Everit M. Cracknell to the *Barbadian Diary of Robert Haynes* (1934), occurs the remark: " Following the burial of Dorcas Chase and of her father Samuel [*sic*], a harsh parent and a cruel slave-owner, strange happenings occurred."   From the contents of this privately printed little volume one gathers that the editor is likely to have had access to information regarding the contemporaries of Robert Haynes, a Barbadian who kept a journal from 1787 to 1836.[1]   In the face of the very definite and consistent statements which are preserved concerning the displacement of the coffins on five separate occasions it is not easy to suppose that we have nothing here but the echo of old wives' tales circulating among a superstitious negro population. On the other hand, the suggestion that a vault at some height above

[1] Already referred to above: only fragments, unfortunately, seem to have been preserved.

sea-level could be repeatedly flooded without anything to betray the presence of water seems difficult to accept, especially if it is true that no disturbance occurred before the first suicide was deposited there, that is to say, for the five years between 1807 and 1812.[1] In any case the recurrence of a series of earthquakes which moved the coffins but otherwise passed unnoticed is altogether out of the question.

For yet one other recorded example of a similar disturbance we have to turn to the Island of Oesel, now called Saare Maa. It is situated in the Baltic, and though formerly included in the Russian dominions, then belonged to Estonia.[2] It has one town, Ahrensberg, and there a cemetery, adjoining a main thoroughfare, displays facing the road some rather pretentious private vaults. One of these, belonging to the Buxhöwden family, was, in the year 1844, the scene of mysterious happenings closely resembling those at Christ Church, Barbados, which have just been narrated. Attention, however, was directed to the matter in this case by horses tethered in the road near by, which became perfectly frantic when some kind of loud crash seemed to proceed from the tomb in question. This occurred more than once and particularly on an occasion when one of the family was about to be interred in the Buxhöwden vault. On opening the subterranean chamber the coffins were found in great disorder, not only scattered but lying in some cases one upon another. Only three were undisturbed, one that of a very devout old lady, and two others of young children. Considerable popular excitement not unnaturally resulted, and it was thought desirable to appoint a commission to investigate the matter. A local magnate, Baron von Güldenstubbe, was appointed president, and among others who took part were the Lutheran bishop—the majority of the islanders were Lutherans, not Greek Church—the burgomaster, one of the syndics and a physician. The coffins were replaced in proper order, the pavement taken up to make certain that there was no subterranean means of ingress, the floor and steps covered with fine ashes, a guard of soldiers set which kept watch during the night as well as in the daytime, and at the end of three days the vault was again opened. According to the writer of the only available account, the condition of things was even worse than before:

[1] It must be remembered, however, that if there were only one or even two coffins in the vault a change of position might easily pass unperceived. It is only when they get thrown about in disorder or piled on one another that much notice would be taken.

[2] Now absorbed in Russia. Ahrensburg is now known as Kuresaare. J.H.C.

Not only was every coffin, with the same three exceptions displaced, and the whole collection scattered in confusion, but many of them, weighty as they were, had been set on end, so that the head of the corpse was downward. Nor was even this all. The lid of one coffin had been partially forced open, and there projected the shrivelled right arm of the corpse it contained, showing beyond the elbow.[1]

No trace of any footstep was to be discerned upon the ashes spread for the purpose of detecting intruders, and nothing in or about the coffins had been carried away. On the other hand, subsequent inquiry showed that the dead man whose arm was thrust out had died by his own hand.

The matter [says Mr. Owen] had been hushed up at the time through the influence of the family, and the self-destroyer had been buried with the usual ceremonies, but the fact transpired and was known all over the island, that he was found with his throat cut and the bloody razor still grasped in his right hand.

This would be a very thrilling story if only it were a little better attested. Mr. Dale Owen declares that he heard it in Paris in 1859 from the lips of Mlle. von Güldenstubbe, the daughter of the Baron who presided over the inquiry, and that the facts were subsequently confirmed by her brother. Apparently the family took the decisive step of burying the coffins separately, after which no further trouble was experienced. We are also told that the commission drew up a formal report of the proceedings which was lodged with the Lutheran Consistory, but in 1899, when Count Perovsky-Petrovo-Solovovo, a well-known member of the English Society for Psychical Research, wrote to Riga to make inquiries it was alleged that no such document could be found. On the other hand, at a later date Count Solovovo did obtain from a member of the Buxhöwden family a definite assurance that the sensational episode of the coffins was still remembered in Oesel and that many of the islanders professed to know that an official report had been drawn up. This, no doubt, is not very satisfactory, but it is sufficient to persuade us that Mr. Dale Owen at any rate was not merely romancing.

---

[1] R. Dale Owen *Footfalls on the Boundary of Another World* (1861), p. 191.

CHAPTER XV

A RARE TYPE OF POLTERGEIST[1]

R EADERS will probably have noticed that the agency which produces poltergeist disturbances, whatever it be, though far from noiseless in its operations, is hardly ever heard to speak. Exceptions are, no doubt, on record,[2] but they are rare. If the racketing spirit attempts to communicate, its purpose is most commonly effected by chalking up some message on the wall or by writing on a blank sheet of paper. The departure from this rule of silence, which is so conspicuous a feature in the story which follows, may reasonably be held quite apart from the other extravagant features, to throw doubt upon its accuracy. Unfortunately also, as the incidents occured forty-six years ago in a remote part of Canada, it is hopeless to think of obtaining any verification. It can only be said that stories published in local journals and containing the names of many people living in the district can hardly be pure inventions. An editor is apt to be sensitive to the ridicule and loss of credit which follows when he is publicly made a fool of. This premised, I may proceed to abridge the tale from the very full account printed in *Light* in the course of December 1889.

On 15 September 1889, the family of George Dagg, a farmer living in the township of Clarendon, Province of Quebec, began, we are told, to be troubled by some strange spirit of mischief which played havoc with their peaceful home and drove them nearly distracted. The family consisted of George Dagg, aged thirty-five years, his wife Susan, little Mary Dagg aged four, little Johnny Dagg aged two, and Dinah Burden McLean aged eleven.[3] This little girl Dinah, an orphan ,was sent out from Scotland by Mr. Quarrier, and had been adopted from the Belleville Home by Mr. Dagg five

---

[1] *The Month*, January 1936

[2] The most striking case known to me of a talking poltergeist is that of Mâcon in 1612, described in great detail by a Huguenot minister, M. François Perrault, who was himself the victim of this infestation (see above, p. 39).

[3] There were also relatives bearing the same name, Dagg, who seem to have lived not far off.

years earlier.   Previously to the commencement of these troubles,
she was a stout, rosy-cheeked Scotch girl.   " Now, " says the report,
" her cheeks are sunken in, dark rings encircle her eyes, and she is a
mere shadow of her former self. "   As constantly happens in such
cases, the farmer folk of the surrounding country believed that some
sort of witchcraft or magic must be at the bottom of the troubles,
and a certain Mrs. Wallace and her children fell under suspicion.
The one fact which was a matter of observation was that when
Dinah was away from the house the disturbances ceased.

The account of the case, which was printed in *The Recorder* of
Brockville, Canada, was furnished by a certain Mr. Woodcock,
described as an artist well known in the Dominion, who had also
lived in New York and in Paris.   He visited the Daggs on Friday,
15 November, and spent most of his time with them until the Sunday
evening.   During these three days he made notes of what he could
learn from the family and the neighbours, and seems to have
convinced himself that the physical manifestations, alleged to have
taken place during the previous two months, were unquestionably
authentic.   Among other things he was informed that on 15 September, Mr. Dagg had brought home a five-dollar bill and a two-dollar
bill and gave them to his wife, who placed them in a bureau drawer.
In the morning a little boy named Dean, an orphan, who was
employed by various farmers as " chore boy, " and who was
temporarily in the service of the Daggs, came down from his bed in
the garret and proceeded to light a fire in the cooking stove.   Seeing
on the floor a five dollar-bill he took it at once to Mr. Dagg telling
him where he had found it.   Mr. Dagg, being suspicious, looked in
the drawer and discovered that the two-dollar bill was also gone.
So sending the boy out of doors to milk, he examined his room and
found his missing bill in his bed.   Although convinced that the boy
was guilty, they said nothing until later in the day when, on returning from the milk house, Mrs. Dagg found on the floor of her house
from back to front a streak of filth.   This, with the theft of the money
was too much for Mrs. Dagg and she immediately ordered the boy
Dean out of the house.   The boy stoutly asserted his innocence, but
had to go.   Mr. Dagg took the boy to Shawville before a magistrate,
and while they were away the same thing happened again and filth
was found in various places, in the eatables, in the beds, etc., showing conclusively that the boy was in no way connected with it.   This
continued for about a week and was accompanied by various other
antics.   Milk-pans were emptied, butter was taken from the crocks
and put into the pans.   As a precaution the milk and eatables were

then conveyed to the attic for safety, but just the same annoyances occurred there as had happened before. This attic had no doors or windows and no entrance except by a stair which led up to it from the kitchen, and no one could enter the place without being seen, as these things were done in the daytime. The worry about eatables was succeeded by the smashing of windows, the outbreak of fires, the pouring of water and much other mischief. One afternoon little Dinah felt her hair, which hung in a long braid down her back, suddenly pulled, and on her crying out, the family found her braid almost cut off. It had to be completely severed. Incidents of this kind recurred during two months, and then a new type of manifestation developed. A gruff voice, which at first was heard by Dinah alone, began to be audible to all who were present.

On the Saturday morning of Mr. Woodcock's visit, he tried to have a private talk with Dinah and took the child to an open shed at the back of the house where she declared she had seen something. Dinah said: " Are you there, Mister ? " To Mr. Woodcock's intense astonishment, "a deep, gruff voice, as of an old man, seemingly within four or five feet from him, instantly replied in language which cannot be repeated here. " The visitor, recovering from his astonishment, said: " Who are you ? " To which the reply came: " I am the devil. I'll have you in my clutches. Get out of this or I'll break your neck. "

From these beginnings a conversational wrangle developed which went on, we are told, for several hours. The voice used foul and obscene language, but in deference to the remonstrances of Mr. Woodcock and George Dagg, after a while showed more restraint. The account insists that the gruff voice could not have been that of the child, which was rather exceptionally high-pitched, and also that there was no possible place of concealment where a practical joker could have hidden himself. As Mr. Woodcock had heard of writings having been found about the house, he challenged the spirit to write something. Putting a sheet of paper and a pencil on a bench in the shed he saw the pencil stand up and move along the surface. As soon as the pencil dropped, he stepped over, and examining the paper said: " I asked you to write something decent. " To this the voice replied in an angry tone: " I'll steal your pencil, " and immediately the pencil rose from the bench and was thrown violently across the shed.

In the report given of the dialogue between the voice and its questioners, we find passages like the following:

Mr. Dagg:	" Why have you been bothering me and my family ?"
Answer:	" Just for fun."
Mr. Dagg:	" It was not very much fun when you threw a stone and struck little Mary. "
Answer:	" Poor wee Mary! I did not mean to hit her, I intended it for Dinah; but I did not let it hurt her. "
Mr. Dagg:	" If it was only for fun why did you try to set the house on fire ? "
Answer:	" I didn't. The fires came always in the daytime and where you could see them. I'm sorry I did it."

In the end a promise was obtained from the spook that it would say good-bye and leave the house for good on the following night, the Sunday.

News of this spread, and there was great excitement throughout the neighbourhood. People began arriving early in the morning, and all the afternoon the place was thronged. The voice was on its good behaviour, as had been promised, but it answered questions and made comments on different people as they entered the room. Some remarks were very amusing and displayed an intimate knowledge of the private affairs of many of the questioners. One of the visitors commented on the change for the better in the language used. The reply thereupon came: " I am not the person who used the filthy language. I am an angel from Heaven sent by God to drive away that fellow. " This character was maintained for some time, but Mr. Woodcock declares that the voice was the same as that which they had previously heard, and, as the day wore on and many questions were asked, the spook contradicted himself, and getting entangled, lost his temper, saying many things quite out of harmony with his supposed heavenly origin.

Before ending his visit on the Sunday, Mr. Woodcock drew up the following report:

" *To whom it may concern:* We the undersigned, solemnly declare that the following curious proceedings which began on the 15th day of September, 1889, and are still going on on the 17th day of November, 1889, in the house of Mr. George Dagg, a farmer living seven miles from Shawville, Clarendon Township, Pontiac County,

Province of Quebec, actually occurred as below described.

1st. That fires have broken out spontaneously throughout the house, as many as eight occurring in one day, six being in the house and two outside; that the window curtains were burned whilst on the windows, this happening in broad daylight, whilst the family and neighbours were in the house.

2nd. That stones were thrown by invisible hands through the windows, as many as eight panes of glass being broken, that articles such as a water jug, milk pitchers, a wash basin, cream tub, butter tub and other articles were thrown about the house by the same invisible agency, a jar of water being thrown in the face of Mrs. John Dagg, also in the face of Mrs. George Dagg while they were being about their household duties, Mrs. George Dagg being alone in the house at the time it was thrown in her face; that a large dining table was thrown down; a mouth organ, which was lying on a small shelf, was distinctly heard to be played and was seen to move across the room on to the floor, while immediately after, a rocking chair began rocking furiously; that a washboard was sent flying down the stairs from the garret, no one being in the garret at the time. Further, that when the child Dinah is present a deep, gruff voice, like that of an aged man, has been heard at various times, both in the house and out of doors, and when asked questions has answered so as to be distinctly heard, showing that he is cognizant of all that has taken place, not only in Mr. Dagg's family, but also in the families in the surrounding neighbourhood; that he claims to be a disincarnated being who died twenty years ago, aged about eighty years; that he gave his name to Mr. George Dagg and Mr. Willie Dagg, forbidding them to tell it; that this intelligence is able to make himself visible to Dinah, little Mary and Johnny, who have seen him under different forms at different times, at one time as a tall, thin man with a cow's head, horns, tail and a cloven foot, at another time as a big black dog, and finally as a man with a beautiful face and long white hair dressed in white, wearing a crown with stars in it."[1]

This document is signed by seventeen witnesses, beginning with the Daggs, all of them responsible people living in the district. No women's names are included, and Mr. Woodcock declares that he

---

[1] It seems pretty obvious that though this document purports to have been signed on the Sunday, there has been added to it a reference to the venerable white-haired figure which only manifested on the Monday morning. This indicates a rather lax conscience in dealing with evidence. But the names of the seventeen witnesses are all printed in full, and the interpolation was probably made with the knowledge of the Daggs and perhaps with the consent of some others of the signatories.

might have had twice as many signatures had he wanted them.

Perhaps the most extraordinary feature of the story is the fact that the spook after all took his departure in a blaze of glory. Though Mr. Woodcock left the house on the Sunday evening to return to his own lodging, a number of people seem to have remained behind with the Daggs, hoping to witness the promised leavetaking of the author of all the disturbance.   By this time he had, so far as appearances went, completely changed his character.   He suddenly laid aside his gruff tones, declared that he had only maintained this harsh accent because otherwise people would have believed that Dinah was doing it, and then proceeded to sing hymns in what is described as a very beautiful flute-like voice.   The group of visitors present were enchanted, and completely convinced by this reassumption of angelic attributes.   So far from hastening the departure of the spook, they pressed him to stay, and this strange séance was prolonged until 3 a.m.   The spirit then said goodbye, but promised to show himself to the children later in the morning.

Early in the forenoon of the Monday Mr. Woodcock himself came back to the Dagg's house to take leave.   He describes how, as he got there, " the three children, who had been out in the yard, came rushing into the house, wild-eyed and fearfully excited."   I can only copy the exact terms of the statement which follows:

"Little Mary cried out 'Oh, Mama! the beautiful man! He took little Johnny and me in his arms, and, Oh, Mama, I played on the music and he went to Heaven and was all red! " They, the Daggs, rushed to the door, but nothing unusual was to be seen.   On questioning the girls they both told the same story.   Their accounts said it was a beautiful man, dressed in white, with ribbons and pretty things all over his clothes, with a lovely gold thing on his head and stars in it.   They said he had a lovely face and long white hair, that he stooped down and took little Mary and the baby [Johnny] and said Johnny was a fine little fellow, and that Mary played on the music-thing he had with him.   Dinah said she distinctly saw him stoop and lift Mary and Johnny in his arms and heard him speak to Johnny.   Dinah said he spoke to her also and said—that man Woodcock thought he was not an angel, but he would show that he was, and then, she said, he went up to Heavan.   On being questioned, she said he seemed to go right up in the air and disappear.   He was in a kind of fire and the fire seemed to blaze up from his feet and surrounded him until he disappeared.   No amount of questioning could shake their stories in the least. "

12

Personally I find it hard to believe that Mr. Woodcock invented this. It runs so counter to the very uncomplimentary view of the spook which he had expressed the day before. Extravagant as the description is, it seems to me that as a documentary illustration of child psychology it is not without its value. Was it all a fiction which Dinah mendaciously invented and stuck to, impressing it on the minds of her younger companions? If there is truth in the statement about the three " rushing in, wild-eyed and fearfully excited," this explanation seems unlikely. A more probable theory would suggest that some telepathic influence affected simultaneously the susceptible mental faculties of the children, enabling them to visualize a scene which existed only in their own imagination. Fancy and reality lie nearer together in the mind of the child than in that of the adult, and, even in the case of adults, they commingle strangely in our dreams. But what could be the source of this telepathic influence? One speaks very much in the dark, but, accepting as I do the existence of a spirit world, angelic, demonic and possibly nondescript, I should be more inclined to look for the impulse there than to identify it with any terrestrial agent. Children may very probably be more susceptible to such telepathic influences from outside than the normal adult is! We must, I think, recognize that some individuals possess psychic faculties, often involving a certain power of clairvoyance. It is alleged that people so gifted are able to see auras, faces, forms or hands, apparently materialized, which others, not so endowed, are incapable of perceiving. Whether that which is discerned on these occasions exists objectively and is localized at a point in space which can be determined by fixed co-ordinates, we do not know. It may be that there is, after all, nothing but a subjective perception, and that this is induced by telepathic suggestion from outside. But, however this may be, it is unquestionable that in a considerable number of accounts of poltergeist phenomena, the spook, while remaining invisible to all grown-up people, is said at times to have revealed himself, often in a highly fantastical guise (*e.g.*, under the appearance of a man they have never seen, an old witch, a black dog, etc.), to some child medium involved in the disturbances.[1]

At a later date (November, 1890) *Light* published some further details connected with the Dagg poltergeist.[2]

[1] See, for example, the Cideville case (p. 81 above) the Molly Giles (Bristol) case (page 19), the Poona case (*Psychic Research*, May, 1930, p. 227), and a number of others.

[2] *Light*, 22 November, 1890, p. 567.

Mr. Arthur Smart, a resident in the neighbourhood, who is described as a most trustworthy witness, testified to these facts which he had himself witnessed.

He sat in front of a little cupboard at a distance of not more than four or five feet and directly facing it. There he saw Mrs. Dagg put in two pans full of bread which she had just taken from the oven. After doing so she took a pail and went out to milk, while he continued to sit facing the cupboard. In about ten minutes Mrs. Dagg, on coming in with her milk found one of the pans full of bread in the back kitchen, and, on her expressing her surprise, he opened the cupboard and found only one there. This, he said, was the first thing which fairly staggered his unbelief.

In the absence of Mr. Dagg, who was away from home with his threshing machine, Mr. Arthur Smart used to be invited to sit with the family, as they were afraid to stay alone.

On one of these occasions, while they were sitting round the stove in the evening, a match was heard falling on the floor, which was uncarpeted, then another and another, and this continued till the floor of the room was pretty well covered. Mr. Smart watched with all the care possible to see if he could see the matches leaving the safe,[1] which hung against the wall, but failed to see them, nor could he see them fall until within a few inches of the floor. After the shower was over he examined the safe and found it empty. He then proceeded to gather up the matches and got enough to fill the safe.

From Mrs. Dagg herself, another investigator (Robert Grant, a teacher, much respected in the neighbourhood), had the following account of one of the most striking incidents of the phenomena which took place in the presence of the same little medium, Dinah McLean. Mrs. Dagg told him:

One day, just after dinner, I and Dinah were standing at the window on the side of the room opposite to where the dining table

[1] The word " safe " does not seem to be used in England in this sense, but the Oxford English Dictionary, under " match," recognizes it as current in the United States, and both the Century Dictionary and Webster mention " match-safe." The safe was probably at some little height above the ground to keep it out of the reach of the children.

stands, when we saw it slowly turning over towards her till it fell on one side.   It then made a second turn and lay with its legs pointing to the ceiling.   This occured at about 1 o'clock p.m. on a clear, sunny day when no one was near except myself and the family.

Mr. Grant reports that he examined the table carefully.   It was about 8 feet long and 3½ feet wide, a very heavy, strongly-built table.

There are two features in the above story which lead me to think that, despite its extraordinary character, the narrative may have been written in good faith, and that if a certain allowance be made for the embellishments nearly always introduced by people who are very much startled, it may correspond pretty closely with the facts.   The narrators do not betray any knowledge that what they record corresponds with the observations made in numberless cases in all parts of the world, and they do not, as they would almost inevitably do if they possessed that knowledge, emphasize these points when they speak of them.

The first matter to which I refer is the assertion of the spook that when he threw a stone, which hit little wee Mary by mistake, he " did not let it hurt her."   The fact that Mary was not hurt was confirmed by the Dagg family, who seemed a good deal surprised at her escape.   It also appears that though a number of fires were started the spook claimed that " the fires came always in the daytime and where you could see them."   The same peculiarity, viz., that though mischief is done it is not of a character dangerous to life or limb, recurs over and over again in poltergeist phenomena.   Several examples have been cited here in previous chapters both of objects flung with violence which missed the human target by a hair's breadth, and of others which were strangely arrested in full career and fell harmless like spent bullets after inflicting a mere tap.   With regard to the fires spontaneously breaking out, the case of the Indian poltergeist, referred to above (page 62), is particularly impressive. Mr. Thangapragasam Pillay was terrified out of his wits at these recurrent excitements, but no damage was done to the fabric of his house.   There was always someone at hand to notice and extinguish the fires.   Giraldus Cambrensis in the twelfth century, speaking of a Welsh poltergeist, declared that in pelting people with all sorts of unpleasant missiles it only meant to tease them without really doing any hurt.[1]   Fifty years later

[1] See above, p. 7.

William of Auvergne, Bishop of Paris, speaks as if such cases were not infrequent and makes a similar comment.[1] So, again, in Queen Elizabeth's time we read in Reginald Scot's " Discoverie of Witchcraft" that " they [the spirits] throwe downe stones upon men, but the blowes therof doo no harme to them whome they hit. "

The other circumstance which seems strikingly in accord with what has been noticed in poltergeist disturbances where a variety of small objects are thrown, is the curious statement of Mr. Smart that when the matches were falling he could never detect the manner of their departure from the " safe " and could not see them at all until they were within a few inches of the floor. Many parallels might be quoted for this apparent dematerialization during flight, but I must content myself with referring to a case of which an account was sent me some years ago by a Jesuit Father in Presburg, Czechoslovakia.[2] My informant quite obviously, knew nothing about poltergeist phenomena, but in giving a description of the incident which had occasioned much talk in the neighbourhood, he told me how two lads were pelted all along the road with a shower of small stones which did not even cease when they sought refuge in a wayside tavern. The interesting point here is that the stones could not be seen until they were about a foot away and did not strike the boys with any violence.

---

[1] He ascribes these assaults, of course, to diabolical agency, but he says that the demons " hujusmodi jactibus homines vel rarissime vel nunquam laedunt." *Opera*, Vol. I, p. 1062.

[2] See above, p. 6.

CHAPTER XVI

SOME FIRST-HAND ACCOUNTS[1]

THE three following stories have all, I may say, come to me at first hand in the form in which they were written down by the eye-witnesses who describe the part they themselves played in the manifestations. The stories are none of them of very recent date, and they are to that extent open to the objection that there may have been room for the operation of what Mr. Podmore calls " exaggerative memory." Still, I have myself been responsible for part of the delay in publication, mainly because I hoped for an opportunity of searching for confirmation in contemporary newsprints. Unfortunately, however, the pressure of other work has prevented this, and as I have every reason to trust the perfect good faith of the narrators, whose names and addresses are known to me, and whose character is vouched for by friends, I publish the stories now for fear they should grow still more out of date, and be in the end entirely forgotten. As the reader will see, the first of these experiences is an Irish case, the second French, and the third, which belongs to the last century, comes all the way from Madras. I can only return my hearty thanks to the writers of these accounts for permitting me to make use of them. Here and there a slight curtailment has been made, or a trivial modification of the wording, such as a hurriedly written manuscript often requires before being sent to the press, but the substance of the facts narrated has not in any way been tampered with. In each case it seemed preferable to allow the writer to speak for himself in the first person.

I

I was a sergeant in the Royal Irish Constabulary in charge of a sub-district in or about November, 1916. I had an official document which required the signature of a certain farmer in my district.

[1] *The Month*, March 1936 and July 1932

Being on duty in the market-town on a Fair Day, I happened to meet the farmer on the street and told him to call at my station at his earliest convenience to sign the document in question. The farmer replied saying: " Sergeant, I am in great trouble. I came to town to-day to arrange for the funeral of my youngest child. I am suffering terrible annoyance in my house night and day for almost a week. Some unseen spirit is wrecking my house, throwing cooking utensils about and breaking delf. It flung a bottle of ink over my dying child, hurled a heavy glass salt-cellar at a mirror in the sick-room and broke a valuable tea set of old china that my wife was carrying downstairs for safety. She was about half way down the stairs with the china in her apron when the whole lot was completely smashed in my presence as well as in that of a few friends who had come to the wake. The day previous to the death of the child, myself and servants were churning in the kitchen, when the butter was taken from the churn and some of it thrown against the ceiling ten feet high. I found some of the broken china in my byre some thirty yards distant."

I sympathised with the farmer, who was a strong, active man, aged about forty. He had a farm of eighty acres or so, kept twelve or fourteen cows, with two horses, young cattle and some sheep. He usually employed a manservant as well as a maid, and appeared to be in comfortable circumstances. His two-storied house, with eight or ten rooms, had a wide hall and a large kitchen. The entrance to the kitchen from the back door was along a passage across which a wall had been built to keep the draught from affecting the kitchen fire, as may be seen in most houses in Ireland.

I told the farmer not to come to the Barrack as it was three miles distant from where he lived, and that I would call on him at his house the day after the funeral. In accordance with this arrangement I went there a day or two later, and was shown the damage done, which was being added to hourly. I saw the butter, some of which was still on the ceiling, and went into the bedroom, a large room, in which the child died. I was shown the mirror which was hit exactly in the centre with such force as to leave a mark like the bottom of a salt-cellar. The mirror-glass was broken in a thousand streaks radiating from the point of injury. It was a good-quality dressing table and the mirror attached was of the heavy bevelled glass kind.

Having seen all the damage, I sat down in the kitchen in the presence of the farmer, his wife, two children (a boy about seven and a girl about ten) and the servant maid. I was adding some words to the document I had brought, when the little girl drew her mother's attention to a towel or kitchen-cloth being thrown across the kitchen towards the legs of the table near where I was seated. Whereupon the wife said: " Maybe you'll believe it now, Sergeant." Being engaged in writing I had not noticed anything and said so. The document having been signed, I listened to a full account the farmer gave me, in the presence of his family and servant, of the strange things which had been happening. The most striking part of the story was that the spook seemed to single out the wife and the little girl for all the punishment; the man himself was in no way molested. There was in the kitchen during the dialogue a strange tenseness, although it was not more than 2.30 p.m. Being an old warrior, I was still unsatisfied with what I saw, and I came to the conclusion in my own mind that if some one of the seven or eight flitches of bacon that were suspended near the ceiling, or if one of the two horse-collars which were hanging on pins in the wall over the fireplace should be thrown down, I should then be satisfied as to the reality of the spook; but I took care not to betray what was passing in my mind, either by look or otherwise, to anybody that were present.

After addressing a few words to the wife about her making restitution,[1] I stood up to go. The woman and children said they would not remain when I left, so they started for the back door—the servant first, followed by the two children, then the farmer's wife, next the farmer, and I bringing up the rear. I had got across the kitchen near the end of the obstructing wall and was turning into the passage, but still in full view of the kitchen, when suddenly one of the horse-collars was flung from its position, high up on the wall, the whole length of the room, landing on the floor with a smack. The farmer turned, and after we had both examined the collar, he said: " You must now believe "; to which I assented. We passed into the yard, going towards the road, when a graip (dung-fork) was thrown across the yard by unseen hands.

These people were Catholics, and I advised the farmer to have Mass said in his house. Some days later I learnt that the curate had said Mass there, and that even while Mass was being said there was some disturbance. I was further informed that immediately after my departure the wife, children and servant sought shelter in the house of a neighbour. They were pursued by an unseen agent

[1] There is nothing to explain this. Possibly the Sergeant's visit was connected with some police-court charge in which the farmer's wife had been bound over.

and pelted with turf and stones right up to the door. Much later, after I had left the R.I.C., I was told that the farmer had had to build a new dwelling at some distance from his original residence. The belief in the neighbourhood was that some time before this date a man, who believed he had suffered a grievous wrong, vowed to have revenge on the farmer's wife and her child. It was said that he lost his life in America just about the time the disturbances commenced.

(Signed) E. O'C.

II

The narrator, in this case a lady, writes as follows:

I live with a friend, an American, in a little village in the north of France, Monneville (Oise), and one winter, a good many years ago, she went to America in November and I came out to Monneville to put in a months' work (painting) before going to England for Christmas. It was very bad weather, wet and dark and the roads seas of mud; there was no one in the village but the little shop-keepers and farm labourers; the two better-class families who spent their summers in the country had gone back to Paris weeks before, so I was left very much to my own resources.

One morning I was told that strange things were happening in the house of an old woman who lived not five minutes off. She dwelt alone with her grandson, a boy of about fourteen years, who was rather feeble-minded and who complained that someone upset his bed every night so that he fell out on the floor. So the grandmother took him into her bed, and then her bed began to rock, too, so that they both nearly fell out together. She told some neighbours of mine and invited them to come round in the evening and see for themselves. So they asked me if I would like to accompany them.

We went about eight o'clock and found the old woman and the boy in bed in a big bedstead set with one side against the wall (the boy inside) both of them in a great state of alarm. Though not very much happened that night, so far as I remember, there were knockings, taps on the walls, on the ceiling and on the floor, others heard in the armoire and even in the stove, there were also saucepans rattling, and so on. We stayed with her an hour or two, and then, as the knocks seemed to have stopped, we came home.

The next night we went again, and more happened.   I distinctly saw the bed rise up on the side so that the leg of the bed was nearly a foot off the floor.   The old lady was terribly frightened and begged us to stay with her all night, but we came away and left her.

Then the neighbours began to hear of it, and more people came; there would be five or six people in the room and as many as thirty in the little court outside looking through the window. Further, the more people came, the more the knockings, etc., increased in violence.   One night besides ourselves—by which I mean Clovis (the " chantre " at the church) his wife, Armantine, his daughter Madeleine and me—there were in the room the village butcher and a Belgian youth called René, who was a strong, thick-set fellow.   He and the butcher placed themselves by the bed and tried with all their strength to keep it from rocking, but it rocked in spite of all their efforts, the legs rising about a foot off the floor. Then Armantine had an idea and said: " Let us try if we can get it to answer us."   Clovis was willing, but he said: " Be sure to call it ' tu ' not ' vous ' ; these things are our inferiors and we must treat them as such."   So Armantine stood forth in the middle of the and told it to knock once for " no " and twice for " yes," and then started her questions with: " Es-tu le bon Dieu? "

Answer a very decided no.

" Es-tu le diable ? "

A hesitating no.

" Es-tu de sa famille ? "

A very decided yes.

Then they thought they would like to know who sent it to bother the old woman, so they asked it: " Was it a man who sent you ? " " No."   " A woman ? "   " Yes."   " How old is she ? "   Thirty-four knocks.   " How many children has she ? "   Five knocks, etc., etc.

Now I found out afterwards that nearly everyone there but myself had made up their minds that a certain woman had sent it, and the answers were all correct as regarded that woman and were what everyone but myself was expecting.   They asked it a great many questions such as the time by the church clock, which it gave to the minute, though as it was pitch dark and the church clock is very erratic, we had to wait till next day to find out just how much differ-ence there was between it and our watches.

They told it to imitate various noises, such as sawing wood (you heard the saw and then the two bits drop), beating a drum, whetting a scythe, crowing like a cock. Each time it responded perfectly, also if they told it to tap on the ceiling, on the floor, or in the armoire, it did it almost before the words were out of their mouths. Then I had a try in English, and it did everything I told it to do. I was the only person in the room who understood English. Then René spoke to it in " Flamand," and he told us it did everything he said.

This sort of thing went on every night for a fortnight, and the village got more and more excited; reporters came from Beauvais— even from Paris; so the " Maire " was very much annoyed and sent the gendarmes, who forbade anyone to go to the house, but as the gendarmes came from Chaumont, ten kilometres away, and were never here after dark, that did not make much difference.

Unfortunately, I was obliged to leave and go to England, so I do not know exactly how it came to an end. When I got back in the spring I heard a great many stories of what happened, but this is all I know of my own knowledge.

(Signed) M.S.L.

III

As well as I can remember I was about nine or ten years of age at the time this story begins, in 1872 or 1873. We lived at St. Thomas's Mount, a military station (for artillery), a few miles from Madras, with my mother, who brought us down to attend school. The family consisted of my eldest brother Tom, aged about thirteen years, Herbert eleven, and myself nine and a half, Bertie seven and a half, Mercy five, and Dan.

My grandfather—Thomas Cronan, retired—lived some distance from us. The Cronans had at the time two sons, Fred and George aged about twelve and sixteen. We went across as usual to see our grandparents with our mother, and while we boys were playing together, sailing boats in a rather large-sized tub, a pebble fell in the centre of the tub, making an unusual noise for so small a stone. We began to accuse one another as to who did it—each one in turn, of course, denying—when a larger stone fell into the tub. This rather startled us, and in a short time a few more fell. So we ran away to our parents, who were sitting out in the garden. While we were trying to explain what had happened, another stone fell in our midst.   This broke up the gathering and, as it was dusk, we went home.

Nothing happened for a few days, but on our next visit to our grandparents the stones fell again, this time larger and at shorter intervals.   Nothing further occurred that night, but the next evening we stayed in, and the stones started falling around us inside the house.   Each day they got worse, larger and more frequent, but for some time no damage was done.   The officer commanding the station at that time came over and placed a guard round the house, and even put men on the roof—the stones fell around them.   When the doors were closed, stones, then a brick, fell, as though coming from the roof, but no one saw the brick fall nor from whence it came, and as it fell it remained in the same place.   The more the house was guarded with troops, the worse the trouble became, so the Colonel withdrew his men.

One morning we found everything from the dressing table, lamps, ornaments, etc., laid on the ground, in the same way as they had previously been arranged on the table; this went on for some days.   After this stopped, many things used to disappear from the house for a day or two, and then again be replaced.   So far, no damage had been done, until one day the glass stopper flew out of a scent bottle, fell on the ground and broke.   Then everything went, one thing after another; for instance, the table would be laid, but as we sat down to our meals, the plates would disappear, and a crash would be heard in the next room where the plates were found in pieces.

At this stage my uncles, Thomas and James Cronan, visited us; when the younger, Thomas, seeing all these things happen, took down a large crucifix from the wall, placed it on a chest of drawers and said: " I defy anything to touch this cross."   But as he was leaving the room he was struck on the back by the same cross, which fell behind him on the ground.   This convinced Thomas Cronan that nothing could be done.

Both brothers, however, concluded that my eldest brother Tom was not looking well, and decided to take him with them to Madras.   On the way a marble paper-weight which was in our house fell into the carriage, which at once settled the matter that Tom was the victim or medium, as from the time he left the house at St. Thomas's Mount, nothing happened there.   The third day after he arrived in Madras, on awaking in the morning, all the doors were found removed from their hinges and laid against the wall.   The next day Tom got a severe fit—to be followed by many which invariably came on at midnight. The day previous to these paroxysms Tom would be unusually quiet, keeping absolutely to himself, at night he would retire early; when the fit was coming on he would sigh very heavily in his sleep, then stretch himself and open his eyes. During these periods, one could hardly recognize him as the same boy, every limb appeared to grow larger and his face was distorted and ugly. He would answer any question, and foretell every event that would take place before the next fit came on. The duration of the fit would be from one and a half to two hours, and when it was leaving him he would fall asleep for a minute or two, and then make a desperate plunge with the object of destroying himself. Every precaution had to be taken to prevent him from taking his life. He would then fall into a swoon for a few minutes, and, when he came to, would ask what we were all doing around his bed, and why we were not alseep, For the next few days he would be very limp. It was when in this condition that he made known why my father was " spelled " and the name of the man who did it.

After this in Madras the priest, Father Lee, was asked to bless the house, and Tom, I believe, was taken to the church, placed before the altar, and endeavours made to drive away the evil spirit. but with no result. Several things happened when he was in my uncle's house similar to those that had taken place in ours, but after a month he returned to St. Thomas's Mount.

In Madras Father Lee, as just mentioned, was called to bless the house. When he was doing so he was pulled by his vestments, and when he put his Rituale down after the blessing, it was immediately taken up to a corner of the roof, the cover sticking to the roof and the pages fluttering as through a great wind was fanning the leaves. Again, when Father Ford blessed the house in St. Thomas's Mount, the same thing happened there; also an egg stood up on the small end, and when he tried to remove it he could not do so, but after he removed his hand from the egg, it just turned over in its normal position. Father Ford, of course, was an eye-witness of all, or the most, of the things which happened in St. Thomas's Mount and which are here described.

In the meantime, we had moved near to our grandfather's house. For some time after Tom's return nothing happened, till we awoke one morning to find that none of the doors could be opened. On calling for assistance from the passers-by, we were told that large boulders of rock which could not be carried by any man were carefully stacked against the doors; grandfather was sent for and men were engaged to remove these. The police were informed, but nothing could be done. The trouble started again. The chairs, small articles of furniture, crockery, etc., were all broken in the way already explained.

My father, who was an engineer, and was at the time building the Palar Bridge, residing near his work, wrote to my mother, and told her to come up to him. There was then no railway, and we had to travel by bullock carts. We were left in peace for about two months, till one morning, about 4.30 or 5.0 a.m., the time my father used to rise, the hand-bell was discovered on the roof of the house ringing for all it was worth, while father could not find his boots, which were also suspended from the roof. My dear old mother said: " Oh, Paddy, the trouble has started here. I hope you will now believe when you see and hear for yourself." This was said because my father would not believe anything we told him. After this there were extraordinary happenings each day. Things got so bad that while the food was being cooked filth was at times thrown in by some unseen hand. Tom also got two more fits which were witnessed by my father and two assistant engineers.

It was at this stage a man of the Lubbay caste came to my father and told him he would remove the spell from my brother, but stipulated for a fabulous remuneration. Tom, in his last fit, had said he would get one more when he would be slapped and would bleed to death. This man declared that he could and would prevent it if my father agreed to his terms. He explained that he would have to make three midnight sacrifices, when he would offer to the spirits who had possession of the boy double the amount of sacrifices offered by the man who had imposed the spell. All was agreed to, and a week later the first orgy was held; it began about 10 p.m.

A large circle was drawn in the centre of the room, around which were placed bottles of liquor corked and sealed as purchased, boiled rice, slaughtered sheep, fowls and game of all kinds, the blood of these poor creatures was mixed with the rice. Tom was seated in the centre before a large fire. The family were permitted to sit about three feet outside of the circle with instructions not to come within or even touch the line once the ceremony began, the penalty being death; neither were any questions to be asked. The man, having first had a bath and being stripped except for a loin cloth, entered the ring, and began by calling on the different spirits by name. Answer was made in tones which were terrifying and blood-curdling. Tom was the whole time in a stupor—not recollecting anything of the affair when it was over. It came to an end just before midnight when all the liquor bottles would be found empty, the gradual disappearance of the liquor as the night advanced being distinctly noticeable. There were also other rites including the piercing of a wax image with a nail.

This ceremony was performed three times, after which Tom was given a gold ring with instructions that he was never to remove that ring from the second finger of the left hand; if he did, he was warned he would get one more fit when the promised slap would be given, but if he survived, there would be no further trouble. After some months we were sent to school, and Tom did very well, till one day we noticed that the ring was missing. We asked him what had become of it and were told he had put it in his chest of drawers—a search was made but the ring was never found. That night he got a fit and a severe slap; he bled profusely through the nose, but there was no other evil result.

At the first sacrifice the man showed my father a mirror, whereon he saw clearly reflected the face of a man who was once his contractor and who " spelled " my father because he thrashed him for walking into the bedroom without permission. After the contractor had succeeded in getting clear to a safe distance he stopped and said: " I will give you cause to remember this." Finding the spell did not work he transferred it to his eldest son, who at that time, was living with my father. This is as much as I can remember of the whole unfortunate affair.

(Signed) E.K.

I must leave these stories to speak for themselves, only remarking that the details given in the third case, extravagant and incredible as they may appear, have points of resemblance with other narratives of poltergeist disturbances alleged to be due to Oriental maleficent magic. See, for example, the case of Mr. Thangapragasam Pillay recounted above (page 61.)

IV

In connection with these accounts I venture to submit, for what it is worth, the evidence of another case. It is a specimen of a type of disturbance which is by no means rare, but which owing to such causes as shyness, or fear of ridicule, or illiteracy on the part of the sufferers, rarely attracts public attention. Some time ago Father M.N., a priest in Ireland, and member of a Religious Order, was kind enough to bring this alleged manifestation to my notice, and with the writer's permission to send on the letters he had received upon the subject. One gathers that the writer of the letters is the wife of a decent farmer in a somewhat remote inland district of County Cork. Obviously, as the letters show, there is no thought of self-advertisement, or wish to attract publicity; no familiarity with poltergeist literature. It also seems hard to understand how some of the incidents described could have been the work of any mischievous child. We give the letters in the order they were received by the priest who sent them to me.

M . . . L . . ., Co. Cork,

Dear Father M.N., 5 Nov., 1928.

A very extraordinary happening has occurred in my house and place for the past six weeks and is still going on. I cannot account for it, unless it is what people call a " Pishogue " or a demon sent to annoy us. The inanimate things move within the house, the bedclothes are taken off the bed and go out at the window. Any article taken goes as far as the boundary or my land and is found. I have three children, 14, 12, 10 years. The eldest (a boy) sees nothing; the two younger (a boy and girl) say they see strange people about the farm and sometimes at the window. There is a tapping at the window heard very often, and scraps of paper found around with threats written on them. We were annoyed while saying the Rosary on Saturday night. We got pinches in the the head and balls made of paper thrown as if from the ceiling. These things are recurring all the time. I had our own C.C. [country curate], Father D . . ., say Mass in the house three weeks ago, but still the thing goes on. I have great faith in the Holy Mass to conquer this thing, whatever it may be. Mrs. J. O. . . . is my sister-in-law and was here yesterday. She advised me to write to you.

The letter is signed in full and ends with a request to the priest to offer Mass for the cessation of the trouble, an alms being enclosed. The next letter, dated 12 Nov. 1928, runs as follows:

Very many thanks for your kind and sympathetic letter. I shall do all those things you mention. I have given small phials of Holy Water to the children and grandmother who lives with us. It still goes on. Yesterday it was very active; the knives, clothes, pieces of soap thrown around the house. Grandmother's cap was pulled off while we were at the cows, and she is much annoyed as she is almost eighty years. About the same time my two younger children were out in the front field where there are some stacks of straw. An old woman took the overall she [presumably the little girl] had on and told her she would take her dress off if she were around again, as she wanted it for her own. The little brother was with her. They tell me there were a great many around the straw; they thought only a few men with flowing grey beards wearing high hats. The most were women and small boys barefooted; they thought some dressed in white. All had leather belts round their waists. One seemed to be walking on his head; they thought he had no feet. I now keep them inside as much as I can. The overall was on the gate next morning. She had an Agnus Dei in the pocket and (it) was not touched. Very little of the straw was found burned.

I had a servant maid since January until this thing commenced in September, when she was reprimanded about some meat found outside on the field; she left that evening. The servant boy tells how she was up at nights previous to that, he heard her laughing and crying at intervals. The threats come in scraps of paper and signed with this girl's name [K . . . O'N . . .]. In one, " We will work it on you while the three of you are there. " " It is a pity I cannot work it harder. " " I will come down the chimney to-night and take Nana's glasses, " and several other threats saying: " It is over now, it is on for five weeks. "

On Saturday last I took my three children to confession. Our C.C. Father D . . .would not give absolution to my eldest boy, as he would not admit he was doing these pranks on us. I am quite positive that this thing is a charm or something worked by the girl I had. I shall take the child to another priest, on Saturday, and before he hears his confession I will explain what Father D . . . did. Will you offer holy Mass that this thing may come to an end.

A third letter was written a week later (23 Nov.). It runs as follows:

Very many thanks for your letter. The trouble still continues, but not as active as it was. The written scraps of paper are still

13

coming.   It was only yesterday we were forced to take any money we had in the house to the bank, as it was written on one of the scraps of paper we would be left without a penny.   There were some few shillings taken, and I got written slips saying it was they took it.   I also had my younger boy home from school and was told if I did not take him along he would be well pulled while I was away.   He got several pinches that morning.   One Saturday evening about 4 o'clock, my little daughter, aged 10½ years, said she saw the servant maid I had employed ride up the yard on a horse, her mother following after on a motor bicycle, and then followed a long train of red coated figures on horseback.   The servant said, when passing the child, " Good-bye, May, for ever. " In the slips of paper found in the house it was written that they were going to C . . ., that is a farmer residing about half a mile away, but within the parish.   I have heard that these occurrences have started there now.   Some of the slips of paper are signed: " K ... O'N ... " That was my servant maid's name.   They seem to hear every word that is spoken in the house, because answers are written on some of the slips.   I do anything you desire me; my relatives have joined me in the Novena to St. Gerard.

The next letter forwarded—there is nothing to show whether the series is complete—is a very brief document, dated 22.12.28, written in a different handwriting and with faults of spelling.

Dear Rev. Father,

Just a line to let you know that work is gone from us, T. God.   I am continuing the Novenia [*sic*] over and over again to St. Gerard. Many and greatful [*sic*] thanks for your prayers.   I never will forget your kindness.   Wishing you a very happy Christmas and very many happy returns.   I remain yours sincerely M... K...

The last letter (which is in the same handwriting as the first three) runs thus:

19 Jan. 1929.

Rev. and very dear Father M.N.,

Many thanks for your letter of the 5th which I duly received. You can send my letters to Father Thurston, and should he want any further details I shall let you have them as well as I can.   The trouble now seems to have disappeared; we have seen nothing for more than a fortnight.   The last thing we had was a queer looking black cat. It would seem very small at times, and very big at other times with very long hind legs. It would get into a bed during the day and give annoyance. In the evening the younger children could see it get out of the window, though it was shut. It would get into a hen coop sometimes as if killing a rat, but in reality the eggs were taken. Some time before this cat appeared, we did away with our own two cats. There was also a pickaxe taken from us and returned broken with the broken pieces also " saying how it was used at the other house and they could not help breaking it, " that was in one of the old scraps of paper.

My husband was coming from the farmyard after looking up the cattle before going to bed, and when coming near the house, he would hear a great many voices, as if there were a number of people in the yard. Although he was nervous to come on, as he was alone,[1] but when he arrived at the house he saw nobody, but he did not go alone after that, as he was afraid. That was also when the trouble was coming to an end. I shall never forget your kindness to me and my family, etc.,

M . . . K . .

Extravagant and preposterous as much of this must seem there are curious features of interest in it. If the first letter stood alone, one would be inclined to say that it conformed in many respects to a type of poltergeist story which is quite well attested.

The pulling off of the bedclothes is one of the commonest features (witness the Enniscorthy case recorded by Sir William Barrett) and so also is the movement of inanimate objects. When the writer says, " we got pinches in the head, " she seems to include herself, and one wonders if a child could play such a prank upon the mother without detection. Father D . . . obviously believed that the elder boy was the culprit, and he probably knew the family well.

On the other hand, it is possible that in such cases when some strange excitement, such as unaccountable movements, knockings and whiskings off of bedclothes, comes to enliven the monotony of everyday life, the children are tempted to join in the fun and let their imaginations run riot. This may well have been the case with Molly and Dobby Giles at Bristol (see page 19). But on the other hand we cannot altogether shut our eyes to the fact that this peculiar sensitiveness of young children to phantom appearances is often

---

[1] *Sic:* it looks as if something had been left out. Is this letter the original, or a copy ?

alleged.   The Grosserlach poltergeist of 1916 supplies a notable instance.   In the case before us, the ready credulity of all concerned, and of the father in particular, is a very conspicuous element in the story, and children are quick to take advantage of such a disposition in their elders.

CHAPTER XVII

POLTERGEISTS IN EARLIER CENTURIES[1]

THE very wide range of alleged poltergeist phenomena has often been pointed out and cannot in fact be disputed. We hear of cases in Russia and in Finland, in Java and Sumatra, in India and in China, as well as in every part of the American continent, in South Africa and in Mauritius; while, of course, in the better known parts of Europe hardly a week passes without some such story being reported in provincial newspapers, though they are now too common to attract wide attention except in a few rare instances. What, however, is not so generally familiar is the fact that there are considerable traces of similar disturbances occurring in medieval times, long before any agency existed for recording them or bringing them to the notice of the curious. A few of these cases have been noted in such books as Görres' *Mystik* or Pertz's *Mystischen Erscheinungen,* but I have long been of opinion that some little care spent in looking through monastic chronicles and other similar literature would not be barren of result. I propose in the present chapter to give details of some few early examples of " thorybism "—to use M. Sudre's convenient phrase—which I have come upon in the course of a not very protracted search.

The first in point of time has more than once been noted before. It occurs in Cyprian's life of St. Caesarius of Arles, a document which that most critical of scholars, Bruno Krusch, pronounces to be the unquestionably authentic work of a contemporary. The record is very brief. We only learn that about the year 530 the deacon Helpidius, a well-known man who on account of his medical knowledge held an official position as physician to King Theodoric, the son of Clovis, found himself the victim of a " diabolic infestation " —at that date, of course, all upsetting disturbances were ascribed to Satanic agency—and he accordingly appealed to the saint to provide a remedy. The deacon complained that he was worn out by the tricks and wiles of a fiend who assailed him, and that in

[1] Hitherto unpublished

187

particular he was frequently bombarded by showers of stones within his own house. St. Caesarius, accordingly, went to him, blessed the house with holy water, and we are told that thenceforth Helpidius suffered no further annoyance.[1]

The next example in chronological order occurs in Alcuin's life of the English missionary St. Willibrord (658-739) who was the first bishop of Utrecht and apostle of Friesland. Alcuin was hardly a contemporary, for he was born only three or four years before Willibrord's death, but he was a famous scholar and had access to authentic materials. Moreover, he was himself of English birth, having a family connection with the saint, though like him he spent a good deal of his life on the Continent. Anyway, the account we are here concerned with runs thus:

A certain father of a family and his household suffered grievous trials from a mocking demon, the presence of the spirit of evil in the home being made manifest by the fright he occasioned and by his malicious tricks. On a sudden he used to carry off food, clothing and other necessary things and throw them into the fire. He even took a little child while it was lying in bed between the father and the mother, they being fast asleep, and threw it likewise into the fire. But the parents, being aroused by the infant's wailing, were able to rescue it, though only just in time. The outrages which the family endured from this horrible spirit took many forms. Neither could it be driven out by any of the priests, until the holy bishop at the father's request sent him some water which he himself had blessed. He directed that all the household gear should be taken out of their dwelling and sprinkled with this water, for he foresaw in spirit that the house itself was about to perish in flames. These injunctions have been complied with, a fire, which broke out in the place where the bed had stood, attacked the empty building and entirely consumed it. When, however, another house was built on the same site and blessed with holy water, there was no recurrence of the trouble previously experienced.[2]

It will be remembered that not only the sudden disappearance of food and of other things badly needed, but also spontaneous outbreaks of fire are amongst the most common phenomena of poltergeist disturbances. In the famous " Amherst Mystery " of Nova

[1] See the *Monumenta Germaniae Historica; Scriptores rerum Merovingicarum;* vol. III, p. 473.

[2] See Alcuin's *Vita Willibrordi* in Jaffe, *Bibliotheca Rerum Germanicarum,* vol. vi, p. 29.

Scotia fire played a prominent part, but a much better authenticated example is the case of Captain Jandachenko at Liptsy in the district of Kharkoff (Russia). The whole story was there investigated by a legal tribunal, the records of which have been printed.[1] In this instance the main dwelling with a number of outbuildings was burnt to the ground.

It is not necessary to dwell upon the disturbances chronicled in A.D. 858 at Bingen on the Rhine, because this case has been often discussed. It is noteworthy, however, that not only were there thundering noises and showers of stones, but a human voice was heard which revealed the secret misdeeds of people who were present; while the troubles culminated in the destruction by fire of the possessions of the principal offender, all ecclesiastical exorcisms having previously proved ineffectual in banishing the supposed demon. The original source from which the facts are derived is the chronicle known as the *Annales Fuldenses*, from which Sigebert of Gembloux, who is commonly cited as the main authority, has condensed his account.[2]

From Germany in 858 we must pass to Wales in the latter part of the twelfth century. The story of the dirt-throwing spirit which—if we may trust the Annals of Margam (Glamorganshire) apparently referring to the same episode—belongs to the year 1184, is told by Giraldus Cambrensis in his *Itinerarium Kambriae* and has been given above (p. 7).

Giraldus confesses that he had no explanation to offer of these strange happenings, except that he suggests that it might be a presage of some change of fortune for better or worse; and he implies that the two persons above-named afterwards came upon evil days. But what surprised him still more was that the ritual of the Church seemed to be of no avail in dislodging these mocking or evil spirits. The priests of the parish came very devoutly with their processional cross and a vessel of holy water, but no sooner had they appeared upon the scene than they before all the rest were bespattered with filth.[3]

There is a certain note of sincerity about this. It does not sound like a story which Giraldus was telling merely to amuse his readers, but as a thing that had puzzled him because he was satisfied that it

---

[1] See Aksakoff, *Vorläufer des Spiritismus*, pp. 51-165. A summary is given in S.P.R. *Proceedings*, xii, pp. 319 *seq.*

[2] See Pertz, *M. G. H. Scriptores*, vol. i, *sub anno* 858.

[3] Giraldus Cambrensis, *Opera* (Rolls Series), vol. vi, pp. 93-94.

had actually happened. Needless to add that the tearing of clothes, even in a locked cupboard, is a by no means uncommon feature in poltergeist disturbances.

Only a few years later we have record of another curious manifestation, this time in East Anglia, which seems to have excited a certain amount of attention. It is recounted by Ralph of Coggeshall as follows:

In the reign of King Richard (I) at Dagworth in Suffolk, in the house of Sir Osberne de Bradewelle, a certain whimsical (*fantasticus*) ghost appeared on many occasions and for a long time together talking with the family of the aforesaid knight, and imitating in its tones the voice of a baby girl. She called herself Malekin and said that her mother and her brother made their home in a house near by. Moreover she declared that she was frequently scolded by them because she left their company and made bold to talk with human beings. She both did and said things which were extravagant and amusing, and sometimes she revealed the secret doings of other people. When she first was heard to speak, the knight's good lady and the whole household were very frightened, but afterwards, when they had become accustomed to her diverting tricks and speeches, they talked with her familiarly and confidently, asking her all sorts of questions. She spoke in English, using the local dialect, but sometimes also in Latin, and she would debate about the Scriptures in all seriousness with the chaplain of the aforesaid knight as he himself informed me. She could make herself heard and felt, but was never seen; though on one occasion a little waiting maid beheld her in the form of a tiny babe clothed in a white frock. This girl has previously begged and implored the spirit to make herself visible, but she would not consent until the child swore by our Saviour that she would neither touch her nor detain her. She confessed that she had been born at " Lanaham," and that while her mother took her with her into the fields when she was reaping with a number of others, the little one, who had been left by herself in a corner, was seized and carried off by another woman. She had now been seven years in this woman's company, but she said that after another seven years she would return to live with mortals again as before. She also made known that she and others wore a sort of cap which rendered them invisible. She frequently demanded food and drink, which, being left on top of a certain chest, disappeared and were seen no more.[1]

[1] Ralph de Coggeshall, *Chronicon* (Rolls Series) pp. 120-121.

The story obviously does not quite hold together. If the child ghost had been carried off by another woman, how, one asks, could she say that her mother and brother scolded her for venturing to talk with human beings ? Still, it does not seem likely that the tale is all pure fiction. During the reign of Richard I the chronicler Ralph, a Cistercian abbot, reputed in historical matters a sober and trustworthy authority, was undoubtedly living at Coggeshall in Essex. This, as the crow flies, is about twenty-five miles distant from Dagworth in Suffolk, and Ralph probably learned the whole story from Sir Osberne's chaplain, who we may assume did somewhat more than justice to its marvellous features. But such talking poltergeists are not without precedent. Apart from the Bingen case and the Giraldus case, the spirit with which the Huguenot minister, M. Francois Perrault, conversed at Mâcon in 1612; the gruff voice which talked for many hours at the Dagg's farm in the province of Quebec (Canada) in 1889, and the group of cases brought together by Professor Bozzano in his *Fenomeni d'Infestazione* are all instances in point. Most curious of all, the Mary Jobson story at Sunderland in 1840 makes it difficult to doubt the occasional association of a human voice with physical phenomena of a rather boisterous kind.[1]

---

[1] The Poltergeist story in St. Augustine—and it certainly seems to be a true case o Poltergeist infestation—is earlier in date than any of the instances here given. It is told in *De Civitate Dei* (22.8: p. 602 of Vol. II in the Vienna Corpus).

There is in our country one Hesperius, a man of captain's rank. He has a property called Zubedi in the district of Fussala, and there, when he discovered by the molestation of his cattle and his slaves that his house was being assailed by the evil influence of malign spirits, he asked our priests, in my absence, that one of them should go thither and by his prayers drive out the evil. One of them went and offered there the sacrifice of the Body of Christ, beseeching with all his might for the cessation of the mischief, and by the mercy of God it ceased forthwith. Hesperius was given by a friend some hallowed earth that had been brought from Jerusalem, the scene of Our Saviour's death and resurrection on the third day, and this he hung up in his room to ensure that no mischief should befall himself.

It is not unreasonable to see poltergeist activity here. Hesperius would not have supposed that cattle-maiming done by human hands was the work of spirits. The molestations must have been such that he could in no way explain them. His fear for an extension of the mischief to his own room points to the same conclusion.

The examples given in classical authors are much less characteristic of the true Poltergeist.   Suetonius (*Otho*, 7) relates that the emperor Otho was once pulled out of bed by what he thought was the ghost of Galba, but this isolated happening might have had many causes. Pliny (*Ep*. 7. 27) has a tale of a house at Athens where clanking of chains was often heard until excavation showed that a corpse bound by chains had been buried there,   Here again there is little that is proper to the Poltergeist. J.H.C.

CHAPTER XVIII

SOME CONCLUSIONS[1]

IT might be objected that most of these things happened many years ago and that they are therefore as untrustworthy as the portents of Roman history. Nevertheless, there are allegations taken from official court records, and the witnesses were speaking of incidents which had then occurred quite recently. Indeed, in citing such cases of old date, we have certain notable compensations as compared with the evidence for modern examples. Nowadays almost everybody has heard of poltergeists. People know what to expect, and consequently they also know the kind of phenomena they may safely invent to lend plausibility to an otherwise unconvincing tale. On the other hand it must be remembered that for newspapers on the look out for sensation the flimsiest rumour supplies matter for a paragraph. It is surely misleading to append to such journalistic notices the comment " never explained," and virtually to suggest thereby that fraud and malobservation may be ruled out. In most instances there is no reason to suppose than any critical inquiry has taken place. No doubt some recent examples may be cited for which first-class evidence is producible, but poltergeist phenomena have now become so familiar since the Press has taken to giving prominence to every reported case, that almost everybody knows beforehand exactly what a poltergeist may be expected to do, and further, it follows that any mischievous young person or hysterical imbecile understands exactly what kind of tricks can be performed with the gratifying assurance that they will produce a sensation. We do not need to invoke a poltergeist to explain the epidemics of shop-window smashing or window scratching which occasionally break out in our big towns. Professor William James the psychologist *who believed in poltergeists*, stated his conviction that " this type of phenomena is a natural type which recurs sporadically in various places without connection," but he added, " it is also an imitated type—imitated

<hr />

[1] *Times Literary Supplement*, 29 February 1936 and *Studies*, March 1935

by the perversity of eccentrically constituted individuals."
There is therfore much to be said for reports drawn up in an age
when there was no understanding of the likelihood of such disturbances. The narratives published two hundred years ago by
intelligent people who evidently considered that their own unpleasant experience was without a parallel in history seem often to
be evidentially more valuable than accounts of modern date. Let
us take by way of illustration an eighteenth century case. The disturbances occured in the house of a physician of good standing at
Dortmund in Westphalia. Several medical dissertations still extant,
which were published some by Berthold F. Gerstmann the father,
and others by his son, prove that the family enjoyed a considerable
reputation. It was the son who in the year 1714 sent to the press a full
account of the spook phenomena from the diary he kept at the time.
It has a long title which, after the manner of those days, almost fills
the front page, beginning thus: *F. B. Gerstmann's Vorstellung des
Gespenstes and Polter Geistes welches in der Stadt Dortmundt und zwar in
dessen Vatters Hause* etc., etc. From this, and from a separately
printed narrative by a Lutheran minister named Starmann (copies
of both are in the British Museum), we learn that on 5 May 1713,
stones began to be thrown at the Gerstmann's house. This was
supposed at first to be the work of mischievous children or tramps.
Several windows were broken, and a watch was set, but nothing
detected; neither could the stones be seen in their passage through
the air. They were only visible when they reached their objective.
All sorts of missiles struck the house, fragments of bricks, slates,
scraps of old iron, potsherds etc. The bombardment was particularly vigorous during the first eight days, but it continued
intermittently until the end of the manifestations. The glass and
porcelain apparatus in Dr. Gerstmann's laboratorium suffered
much damage. The family tried to protect the more breakable
articles by putting them away in cupboards, but the glass retorts and
beakers were often struck in the very act of removing them. A much-
valued mirror, when actually clasped in the arms of the youngest
boy, who was taking it to his mother, was shattered by a missile,
and while the eldest son was reading a Greek New Testament in the
summerhouse a sharp stone struck it and tore out two pages.
     Passing over certain unpleasant and unprintable forms of
annoyance which are often characteristic of such infestations, we
may note that an ink bottle was whisked away from one room to
another smashing against the wall upon which it left ineffaceable
traces, that domestic utensils laid aside for a moment could not be

found when the need of them recurred a minute or two afterwards, and that the harassed master of the house was denied even the consolation of a smoke because his pipe had unaccountably disappeared. Further his wig was so tangled and befouled that he had to buy another, and when the new one arrived it was soon after taken from the peg upon which he had hung it, and thrown into a kettle of hot water. Infuriated by the annoyance of the invisible aggressor the Gerstmanns took to slashing at it blindly with a sword, but when they wanted to replace the weapon in its sheath, they found that the sheath was useless because it had been stuffed full of dirt and the sword itself later on was discovered broken to pieces in an out-of-the-way corner. It was also noticed that abuse and maledictions directed against their tormentor seemed to be fully understood and provoked prompt retaliation. The visitation lasted for twenty-five days ending on 2 June, but the spook as a parting shot tore the clothes of the doctor's youngest son, aged twelve, (we may perhaps suppose him to have been the medium) slashing them in a dozen different places. One curious feature of the case is that at the very last a voice was heard announcing in the following words that the disturbances were over: " Beschlus; Heute Beschlus; schlechten Beschlus; Stink Beschlus." (The end, the end to-day of mischief and stench). These loud cries, the origin of which could not in any way be traced, were several times repeated.

Incredible as these details must sound, it is difficult to suppose they were a pure invention. The Gerstmanns were people of some consequence who had nothing to gain by a fabrication of this sort. They professed to be devout Evangelicals, and, as seems to have been the case with a dozen similar narratives preserved to us from the seventeenth and eighteenth centuries, their statement was really printed as an apologia. Such disturbances were then universally ascribed to the action of the devil and some degree of unpopularity was likely to be incurred by people who were unpleasantly mixed up with weird phenomena. A diabolic visitation was suggestive of an unholy familiarity with witchcraft and sorcery. It is noticeable that most of the early published accounts come from ministers of religion, in some cases Protestants, in others Catholics, who had themselves been the victims of similar hauntings. There seems no reason to suppose that the clergy were more tormented then other people, but they probably felt that they had to protect their reputation from misleading rumours, and being educated men they had no such difficulty as peasants would have had, in printing an account of what had happened to them. Several of these booklets are prefaced by a dedication to higher ecclesiastical authorities as well as by a solemn protestation of the exact truth of the story recounted. In many cases the signed testimony of witnesses is added. Further it must be confessed that in spite of the seemingly extravagant contents most of these narratives have a ring of sincerity which it is very hard to resist.

One specially interesting account of a long continued poltergeist manifestation, that of M. Perrault, a Huguenot minister at Mâcon, has been given above. The Hon. Robert Boyle, one of the founders of the Royal Society, had it translated and printed in English. He had met the author at Geneva, and Boyle while protesting his "backwardness of assent to the many fictions and superstitions which are wont to blemish the relations where spirits and witches are concerned," declares that the inquiries he made concerning M. Perrault and his story "did at length overcome in me (as to this narrative) all my settled indisposedness to believe strange things." They were strange things indeed which the minister had to record, beginning on 14 September 1612, the disturbances lasted for more than two months. They included the pulling off of bedclothes, the throwing of stones, a veritable *charivari* (this is Perrault's own word, retained in the translation, an older instance than any given in the *O.E.D.*) of stools and fireirons and metal dishes, causing an unearthly clatter, with many other phenomena. But the most curious feature of the case was that for several weeks a number of M. Perrault's friends and neighbours used to gather in his house to carry on a lively conversation with the invisible spirit. It answered audibly manifesting a most uncanny knowledge of their private affairs, and sometimes of occurrences at a distance. In this instance no material damage was done. M. Perrault declares that not so much as a pane of glass was broken, but still he seems to have been extremely relieved when the visitation ended. He would have echoed heartily a distich we find quoted in the Gerstmann book:

> Polter-Geist sey wer er sey,
> Ich bin froh dass ich bin frey.

From an evidential point of view no one who compares the details of any considerable number of poltergeist hauntings, ancient and modern, can fail to be impressed by certain features which, though not present in all, are apt to recur in surroundings separated from each other by thousands of miles of space and many centuries of time. The statement made by Giraldus Cambrensis and William of Auvergne, Bishop of Paris, in the thirteenth century that in spite of great violence and damage to property men sustain no bodily hurt—*homines hujusmodi jactibus vel rarissime vel nunquam laeduntur*, to quote the words of the latter—are borne out by the cases reported to-day not only from Europe but from every part of the world.   By the testimony of witnesses in countries widely remote the mysterious movement of stone, or other flying objects seem to be under perfect control.   Such missiles travel as if they were animated things able to direct their own movements.   Sometimes they come with terrific speed, sometimes they pursue a leisurely course, sometimes again, in defiance of the laws of motion, they turn corners, twist about or wobble up and down.   We hear also of their grazing so narrowly the head of the human target that he feels on his cheek the wind produced by their passage and his hair is blown about.   At other times they strike him, but in that moment their movement is suddenly arrested, they inflict no more than a tap, and fall spent at his feet.

The particular feature of silent movement is a relatively rare characteristic of poltergeist activities.   The very word " poltergeist " seems to lay stress upon noise and violence as being most usually associated with such disturbances.   Objects are projected with alarming velocity, and often seem directly aimed at some human target, but for all that there is hardly a single well-attested instance of injury resulting to life or limb.   Mockery and mere annoyance seem to be the main purpose of these assaults.   Consequently the missiles which often fly so swiftly and so menacingly either do no more than graze the victim against whom they are directed, or are mysteriously arrested in the moment of impact and do little or no damage.   In a case where I had the opportunity of questioning a number of eye-witnesses, a maid, about seventeen, seemed to be the focus of all the disturbance, and she was repeatedly struck on the head by objects as various as coal-scuttle covers, alarm clocks and plum-puddings, all of which seemed to fly at her with hostile intent.   I afterwards saw a letter she wrote to her mistress, in which she said: " Really and truly I had the terrible feeling that in the end something would have hurt me; I think my head must have been made of wood, nearly; don't you, madam ? " It is plain that she had really suffered no damage, and there seem to be many similar cases on record of little children who have been struck by quite big stones without being any the worse for it.

Another peculiarity is the wavy path, quite irreconcilable with gravitational laws, which these projectiles often seem to follow. They turn corners, swerve in and out, and behave, in fact, like a bird which is free to pick its own way. Not less surprising is the assertion repeated by many credible witnesses, that the stones and other missiles are for the most part invisible at the beginning of their flight. They do not come into view until they are just a few feet off. They enter closed rooms and seem to drop from the ceilings or to penetrate doors and windows without leaving a trace of their passage. Spiritualists would probably urge that they are first de-materialized and only re-materialized in the process of flight. From this transformation it is said to result that they are sometimes very hot, a feature noticed in medieval and other early cases by observers who therein found proof of their infernal origin.

In a considerable number of instances we are told that the missiles can never be seen flying, they only become visible just as they land. Sir William Barrett, Mr. Andrew Lang and others seem justified in arguing that the concurrence of testimony regarding these abnormalities in the movement of material objects requires explanation and that no adequate explanation is forthcoming.

When Mr. Podmore in 1903 made reply to Mr. Andrew Lang, who had criticised his rather peremptory dismissal of the evidence for poltergeist phenomena, he justified his sceptical attitude in these terms: " My position is that, when we succeed in getting the testimony of educated and intellectual witnesses at first-hand, and not too remote, we find that the poltergeist performances were tolerably commonplace; and that the really marvellous incidents in every case rest either upon rumours, or upon the evidence of uneducated and incompetent witnesses, or more rarely upon the evidence of educated witnesses given long after the events." Incidentally let it be said that Mr. Podmore had taken no account of the Derrygonnelly case personally investigated by Professor Barrett in 1877 nor of a good many foreign cases in which it would be quite impossible to describe the witnesses as uneducated. But plenty of fresh information has come since 1903, and to make a small selection out of a large mass of excellent material a word or two may be said of the descriptions of personal experiences which we owe to Professor Lombroso, Baron von Winterstein, and Professor H. Nielsson.

Lombroso after taking a medical degree, had become a director of an important lunatic asylum, had then been appointed Professor of Psychiatry at Pavia and Turin, and had finally filled the chair of Criminology in the University of the city last named. In his book *Ricerche sui Fenomeni Ipnotici e Spiritici*, he tells us how, down to the age of forty-six, he had regarded all spiritualistic manifestations with utter contempt. Then in 1882 his professional duties brought him into contact with a case of transference of sense perceptions which upset his purely materialistic outlook. In Turin towards the close of 1900 (address, names and date are given in full), he was invited to investigate a poltergeist disturbance in which chairs, copper vessels and other articles flew about without any discernible cause. It was a wine-shop with an underground cellar and here a number of bottles began to jump off the shelves upon which they were stored leaving under foot a welter of spilt wine and broken glass. Lombroso tells us in particular that standing alone in the cellar he himself watched one bottle after another quit the plank on which they stood, not tumbling violently, but as if they had been lifted down by an invisible hand (*come se fossero portate da qualcuno*). The phenomena which were very varied lasted for three weeks (16 Nov. to 7 Dec.). A confirmatory statement by a competent eye-witness dated 9 Jan. 1901 has also been printed.

So again at the International Congress for Psychic Research held at Athens in April 1930 Baron von Winterstein, who is the President of the Austrian Society for Psychical Research described the phenomena occurring in the presence of the girl Frieda Weissl. They had been observed by Professor Dörfler, by himself and by a number of others not more than five months previously. Although nothing exceptionally sensational was witnessed, they saw small objects fly through the air spontaneously in daylight, keys jumped from their keyholes, people including Frieda herself, were slightly wetted with water, and strange imitative noises were heard, particularly the clicking of a typewriting machine. The manifestations, which had been more pronounced in the girl's own garret at Eggenberg, continued though less violently when she came by invitation to spend a week or two, first at Gratz and then at Vienna in conditions which allowed the Society to keep her under close observation.

Much more remarkable than this last was the case of Indridi Indridason, a quite young man whose extraordinary phenomena were in 1907-8 carefully investigated by the Icelandic Society for Psychical Research. As the one accessible account of what occurred was only made public in 1924 at the Warsaw International Congress, it might be thought that Mr. Podmore's suggestion as to the effect of " exaggerative memory " must detract considerably from the value of the report, seeing that the manifestations had taken place seventeen years earlier. But the Rev. Professor Nielsson of Reykjavik—his paper was written in English—took pains to explain that his account was derived from the Minute Book of the Icelandic Society in which the incidents were recorded as they occurred, and that these Minutes were regularly attested by the officials of the Society and other witnesses. Moreover, both Professor Nielsson himself and Mr. Kvaran, the President, who also took part in the Congress, had been intimately associated with the manifestations when they occurred. The phenomena many of which occurred in artificial light were certainly astounding. We are told that the young man Indridi was pulled out of bed with such violence by an unseen force that neither his own resistance nor the help of a friend who exerted all his strength in the effort to hold him could prevent his being dragged on to the floor. The account given above (page 9), which I repeat here for convenience, describes an absolute pandemonium, more than once renewed.

The medium Indridi is frightened and calls for help. Mr. Oddgeirsson goes into the bedroom, but a chair is then hurled against him and falls down beside the stove. Mr. Oddgeirsson swerved to avoid the chair but went on. He finds Mr. Thorlaksson lying on the medium's chest. Mr. Oddgeirsson threw his weight on to the medium's knees, who was at the moment all on the move in the bed. Then a bolster which was under the medium's pillow was thrown up into the air. It fell down on the bedroom floor. Simultaneously the candle-sticks which were in the outer room came through the air and were flung down in the bedroom.

It needs an effort to remind ourselves that the writer of all this was not a counterfeit Hans Anderson, but an exceptionally cultured professor of theology. His uncle, the Right Rev. Dr. Sveinsson, was Bishop of Iceland, and the Bishop also, we are told, took great interest in the psychic phenomena which occurred in the presence of Indridi, himself assisting at some of them. The Mr. Thorlaksson just mentioned and Mr. Kvaran, the President of the Society, both held public appointments, but they signed a statement that they had witnessed these scenes and had compared Professor Nielsson's report with the minutes written down at the time when the events took place, finding it " correct in every detail."

Neither must it be forgotten that a certain number of poltergeist cases have come before the Courts. In the Cideville case, given above, the verdict of the Court went substantially, if not formally, in favour of the poltergeist. In others as at Resau (1888-9) a boy accused of breaking windows by throwing stones was sentenced to

14

fine and imprisonment, because the Court, so the President declared, must take its stand wholly and entirely on the ground of enlightened science and refuse to entertain the idea that a magnetic or any other force can play the part of a spook.

But nothing in the least shook the testimony of the Lutheran pastor that in the house where the accused lived he had seen objects take flight of their own accord and travel in curved paths contrary to the laws of motion.

Thorybistic phenomena are frequently encountered also in the lives of the saints. A relatively early English example may be found in the life of St. Godric who died in 1170. If we may trust his biographer, not only was the Saint's hermitage bombarded with showers of stones, but the evil spirit threw at him the box in which he kept his altar-breads, took the horn which contained the wine he needed for Mass and poured it over his head, and ended by pelting him with almost every movable object which his poor cell contained. Whether the Wartburg experiences of Dr. Martin Luther (himself one of the earliest to use the term Poleter-Geister) and of the Wesley family at Epworth should be included in this category may be doubted by some, but by the sufferers in question they were attributed to the same source.

The manifestations as a rule endure for a brief space and then suddenly come to an end. Sometimes the phenomena are all over in twenty-four hours; sometimes, as in the Poona case, they continue for months. What, I think, is hardly appreciated by any but those who have given a good deal of time to investigating the question is the enormous amount of evidence available. Much of this, no doubt, is unsatisfactory, consisting as it does of newspaper reports.

But even in these cases it is often hard to see how simple people, who plainly know nothing of the existence of other similar phenomena, should describe over and over again just the same peculiar happenings which are attested elsewhere by eye-witnesses of the highest credit. The pulling off of the bedclothes from people asleep at night, the dragging across the floor of heavy bedsteads or articles of furniture—feats beyond the phsyical strength of the children suspected of playing pranks—the curved path taken by missiles which sweep around corners or twist in and out as a living bird might do, the gentle descent to the floor in some cases of large pictures or mirrors whose cords and supporting hooks remain intact, the flight of showers of stones which seem to come from space and are only perceptible when quite near, the sudden and harmless arrest of swiftly moving objects which threaten destruction to anything that impedes their progress, the spontaneous bursting open of securely fastened doors in full view of watchful observers, the escape from closed receptacles of articles stored therein without any discernible means of exit,[1] the constant disappearance and hiding of domestic odds and ends specially needed which are often afterwards restored in ways equally mysterious, the sudden outbreak of a conflagration in places where no spark or source of fire existed— these features recur all over the world in countries as far remote from each other as Canada and the Dutch East Indies. Moreover, not to speak of several medieval examples,[2] we find highly respected divines in the seventeenth and eighteenth centuries, Catholics as well as Protestants, suffering from similar visitations and giving identically the same descriptions of the phenomena as those we read to-day.

For my own part I find it impossible to believe that such manifestations as are attested by the late Sir William Barrett, F.R.S., Professor Lombroso, or Baron von Schrenck Notzing[3] had no real existence, but were due to hallucination. There are dozens of other records—some of them based upon the painstaking examination of witnesses before a legal tribunal[4]—which offer every guarantee of

[1] On 30 June, 1928, Miss Kohn records: " My sister bought four dozen eggs, which were counted and put in a basket in the food cupboard in the dining-room. Almost immediately one egg shot in our direction from the direction of the closed cupboard and smashed. We took the basket out of the cupboard, and ascertained that one egg was missing. I had no sooner gathered up the egg-shell and washed the stain from the floor than a second egg came violently from the opposite direction, i.e., not as if coming from the cupboard, and smashed near the spot where the first egg smashed. We again counted the remaining eggs and ascertained that a second egg was missing. Damodar, whom we were closely observing, had not approached the cupboard during the time." Three other eggs were broken in the same way later in the day.

[2] A remarkable case of early date is the poltergeist near Bingen on the Rhine of which an account is given in the *Annales Fuldensis* under the year 858. Showers of stones were thrown, sledge-hammer blows resounded on the walls, a great conflagration broke out, and the exorcisms of the Church produced no effect.

[3] Several of these investigations of Baron Schrenck have been collected by his widow in the volume *Gesammelte Aufsätze zur Parapsychologie* (1929), pp. 240-401.

[4] I may mention as striking examples: (1) the Ylöjärvi case in Finland (1885) of which a full account is given in Schrenck Notzing's *Aufsätze*, just mentioned, pp. 263-283, the evidence tendered regarding the wavering path of the missiles being of exceptional interest; (2) the Yerville case in France (1850), for which see the *Proceedings of the S. P. R.*, vol. xviii (1904), pp. 454-463; and (3) the Jandachenko case in Russia (1853) the whole evidence for which is printed in German in Aksakoff's *Vorläufer des Spiritismus* (1898), pp. 49-165.

genuineness.   Even the newspaper accounts are not likely to have been all written unscrupulously with a view to sensation.   Many give proof of a sane and critical attitude on the part of the reporter at the same time that he finds himself constrained to yield to the evidence which he has collected on the spot.

Although, as the reader will infer, I am myself quite satisfied of the reality of many of these poltergeist phenomena, notably in such a case as that of the Ketkar household at Poona, I have no thought of contesting the fact that nothing more purposeless—one might well say, nothing more childish—could be imagined than these incomprehensible displays of some Puck-like spook bent on every exasperating form of mischief.   In the words of Alice in Wonderland, " he only does it to annoy, because he knows it teases. " Nevertheless these phenomena seem to me to have their value as a proof of the existence of a world of spiritual agencies, not cognoscible directly by our sense perceptions.   For the crude materialist such incidents must surely be very difficult to explain away.   The stones have fallen, for they are solid and still to be seen; but who has thrown them ?   Crockery, chimney ornaments and glasses have been smashed, heavy pieces of furniture have been moved, pictures have jumped from the walls, but witnesses declare that they stood by and saw that no human hand came near them.   Now it would be a very violent supposition to maintain that any human being is so psychically endowed that by taking thought he can make material objects external to himself fly about in eccentric paths, that he can move furniture, spirit away the contents of receptacles closed and locked, or set a curtain on fire by merely looking at it.   What the nature of the agency is that performs these marvels we are not called upon to determine.   Divines of all creeds in the seventeenth century were satisfied that such alarming phenomena could only be the work of the devil.   I am not prepared to declare that they were wrong, though this solution cannot, I submit, be treated as a matter of certainty.   But, be this as it may, we may reasonably call upon materialists who deny the possibility of miracles either to provide a physical explanation of these extraordinary poltergeist disturbances, or to submit some reasonable ground for rejecting the mass of evidence by which their reality has been established.

It may be admitted in any case that nothing could be conceived more purposeless or irrational than the vagaries of the poltergeist. None the less, it seems impossible to reject the evidence which for so many centuries and in every country of the world attests the sporadic occurrence of such phenomena.   To attribute them all to diabolic agency is difficult, if only because we credit the enemy of mankind with a higher level of intelligence than that which seems to prompt these outbreaks. Experience has shown that the exorcism and comminatory rites of the Church are not always, or indeed generally, effective in putting an end to poltergeist disturbances, though they sometimes produce a temporary mitigation. On the other hand, I have come across a few cases in which a special novena or the saying of Mass seems definitely to have got rid of the nuisance.

APPENDIX

THE EXORCISM OF HAUNTED HOUSES[1]

S O far as can be gathered from a study of the Latin *Ritualia*, whether medieval or modern, it would seem that the Catholic Church, at any rate in the West, has never taken very much account of those spectral appearances—ghosts in fact—which are said at times to disturb the peace of some ordinary dwelling house. There is of course, a lengthy ceremonial provided for the exorcism of persons possessed by the devil. But the driving out of the demons who have obtained control over a human being has abundant scriptural warrant and always been recognized by the Church as a function of her ministry. In accord with this the form of words employed in the ordination of an exorcist speaks only of the expulsion of unclean spirits from the bodies of living men—" *pelluntur spiritus immundi a corporibus obsessis* "—and the candidate is empowered to impose hands upon energumens, whether already made Chritians by baptism or preparing to receive it. Thus there is mention only of the exorcism of persons, not of places; and indeed we might doubt whether the Church had ever contemplated such a task as the purifying of any locality from malign influences, if it were not for the observances which are enjoined as a preliminary to certain other liturgical functions. In such offices as the consecration of a church, the solemn blessing of a grave-yard, of the reconciliation of a sanctuary that has been desecrated, the ceremonial begins with what we may call a form of exorcism, intended apparently to banish from that spot the activities of all the powers of darkness. Holy Water is blessed with that express object, the site is then abundantly washed and purified, and on occasions of greater solemnity it is finally fumigated with incense. Indeed we may note that something like the same procedure is observed not only in the ritual of Baptism, but also when Extreme Unction is administered or even when Holy Communion is taken to the sick.

But in all these exorcisms it is the activities of Satan and his

[1] *The Month*, January 1935

myrmidons which are the direct object of attack.   There seems to be no recognition of ghosts, or of the spirits of the dead as such, and there is no suggestion that the souls of men are likely to return to haunt the scenes amidst which they formerly dwelt on earth.   It is true that in the dedication of a church, when the bishop comes to the threshold of the building to be consecrated, he marks a cross there with his pastoral staff, exclaiming: *Ecce crucis signum, fugiant phantasmata cuncta* (behold the emblem of the cross, let all spectres flee away).   One may doubt, however, whether anything more is intended by this than to contrast the realities of true belief with the mocking shades of error.   Speaking generally we may assume that the building where people come to pray is not looked upon as a favourite lurking-place of ghosts.

In any case the fact remains that in the ordinary service-books approved by ecclesiastical authority no provision is made for dealing with the problem of hauntings (real or alleged) otherwise than by the everyday formulas for the blessing of a house which are contained in the *Rituale Romanum*.   It is certainly curious that in the very large collection of medieval *Benediktionen* which have been brought together in the great work of Adolf Franz,[1] there is apparently no prayer to be found which deals directly with ghosts; neither is there anything of the sort in Martène's *De Antiquis Ecclesiae Ritibus*.   All the same, the belief in ghosts was widespread, not only at the close of the sixteenth century, as the treatises of the Protestant Lavater and the Catholic Le Loyer, with many others, would suffice to prove but also many centuries earlier.[2]   There can be little doubt that Shakespeare counted on his ghost-lore being taken seriously, and Milton also had no fear of ridicule when he wrote in " Comus ":

> Some say no evil thing that walks by night,
> In fog or fire, by lake or moorish fen,
> Blue meagre hag, or stubborn unlaid ghost,
> That breaks his magic chains at curfew time,
> No goblin or swart faery of the mine
> Hath hurtful power o'er true virginity.

Such Catholics as Le Loyer fully admitted that God might permit souls from purgatory to revisit the earth to ask for prayers, though the shapes which they assumed were phantasmal and not solid.   Protestants for the most part denied the possibility of any

[1] *Die Kirchlichen Benediktionen im Mittelalter*, 2 Vols.   Freiburg, 1909.
[2] See, for example, the article on *Broucolaccas* in *The Month* for November, 1897.

return of the dead, and assumed that all spectres were of diabolic origin. Both parties seem to have been agreed that the commonest type of hauntings which caused terror and disturbance were the work of demons. That such infestations by the spirits of another world, often associated with a particular building or household, or again, with some individual seemingly possessed of a peculiar psychic faculty, go on at the present day, there is much evidence to prove. People of sober judgment and scrupulous veracity assert very positively that they have heard astounding noises or seen ghosts, and well-attested stories of poltergeist phenomena are constantly being reported in every part of the world. In such cases recourse is often had to a priest, who is asked to advise what can be done to put an end to this form of vexation. When prayers have been said, and Masses perhaps offered, when the house has been blessed, and relics, pious medals, or other sacred emblems brought to the spot—all without perceptible result—the family so afflicted will sometimes ask that the evil agency which is the cause of the trouble should be solemnly exorcized. For this contingency, so far as the present writer knows, there is no provision made in the Church's official service-books. But after more than one vain attempt to find a form of ritual suitable to the occasion I chanced to stumble upon a document contained in the Appendix to an edition of the *Rituale Romanum*, published with the full authorization of the Council of the Inquisition, at the royal printing office, Madrid, in the year 1631[1] It has struck me that an account of this conjuration formula might be of some interest in itself, and possibly be of service to others who found themselves in difficulty. Hence the present appendix.

The document bears the heading *Exorcismus domus a dæmonio vexatæ* (the exorcism of a house troubled with an evil spirit). The priest is directed to wear surplice and stole and to begin with the words " In the name of the Father and of the Son and of the Holy Ghost. Amen," making at the same time a triple sign of the cross. Then after the versicle *Adjutorium nostrum*, etc., and *Dominus vobiscum* etc., follows the first prayer in these terms:

Almighty and Eternal God who has bestowed such grace upon Thy priests that whatever is worthily and conscientiously performed by them in Thy name is accounted to be done by Thee, we beseech

[1] *Rituale seu Manuale Romanum, Pauli V, Pont. Max. jussu editum, cum cantu Toletano, et aliis quibusdam. Matriti; ex Typographia Regia. Anno MDCXXXI*, pp. 445-450.

Thy immeasurable clemency that where we are about to visit, Thou also wouldst visit, that what we are about to bless, Thou also wouldst ✠ bless, that Thou wouldst lend Thy mighty right hand of power to all which we are about to do, and that at the coming of our humble person (by the merits of Thy saints) the demons may fly away and the angels of peace may enter in. Through Jesus Christ our Lord, etc.

O God of angels, God of archangels, God of prophets, God of apostles, God of martyrs, God of confessors, God of virgins and of all right-living men, O God and Father of our Lord Jesus Christ I call upon Thee and I suppliantly invoke Thy holy name and the compassion of Thy radiant Majesty, that Thou wouldst lend me aid against the spirit of all iniquity, that wherever he may be, when Thy name is spoken, he may at once give place and take to flight. Through, etc.

CONJURATION

I adjure thee, O serpent of old, by the Judge of the living and the dead; by the Creator of the world who hath power to cast into hell, that thou depart forthwith from this house. He that commands thee, accursed demon, is He that commanded the winds, and the sea and the storm. He that commands thee, is He that ordered thee to be hurled down from the height of heaven into the lower parts of the earth. He that commands thee is He that bade thee depart from Him. Hearken, then, Satan and fear. Get thee gone, vanquished and cowed, when thou art bidden in the name of our Lord Jesus Christ who will come to judge the living and the dead and all the world by fire. Amen.

This is followed by the recitation of the first five of the Gradual Psalms (Ps. 119 to 123) which the priest is to repeat, while he visits every part of the house and sprinkles it with holy water, ending his round with a few versicles as an introduction to this appropriate prayer:

Do Thou, O Lord, enter graciously into the home that belongs to Thee; construct for Thyself an abiding resting-place in the hearts of Thy faithful servants, and grant that in this house no wickedness of malicious spirits may ever hold sway. Through, etc.

The second set of five Gradual Psalms are then recited while the priest renews his perambulation of the entire building, again sprinkling holy water and ending with a different prayer:

O God, omnipotent and never-ending, who in every place subject to Thee, pervadest all and workest all Thy Will, comply with our entreaty that Thou be the protector of this dwelling, and that here no antagonism of evil have power to resist Thee, but that, by the co-operation and virtue of the Holy Spirit, Thy service may come first of all, and holy freedom remain inviolate. Through, etc.

Then for the third time the whole house is sprinkled, while the five remaining Gradual Psalms are recited, ending with another prayer:

O God, who in every place subject to Thee are present as guardian and protector, grant us, we beseech Thee, that the blessing ✠ on this house may never slacken, and that all we who join in this petition may deserve the shelter which Thou affordest. Through, etc.

Upon this follows the extract from the gospels concerning Zacchæus, the publican, which is read in the Mass for the dedication of a church. Incense is then put into the thurible, the whole house is incensed, and after the prayer *Visita, quæsumus, Domine, habitationem istam*, etc., the priest gives his blessing, once more sprinkles holy water and takes his departure.

For the exorcism of an energumen, as pointed out in the Codex of the Canon Law (c. 1151), special faculties must be granted by the Ordinary, but this does not seem to apply to the use of such a form as that which has just been summarized, seeing that it concerns not a person but a place. On the other hand no ceremonial of this liturgical character ought to be employed by private initiative or without episcopal sanction.

INDEX

OF PERSONS AND PLACES
CONCERNED WITH POLTERGEISTS